I Can't Believe
My Dog Did That!

Chicken Soup for the Soul: I Can't Believe My Dog Did That!
101 Stories about the Crazy Antics of Our Canine Companions
Jack Canfield, Mark Victor Hansen, and Jennifer Quasha

Published by Chicken Soup for the Soul Publishing, LLC www.chickensoup.com
Copyright © 2012 by Chicken Soup for the Soul Publishing, llc. All Rights Reserved.
The publisher gratefully acknowledges the many publishers and individuals who granted Chicken Soup for the Soul permission to reprint the cited material.

Front cover photo courtesy of Getty Images. Back cover photos courtesy of Photos.com.

Cover and Interior Design & Layout by Pneuma Books, LLC
For more info on Pneuma Books, visit www.pneumabooks.com

Distributed to the booktrade by Simon & Schuster. SAN: 200-2442

Publisher's Cataloging-in-Publication Data
(Prepared by The Donohue Group)

Chicken soup for the soul : I can't believe my dog did that! : 101 stories about
  the crazy antics of our canine companions / [compiled by] Jack Canfield, Mark
  Victor Hansen, [and] Jennifer Quasha.

  p. : ill. ; cm.

  Summary: A collection of 101 true stories from people about the incredible things
their dogs have done, from funny to fearsome, from heartwarming to heroic.
  ISBN: 978-1-935096-93-1

  1. Dogs--Behavior--Literary collections. 2. Dogs--Behavior--Anecdotes. 3. Dog
owners--Literary collections. 4. Dog owners--Anecdotes. 5. Human-animal relation-
ships--Literary collections. 6. Human-animal relationships--Anecdotes. I. Canfield,
Jack, 1944- II. Hansen, Mark Victor. III. Quasha, Jennifer. IV. Title: I can't believe my
dog did that!

PN6071.D6 C457 2012
810.8/02/03629772   2012939989

PRINTED IN THE UNITED STATES OF AMERICA
on acid∞free paper
21 20 19 18 17 16 15 14 13 12   03 04 05 06 07 08 09 10

Chicken Soup for the Soul®

I Can't Believe My Dog Did That!

101 Stories about the Crazy Antics
of Our Canine Companions

Jack Canfield
Mark Victor Hansen
Jennifer Quasha

CSS

Chicken Soup for the Soul Publishing, LLC
Cos Cob, CT

www.chickensoup.com

Contents

❶
~One of a Kind~

❷
~In the Doghouse~

❸
~Let's Play Ball~

❹
~Barking Mad~

❺
~For the Love of Dog~

❻

~Treat, Play, Love~

❼

~Throw Me a Bone~

8

~Love Me, Love My Dog~

9

~Dog Gone Smart~

10

~My Best Friend~

I Can't Believe My Dog Did That!

Chapter 1

One of a Kind

Newsies

*A good newspaper is never nearly good enough
but a lousy newspaper is a joy forever.*
~Garrison Keillor

When I opened the cottage door to call our dogs, Molly, the Nova Scotia Duck Tolling Retriever, and Barbie-Q, the little no-name breed, for dinner, I recognized him immediately. New neighbours had moved in across the road two days earlier and the Pug was part of their family; I'd seen him playing on the deck of their cottage.

He looked up at me, his big brown eyes round and appealing above the black mask that covered his snout. Beside me, Molly paused and looked up. I knew that expression. I glanced over at the neighbour's cottage. No one was around.

"Okay," I answered Molly's silent request. I looked down at the Pug. "Would you like to stay to dinner?"

He wriggled his tail, then pranced up the steps and past me.

He proved to be an appreciative guest, his enjoyment of our doggy cuisine obvious as he burrowed his little black mouth deep into gravy-laced kibble. He even gave a lusty burp and licked his chops with gusto when he finished.

"Bruiser! Bruiser, where are you?" I heard.

He cocked his head, then trotted to the full-length screen door and looked out, tail wiggling. His reaction left no doubt. He was Bruiser. I opened the door for him and followed him onto the deck.

"He's over here," I called across the lane to the young woman in shorts and tank top. "He stayed for dinner."

"Thanks," she said, jogging across the road as Bruiser rushed to greet her. She introduced herself as Nancy as she lifted his squirming body into her arms.

"Bruiser's an unusual name for a Pug," I said, as she tucked him against her side.

"I named him after the dog in the movie *Legally Blonde*." She grinned. "Hope he wasn't any trouble." She waved and headed back across the road carrying the Pug.

"Any time," I called.

The trouble began soon afterward—the next morning, in fact, when Molly dashed out as usual to fetch the morning paper at the end of the drive. At the corner of our cedar hedge where the carrier normally tossed it, she stopped short. No paper.

She lowered her nose and began a serious investigation of the area. After a few minutes of watching my dog's unsuccessful attempts to find the daily news, I scuffled into my moccasins and went to help her.

As I was opening the front door, I saw my new neighbour running across the road in slippers and PJs. She was waving something in a blue plastic sleeve. Under her left arm, Bruiser hung ignominiously.

"Sorry," she said, as she ran up the steps. "Bruiser's been watching your dog fetch the paper for the last couple of days. He must have thought it was a good idea, so he brought your paper to us."

"No problem," I replied, taking the paper and giving Bruiser a little head-pat. "Shows initiative, right, guy?" He licked my hand, snuffled a Pug sound and wiggled his tail.

It's been said you can't outfox a fox. Molly soon proved that the cliché also applied to Nova Scotia Duck Tolling Retrievers. Bright and early the next morning, she posted herself on our front step.

The Pug proved to be a worthy opponent. As I glanced out the front window, I saw a small, black-masked snout peering out from the hedge.

I got my coffee and drew up a chair. This was going to be interesting.

A few minutes later, the carrier's car appeared over the crest of the knoll. Instantly, Molly was on her feet, alert and ready. In the hedge, a small beige-and-black body also came to attention.

The car slowed at the end of our drive, an arm appeared through its open driver's window, and the morning news flew through the air. Simultaneously both dogs lunged.

The collision occurred at the corner of the hedge. A yelp, a squeal and Bruiser went flying. Molly paused for a moment, shook to regain her dignity, then picked up the paper precisely in its middle and triumphantly trotted back to the cottage, the obvious winner in this war for words.

By then Bruiser had scrambled to his paws. He, too, shook himself vigorously, paused a moment, then proceeded to prance behind Molly toward our cottage. When I opened the screen door for Molly, and accepted the paper she carefully presented, Bruiser, his joie de vivre apparently unabashed, trotted inside behind her, the corners of his mouth curled up in a good-natured grin.

The following morning, it bucketed rain and Molly opted to watch for the paper from the front window. Surely, she may have speculated, the Pug wouldn't come out in such inclement weather for a fetch he now knew he couldn't possibly retrieve.

Molly would soon learn never to underestimate the tenacity of a Pug.

I'd gone back into the kitchen for a moment when I heard the carrier's car approaching and Molly's excited whines.

"No rush, girl," I assured her as I headed toward the front door to let the now yelping, prancing dog out.

Then I saw the reason for her distress. Bruiser had darted out of the hedge and lifted his leg. His aim perfect, he peed on her precious blue-sleeved paper.

~Gail MacMillan

Dogleg on the Fairway

Golf combines two favorite American pastimes:
taking long walks and hitting things with a stick.
~P.J. O'Rourke

My back yard overlooks the fairway of a golf course, and frequently errant golf balls land in the grass by my fence. Even in my yard.

So, on Sundays I often hear, "Fore! No! Don't go there! Aw, crap!"

This confluence of bad golf and early morning histrionics is why my two dogs have their own spin on the game. Here's how it goes.

Max, my proud Shepherd and Collie soldier, stands guard on my deck in the morning while I drink tea and read. He gazes over the terrain toward enemy territory, The Valley Beyond The Hill. His eyes are sharp, his body tense. My Cairn Terrier, Brinkley, his right-hand man, searches for artillery that has already landed. He finds two treasures, both of them the six-dollar kind.

Suddenly, four men appear in the valley. Their goal is to take the high ground, one hundred sixty yards away. Max postures for incoming ammunition.

"Fore!"

The artillery soars into the sky. It arcs toward Max. With one giant, graceful leap, he snatches it from the air.

"Aw, dang it!" cries one man. "Max got it and I was going for a birdie this hole!"

The other men laugh. "Just take a drop and move on. The ball is gone."

"No way! That darn ball cost me six bucks!"

"Hi, Gary," I say as he heads my way. "Still got that hook, huh?"

"I'm getting better. I didn't come close yesterday."

Gary jumps the fence and turns to Max. "Hey there, big guy. Are you gonna give me my ball back, or do we go through the entire ordeal?"

Max's tail wags. Brinkley barks when Gary moves. The real game is on.

Max tosses the ball to Brinkley who runs to the deep end of our swimming pool. He places the ball on the pavement at his feet then waits for Gary to make another move. Max trots over by Brinkley.

"Please, boys," says Gary, trying to negotiate. "I can still get par. It's a clean shot from here."

Gary takes a step. Brinkley picks up the ball, leans over the water, and drops it into the pool. He and Max watch it sink to the bottom, both tails wagging in triumph.

Gary sighs. "Okay, guys!" he shouts toward the course. "I'm laying four. I 'found the water.' Again."

Max and Brinkley wait for Gary to pet them. "All right," he says. "We're still friends, but I'm tired of losing my six-dollar balls to you."

"Never considered a cheaper ball until you fix the hook, huh?" I ask.

Gary looks at me. "No. That would be admitting defeat. Me and the guys take lessons now because of your boys. Our pro pays them homage every class."

He heads over to the fence. "Yep, they're a real inspiration for me to improve my game."

Max barks and gently tugs on Gary's pant leg. Gary laughs and pats Max again. "Yeah, I'll miss you too, buddy, but I'll be back next week."

Just then Brinkley trots over with one of his earlier finds and drops it at Gary's feet. Gary leans down to pick it up.

"Aww, thanks little guy. That's so sweet." He turns to me with a grin on his face. "Soggier than all get out."

"It rained last night," I reply.

"Hey! There's my excuse for playing so bad. See you next Sunday."

"See you," I say, as he jumps over the fence.

Max and Brinkley walk over to me and curl up at my feet. Time for a break. And a cookie.

"Good boys," I murmur and grin. "Job well done."

~Pamela Goldstein

Food Felon

A well-trained dog will make no attempt to share your lunch.
He will just make you feel so guilty that you cannot enjoy it.
~Helen Thomson

Toby, a Golden-Retriever-Yellow-Lab mix, loved to eat. As a matter of fact, Toby loved to eat anything. Dog food was fine, but what he really liked was food left unattended by a family member who was doing something like, oh, answering the telephone or getting up to refill his milk glass. Toby would stealthily move from his position on his blanket in the corner of the family room, nonchalantly wander over to the dining room table, and make his move the second he spotted the opportunity.

Toby's thieving ways didn't go over too well with my husband Mark.

"That dog is impossible," Mark said whenever Toby nabbed something off his plate. "When's he going to learn that there is people food and there is dog food?"

I didn't have an answer for him but it seemed pretty clear that not only was Toby never going to learn, he also didn't have any interest in learning. Dog food might be okay, but people food was clearly better. Besides, Toby seemed to truly enjoy his life as a food felon.

Eventually, we all grew a little wiser when it came to protecting our meals. Someone in the family was appointed Guardian of the Dinner Table so Toby was no longer able to sneak a hamburger or a hot dog off anyone's plate. We learned not to leave bowls of potato chips unattended on the coffee table. We especially learned to keep all food scraps in the garbage, which went under the kitchen sink behind a sturdy door.

Toby didn't like our vigilance, but we knew that it was good for his digestive system and also good for our nerves. Mark was especially happy that Toby was no longer stealing food from us, his exasperated, hungry owners. After a while, we no longer had to be quite so vigilant. Toby seemed to be content with the food in his bowl. Family members were able to leave peanut butter and jelly sandwiches on the kitchen counter, leave the room for longer than ten seconds, and return to find their snack still intact. Our kitchen kleptomaniac was apparently cured. Or so we thought.

One night, Mark was making a sandwich to put in his lunch for work the next day. Toby sat watching him, his big brown eyes following Mark's hand as Mark slathered on mayonnaise and sliced some roast beef extra thin. Mark looked at Toby looking at him.

"This looks good, doesn't it, Toby?" Mark said more than a bit smugly. "Well, I'm sorry but it's for my lunch. I'm going to put it in the refrigerator and eat it tomorrow and it's going to be delicious."

Toby thumped his tail in response, drooling just a bit.

"You may have a small piece of roast beef," Mark told him, tossing him some meat. Mark wrapped his sandwich in foil, put it in the refrigerator, cleaned up and then left the room. Toby watched him the whole time.

The next morning when he got up for work, Mark went to the refrigerator for his beautiful roast beef sandwich. He opened the refrigerator door, reached for the foil packet and his fingers met... nothing. Mark leaned down and looked into the refrigerator. His sandwich was gone. After checking every shelf, bin and container he realized that his roast beef sandwich was really and truly gone. He decided that someone else in the family must have eaten it so he grabbed an apple and a cheese stick and shut the refrigerator door.

The subject of the missing sandwich didn't come up for a day or two, not until I was making a sandwich with the last of the roast beef.

"This looks good," I commented as I sliced what was left of the beef into thin slices.

"You should know," Mark responded. "After all, you ate my roast beef sandwich the other day."

"I did not," I responded, shocked.

"Sure you did. It was wrapped in foil in the refrigerator and it was gone the next morning. Didn't you eat it?"

"Not me," I said. "Maybe one of the kids?"

But both of our sons denied touching their dad's roast beef sandwich and I believed them. Neither of them had ever been big fans of roast beef. Later that same evening I found a ball of foil crumpled on the floor of the living room. The moment I picked it up, Toby left the room looking somewhat guilty.

I looked at the ball of foil I was holding. Was it possible? Had Toby managed to get the refrigerator door open, find the roast beef sandwich, and devour it without our knowledge?

Mark and I agreed that it had to be what happened. "I can just imagine what he was thinking," Mark said ruefully. "I was making that sandwich, telling him how wonderful it was going to be, telling him how he couldn't have any of it and he was thinking, 'want to bet?'"

~Nell Musolf

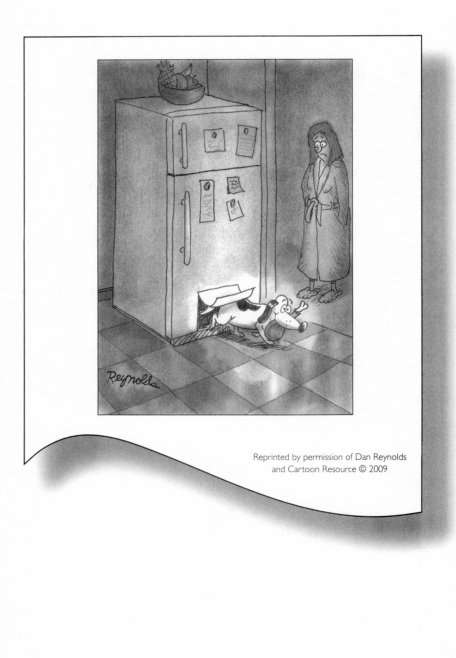

Reprinted by permission of Dan Reynolds
and Cartoon Resource © 2009

Surpris

Even a blind squirrel finds an acorn sometimes.
~Proverb

Our dog, Pepper, loves to chase squirrels. He has never caught one, and more often than not he runs in the opposite direction. But according to him, he is doing his job of protecting us from squirrels.

During summer, he would often stand at the last spot he saw a squirrel or chipmunk and wait for it to reappear and hop into his jaws. Miraculously, this past summer Pepper's dream came true—he actually caught a squirrel.

One afternoon when my son opened the front door to let Pepper outside, he spotted a squirrel hanging on the side of our brick house right by the front door.

He was so surprised he yelled, "There is a squirrel on the house!"

Everyone, including Pepper, came running. Pepper zipped outside and ran right to the big oak tree in our front yard and stood there looking around. Meanwhile the kids and I stood on the front porch staring up in amazement at the squirrel that was indeed hanging on the side of the house.

This should have given the squirrel plenty of time to drop off the house and make his escape into one of the many other trees in our yard, but he didn't. Instead, the squirrel hung there trying to decide what to do. Just as Pepper realized that there was no squirrel in the

back to the house, the squirrel decided to
began creeping toward the ground.
ght sight of him and sped over. Now the squirrel real-
was in big trouble. He was hanging from the side of the
and a big black dog was standing right beneath him.

Panicking, the squirrel raced across the side of the house hoping to lose the dog, but Pepper took off in hot pursuit. They charged down the entire length of the house—squirrel on the house, dog right below. The squirrel turned the corner thinking he was safe, but Pepper found him. We watched in amazement as Pepper herded the squirrel back and forth along the side of the house, trampling all my flowers along the way.

Finally the squirrel figured out that he needed to get off the side of the house. Spotting the gutter, he jumped onto it and attempted to shimmy up to the roof, but quickly realized that it was slippery. The tired squirrel slipped down the gutter and fell right into Pepper's waiting jaws.

Pepper was so surprised that he almost completely dropped the squirrel, but he managed to grab hold of his tail. The kids started screaming in a combination of shock and horror while Pepper ran triumphantly around the yard with his catch swinging from his mouth.

Not wanting the dog to actually hurt the squirrel, I ran over and told him to drop the squirrel. Poor Pepper didn't want to let the squirrel go, but he did. The squirrel, minus a large chunk of tail, raced off to the nearest tree and proceeded to scold us from its highest branches.

I don't know who was more surprised that Pepper caught the squirrel—Pepper, the squirrel, or us!

~Jennifer Flaten

Kitchen Renovation

We could have bought a small yacht with what we spent on our dog and all the things he destroyed. Then again, how many yachts wait by the door all day for your return?
~John Grogan

ur beloved dog Bojangles, or BJ as we called her, seemed to be the perfect family pet. She was adorable and loving, showing what appeared to be gratitude. My stepdaughter Amanda had rescued BJ from certain doom, finding her discarded in the hedges as a tiny puppy. Following Amanda's begging, we accepted BJ into our home.

We didn't know much about BJ other than that she was tiny with fluffy brown fur. Our veterinarian made many attempts at guessing her breed. He determined initially some sort of Beagle mix, then as time progressed added potential Dachshund due to her short legs and long back. Her tail could have been Collie or Sheltie or Terrier. He finally just determined that she was officially a mutt.

BJ was well behaved and we had little trouble housebreaking her. As a small pup, we thankfully could coordinate schedules so she didn't have to spend much time alone. That did eventually change, but BJ had been with us long enough that we felt confident she would be fine spending longer periods of time alone while we were at work or Amanda was at school.

It did not take long to figure out that BJ disliked her time alone and displayed separation anxiety. We could see her running to the front windows as our cars pulled away from the driveway. Within a short period of time, the first one home was greeted by a number of surprises.

BJ began her solitary escapades by finding the hamper. Dirty clothes were strewn throughout the house—down the hallway, into the living room and everywhere in between. This seemed easy enough to handle. The hamper was moved into the closet.

Next, BJ discovered the bathroom trashcan. This time there was a path of tissues down the same hallway and into the living room, just like the dirty clothes. Again, we adjusted and moved the trashcan, placing it on the bathroom counter before we left for the day.

We scanned the house and puppy-proofed as best as we could, but BJ could always find trouble.

One day when my husband Ted and I returned home, BJ greeted us with her usual excitement, but her tail wagging was accompanied by a look of guilt. Although from the door there were no visible signs of destruction, as I walked into the kitchen I immediately called for Ted—and for BJ.

Somehow, our precious family pet had pulled up a corner of the linoleum and our kitchen floor was all but gone. There were patches left, but most of the linoleum was in strips, pieces, and piles throughout the kitchen. BJ had spent the day remodeling. It never occurred to us to puppy-proof the floor!

Yes, we were less than delighted with this disaster, but eventually we had to laugh. I could not fathom how this tiny, adorable fur ball could have totally destroyed an entire kitchen floor. Yet to tell you the truth, I never really liked that linoleum anyway. Perhaps BJ, in her own way, was trying to help.

~Lil Blosfield

Frequent Flyer

If you obey all the rules, you miss all the fun.
~Katharine Hepburn

"What a funny little dog," Mom said to me when I first introduced her to our newest addition. "Her head is much too large for her little body."

"What a horrible thing to say. Gracie Lou is gorgeous. Well, maybe her head is a little big. I'm sure she will grow into it one day."

Gracie Lou came from a Bronx, New York rescue that, during the spring and summer months, brought a small group of dogs from the Bronx to our suburban neighborhood in Connecticut in search of forever homes in the "country."

When we met her, she was a six-month-old pup with stand-up ears, calm brown eyes and, yes, a head that seemed way too big for her body. And, she could fly.

Well, almost. That puppy could jump up and down so high and so often it made my head spin. I thought she would outgrow her high-flying capabilities but I was wrong.

It started about two months after Gracie Lou came to live with us. I would put her in the fenced-in back yard with her brother Sam, a nine-year-old black Lab. As Sam was getting older, we felt he could use a little puppy love to ignite that spark and bring back the inner youth we knew was still there. We were right. From the minute Gracie Lou ventured into our lives, they were inseparable. They would chase one another in the house, up and down the stairs, and outside all around the back yard. After dinner, they would lie paw-in-paw on the same dog bed, even though they each had their own.

Every day I would put them in the back yard, secure the fence, and go back inside. One day I let them out and within minutes, I heard a brushing at the front door. To my surprise, there was Gracie Lou asking to come in.

I went to the back to inspect the fence. All secure, but there was a slight gap in the back corner of the fence. Maybe she was squeezing through there. I found a piece of slate and blocked the hole. Problem solved.

The next morning I let them out in the back yard and watched them through the kitchen window. Around and around the yard they ran. Around and around the pool, onto the patio, passing by the window again and again. Finally, Sam had enough. Yes, age has its demands. He settled into his favorite shady corner for a well-deserved rest. Gracie Lou was not quite done, though. I saw her nudge him for a few minutes and then, after a warning glare from Sam, she too settled down next to him.

Finally, the "kids" were down for a nap.

Upstairs in my office I immersed myself in photos and text, trying to piece together an annual review I was working on for one of my principal clients.

A couple of hours flew by and I went down to get a drink and check on the pups. There was Sam in the same spot, but no Gracie Lou. Where could she have gone? After looking around the house, I ran up and down the street desperately calling her name.

I went back home to get my keys and drive the neighborhood. Before leaving, I quickly checked on Sam and there, behind the locked fence was Gracie Lou looking ever-so-innocent. I thought I must have been losing my mind. Had she been there the whole time? I let them both in the house. Gracie Lou seemed exceptionally thirsty.

A couple of days later, I was in the office and the phone rang. It was my neighbor, Maria.

"Lose something?" she said.

"Not to my knowledge. Wanna give me a hint?"

"She is furry, has cute ears and a big head," she added.

"Gracie Lou? She's in the back yard."

"Oh no, she's not. She's in my house, eating Lily and Nolie's food," she replied.

It turns out Maria came home to find Gracie Lou lying in her living room with her two white Labs.

Gracie Lou had jumped over our fence, run down the street to Maria's, jumped her fence and then went through the doggie door to play with Maria's dogs, Lily and Nolie.

"I was wondering what the dark fur was on my living room rug," Maria said.

"She's done this before, Jeanne," she said as she laughed.

I was so embarrassed.

After Maria's call, I guess Gracie Lou felt guilty leaving Sam behind during her adventures. She rarely jumped and if she did, she would stay on the other side of the fence, nose-to-nose whining, as if coaxing Sam on. You can do it. You can jump it. Come on.

Thank goodness Sam had the sense not to try that game. Or did he?

Up in the office one afternoon, I looked out only to see my two canines trotting down the street. I opened the window and yelled, "Stop." They both stopped dead in their tracks. Caught.

"Get back here," I demanded. By the time I got down the stairs they were both in the back yard. The gate was open now. How in the world? I knew I had secured it.

This happened several times. I just could not figure out how that gate got opened. Maybe the kids left it unlocked, maybe the garbage men, or maybe I was losing my mind.

One day I heard Gracie whining to Sam. I looked out the window and saw them both huddled near the gate, as if formulating a plan. The next thing I knew, Gracie Lou was backing away from the gate, leaping over it and hitting the release lock as she soared. Upon landing, the gate was open and Sam was free to waltz out. Side by side they began their saunter towards Maria's. I couldn't believe the brains.

At first, I thought it was a fluke, but over the next few weeks, I witnessed this several times. Needless to say, I finally had to tie the gate closed.

Gracie Lou will still jump if Lily and Nolie are on a walk with their mom, but she hasn't run down the street—I think she doesn't like to leave Sam behind. Now if Gracie Lou and Sam want to play with their friends, I call Maria and walk them down like a responsible mother.

And yes, Gracie Lou did finally grow into her head. Or should I say she is perfectly proportioned in every way.

~Jeanne Blandford

Click

I think the next best thing to solving a problem is finding some humor in it.
~Frank A. Clark

I heard a strangely familiar click as I rushed off my back porch after my Greyhound, Holly, and Yorkshire Terrier, Caesar, to dissuade them from tag-teaming a panicked, fleeing rabbit. A few seconds later they aborted the chase after the rabbit squeezed itself through two planks of the wood fence.

The dogs returned to the porch empty-handed. Thankful that I wouldn't have to snatch a squealing rabbit from a dog's jowls, I grabbed the door handle to let them back inside. The door wouldn't budge. The earlier "click" now made sense. Excited by the chase, my Belgian Tervuren, Maxx, who had remained inside the house, had hit the locking mechanism with his paw when he jumped onto the glass door.

Maxx wagged his tail as I jiggled the handle.

"Oh, come on," I pleaded, as if Maxx could turn the handle to pop the lock. Holly and Caesar poked their noses into the corner of the door in anticipation while I stood outside in a business suit, pantyhose, and heels. Better than in my pajamas, I supposed.

For security reasons, I neither kept a key hidden outside nor provided one for the neighbor for such emergencies. To complicate matters, my husband wasn't due home from an out-of-town business meeting for three more days, and our nearest relative lived 300 miles north. I was on my own… except for the baby I was due to deliver in four months.

Desperate to get back inside and to leave for work on time for a scheduled employee breakfast, I tugged on a nearby window—locked. Then I tried to open all the back windows—same result. Meanwhile, Maxx darted from room to room, peering through the curtains at me and playing a game of peek-a-boo. Since he remained interested, I planned to lure Maxx back over to the door, hoping he'd jump up and hit the handle and unlock the door.

"Come on, boy," I called from outside and darted to the back door. When I discovered him waiting for me, I thought my plan might work. I held out my hand and said, "Do you want a treat?"

His ears perked up. A good sign. I raised my hand in an upward motion and repeated the word "treat" in hopes of getting his front legs off the ground. Instead, he lay down as I had taught him whenever I rewarded him with a snack. Stupid obedience training.

Holly and Caesar also knew the word and lay down on the patio. Three dogs now stared at me, waiting for a make-believe reward. Whining commenced when I didn't produce the goods. A couple of minutes later, I turned to see Maxx walking toward the kitchen. The word "treat" must've awakened his hunger since he began sniffing the countertop where I had placed the cheesy egg-and-ham casserole for the employee breakfast. The jumping motion—which I had hoped to elicit earlier from Maxx—came to him with ease as he placed his front paws on the kitchen island to investigate the casserole dish.

I pounded the glass door. "Maxx, no! Leave it."

He turned his head sideways and nudged the tin foil, and the casserole fell to the ground. I continued banging as Maxx began to gorge. Knowing that I could never compete with breakfast, I decided it was time to call a locksmith. I headed over to the gate to walk next door to my neighbor's house but, unfortunately, the gate was padlocked and the key was stored in the garage. Why did I have to be such a safety nut?

I sized up the fence. What would be so hard about scaling a four-foot fence? The business suit? The heels? The protruding belly?

I kicked off my shoes—those I could ditch without breaking the law—and started to climb. Once I reached the top of the gate, I turned around and started to lower myself down the other side. I hooked my toes on the cross boards; unfortunately, my toes weren't the only things hooked on the wooden planks. The front of my skirt had caught on the top of the gate and proceeded to rip until I could unhook it. Losing my balance, I hit the ground with a thud. With a torn skirt, toes peeking through tattered hose, a disheveled blouse, and a forehead beaded with sweat, I stood on my neighbor's porch and rang the doorbell.

"Cathi, what on earth happened?" she asked. "Are you okay?"

"Maxx locked me out of the house, and I need to call a locksmith."

After the laughter cleared, I made the call. Twenty minutes later, a white van pulled into the driveway. The man looked at me and asked, "So, what can I help you with?"

I pointed to my front door. "I need to get into my house. I've been locked out." I didn't have the energy to tell him the whole story. Not to mention, would he even believe it?

"Do you have some I.D.? You know, to prove that you live here before I just go and open the door."

I couldn't blame him for asking since I looked like a vagrant. I was certain that I'd appreciate his reticence once the ordeal ended. My mind flashed to my purse on the kitchen island.

"It's in my wallet inside the house," I said, and for the first time that morning, I began to cry. Pointing to my naked toes, my ragged skirt, and my protruding belly, I said, "Sir, I really just need to get inside."

"Will the neighbor vouch for you?" he asked, and I nodded.

Within fifteen minutes, I stood safely in the kitchen amidst an empty casserole dish and a sated Belgian Tervuren. I called my employer, and they graciously gave me the day off work. As I changed out of my ragged clothing and placed a bag of ice on my backside to ease the pain from my abrupt landing, I made a mental note to make a spare key for the neighbor. A sharp bark interrupted my thoughts: a reminder from Caesar that he still wanted his treat.

~Cathi LaMarche

Who's Afraid?

The average dog is a nicer person than the average person.
~Andy Rooney

My mother has a Beagle named Cooper that we rescued from the pound about three years ago. Cooper is very energetic and loves to go for walks up and down our long lane. My mother usually takes him out late at night during the summer.

On one of those walks my father came home from work in his police car. As my mother and Cooper went to greet him, Cooper got very excited about saying hi to his daddy. My father, however, saw this as an opportunity to try something and turned on his intercom.

"Coooooper!" Dad said through the intercom, using a low, spooky voice. Poor Cooper had no idea what to make of the ghost-like voice that was coming out of nowhere. He couldn't tell that it was just my dad.

After a moment of hesitation, in which everyone was silent, Cooper turned around and sprinted back to the house, dragging Mom by his leash behind him. Cooper refused to stop, and Mom, despite losing her pink slippers in the grass, kept running for fear of letting go of the terrified, fleeing dog.

Cooper ran the entire way back up the lane and into the house, stopping only for a few seconds for Mom to undo his leash, and then he ran down the hall. In his haste, the rugs were kicked aside and he skittered sideways on the hardwood floor before finally stopping under my parents' bed.

Mom found him cowering under her bed, and tried to get him to come out. When she couldn't, I shook the treat box. Usually he comes running, but this time he didn't. I had to take a treat to him under the bed. Cooper took the treat from my hand, but then retreated back under the bed before my mother could grab him.

A short time later, he finally came out. He didn't seem to remember the episode. His tail was held high again and the bounce in his step was back. It seemed that he was saying: "Who's afraid? Me? No not me! I'm not afraid!"

My mom looked at me and rolled her eyes while she stroked her "brave" little dog.

I, on the other hand, chose to agree with him completely.

~Aeriel Crook, age 16

Flying Dog

One can never consent to creep when one feels an impulse to soar.
~Helen Keller

It was a warm spring day, with new leaves sprouting on trees and the smell of freshly mowed grass in the air. My daughter's large dog Rocky excitedly pulled on the leash, anticipating a free run when we reached the park. The park was empty of people so I removed his leash. He leapt incredible lengths with his long legs, running hard in circles around the soccer field.

We entered the woods on a paved path surrounded by tall trees, and walked across a short wooden bridge over a slow moving stream. Rocky obediently watched me, never straying far from my presence. The coolness of the shade was refreshing, drying the sweat from my skin. Surrounded by nature and the love of a dog, I was filled with joy.

We exited the woods beside a pond covered with green scum. The scum was so dense it made the water look like an extension of the grass. Directly in front of us was a flock of geese gathered on the land. Rocky stopped. His eyes focused on the birds. He stood motionless for a brief moment, then wiggled his rear end and darted for the geese. Instinct was screaming, "This is dinner!"

Quickly, the geese waddled into the pond as fast as they could, seeking safety and honking loudly. The last one to reach the water was too slow. When Rocky's nose was within inches of the bird, it flapped its wings wildly and flew high over the water.

Rocky leapt off the steep embankment into the air behind the bird, his mouth open wide, prepared to grab onto the flying goose. Several feet from the shore, I saw Rocky flying through the air—until gravity took over. He plummeted and fell deep into the pond.

Rocky is terrified of water—he darts away from the smallest sprinkle of our garden hose. I looked for his head to surface, but there was no sign of him. The horror of how I would tell my daughter that her dog had drowned raced through my mind. She had warned me many times to keep Rocky on the leash.

"Oh my God!" I screamed as Rocky surfaced, his legs thrashing the water with great force, the water splashing high around him. Geese scrambled away in every direction as he tried to stay afloat. I yell repeatedly, "Rocky come here! Rocky come here!"

I couldn't jump in to save him; I could drown. Plus it would be too difficult to climb up the steep embankment. I also didn't want to get in that water with all my clothes on, with that awful scum clinging to my body. But I couldn't just stand there doing nothing, watching him drown.

Rocky began to make progress toward me; it looked like he could swim. Yes, he was definitely swimming. Closer and closer he came. When he got to the embankment, he jumped from the water onto the land.

I exhaled with a sigh of relief and sat down on a park bench to process what had just happened, trying to calm my nerves. Rocky sat on the ground beside me, panting hard while we both looked out over the pond.

Water dripped from his chin, his whole body soaked. Did he think that green scum was grass or did the excitement of the moment make him forget he was afraid of water? Well, the goose got away, Rocky learned to swim, and I survived the shock.

Next time, I hope Rocky leaves the flying to the geese.

~Susan Randall

Sit!

Dogs act exactly the way we would act if we had no shame.
~Cynthia Heimel

I hoped my arm would remain attached to my body while I struggled to contain my energetic gentle giant. The Saint Bernard book I'd read strongly recommended training early while the dog was still a manageable size. But my puppy already outweighed me.

So here we were at a city park, standing in a line at a beginning obedience class for any breed of dog up to six months of age. I noticed that the other participants had attractive jeweled collars with matching leashes.

My baby wore a collar that had been my husband's belt, and I grasped a logging-sized chain in my gloved hand. Even my dog's name, Brute, had drawn a chuckle from the crowd. Brute, according to Mr. Webster, means savage beast. My savage beast had hidden behind me to escape a growling Chihuahua.

In my most authoritative voice, I gave the command again. "Sit!" Brute glanced down at the other sitting dogs, tipped his head and gave me a puzzled look. I could almost hear him say, "You want me to do what?" This was the breed I'd read was highly intelligent and easy to train.

The instructor proposed I hold the chain in one hand, put my finger tips from the other hand on Brute's shoulders, and gently lean and push down with my elbow on his hips. This was easier said than done. I stretched over Brute, but my elbow only went as far as the middle of his back. Brute anticipated me giving him a back rub and excitedly wiggled all over, which set me off balance and propelled me over the top of him. I found myself lying on the grass looking up at an enormous drool machine.

A long string of slobber nailed me on the chest as I got myself up in time to join the group for our second part of the "Sit" command.

This time the dog was supposed to sit and then the owner would back up and say, "Stay."

Brute wasn't actually sitting, but he had flopped on the ground. So slowly I backed up and using my don't-mess-with-me voice, said, "Stay." I couldn't believe it. Brute stayed.

Then a low rumbling noise reached my ears. My massive Swiss breed was sound asleep and snoring.

Class ended. As the instructor suggested additional ideas to try at home, he rubbed the top of Brute's head. Brute's tail started up like a motor and all the papers, pens, and class fees flew off the table.

Deciding to give it one more try, I stared deep into Brute's eyes and ordered, "Sit!"

And Brute sat. Hallelujah! Miracles do happen.

Soon, however, a muffled, high-pitched barking filtered out from under my dog's bottom. Yes, Brute was sitting on the Chihuahua.

~Sharon Landeen

Chapter 2

I Can't Believe My Dog Did That!

In the Doghouse

The House Special

To eat is to appropriate by destruction.
~Jean-Paul Sartre

Walking through a secondhand store on my lunch hour, I saw it—an elegant doghouse with oak shingles layered on every side, in my price range. Just what Yainex, my new four-month-old Golden Labrador Retriever, needed in his dog run. But how would I get it home?

Returning to work, I told a coworker about the doghouse. I sighed and said, "It's too bad my husband is out of town with our pickup."

"Hey, I have my pickup here today. I can help you get it right after work," he graciously offered.

The doghouse was still there when we arrived at the store. We loaded it into his pickup and after reaching my home, he helped me carry it to the dog run.

"Yainex, here is your beautiful new home," I said.

Yainex ignored it. Jumping up and down with excitement, he grabbed his ball to play as soon as I opened the gate to the dog run.

"Oh well, I really like it. Let's go play," I told him.

The next morning when I went down to feed him, I was shocked at the sight of the doghouse. One whole side of the doorway was gone.

"Yainex, what have you done?" I asked.

He had chewed all the cedar shingles on that side. He was eating his beautiful house.

My mind raced back to the first time I realized that Yainex was a serious chewer. Knowing that puppies like to chew and play, I purchased some toys and rawhide bones for him. Then one day his favorite squeaky toy, a bright yellow Tweety Bird, just disappeared. No sign of Tweety Bird could be found. Then, the following morning, bright specks of yellow told the story. He had eaten Tweety Bird. It wasn't long before I had to take away all his toys and rawhide bones.

Bored while I was at work, Yainex began to chew the edges of the boards on the walls of our house that were exposed in his dog run. I nailed up sheets of pressed plywood to protect our home. Yainex tried chewing the edges of the plywood, but didn't like the crumbly texture and stopped.

I wondered if that might work again. Where was the leftover pressed plywood?

Pulling it out of the garage, I used a handsaw to cut it into pieces big enough to cover the oak shingles still left on the right side of the doorway. For good measure, I also covered the whole exposed north wall of the doghouse.

The next morning I gazed in utter amazement at the doghouse. Yes, the pressed plywood had done its job, but now there was a skylight in the doghouse. He had chewed an eight-inch hole in the roof.

"Oh Yainex, what have you done now?" I cried.

Looking inside the doghouse, I noticed that the corner studs and the inside walls had been chewed also.

He was destroying his doghouse. I had heard of horse owners putting soap on fence rails to prevent them from being chewed, so I decided to try that. Soon I had coated the entire inside walls of the doghouse with dish detergent.

"Okay, chew that!" I told him. And then I added another piece of pressed plywood to patch the hole in the roof.

It seemed to work. Yainex didn't like the soapy-tasting wood or the pressed plywood. Morning light revealed no new damage to the doghouse. When my husband arrived home, I showed him the new doghouse and proudly told him of my efforts to save it.

Shaking his head, he dryly said, "If I had known you wanted a doghouse that ugly, I could have made it."

~Yvonne Kays

Mouse Trap

The dog was created specially for children. He is the god of frolic.
~Henry Ward Beecher

I could have avoided all that trouble if only I had remembered to keep the cat in. Five little human noses were pressed curiously against our glass door, each vying for the best view as our loyal old mutt, Pup, squeezed in beside them.

"Mom! There's something out there!"

Recalling the bank robber who was chased down in our back yard last summer, I raced toward the sofa, pushed past the kids, and peered through the locked glass door, ready to defend my young.

Following five little pointing fingers, I saw it. The rear half of a mouse lay neatly on the patio: no blood, no gore, a neat kill. Sassy, our dainty gray-and-white cat, sat smugly near her gift. I sighed in relief. A rodent carcass I could handle.

"Okay, kids, stay here," I said, grabbing a couple of paper towels. I scooped up the remains and headed to the Dumpster, Sassy trailing behind me, yowling her protest.

"Thank you for sharing, Sass, but no thank you."

"Mrroowph!" Sassy snorted.

Excitement over, we all went back to whatever we were doing.

"Mom! There's another one!"

Five minutes couldn't have passed. I resolved to bring in the cat as I grabbed another paper towel and stepped through the door to the patio, but as I reached down for this one, which was still, thankfully, intact, it leaped.

"Eeeeek!" I screamed.

Five screaming kids and our suddenly alert old mutt shot through the open glass door, much to the disgust of Sassy, who marched slowly amidst the pandemonium, tail high, through the open door. She had clearly washed her whiskers of us.

Flabbergasted, I watched our old hound take the mouse between his jaws so that all that could be seen of the tiny creature was a dangling tail that waved up and down while Pup raced in circles to avoid the kids' attempts to catch him. Ugh! The last thing I wanted was for them to see a mouse chewed alive! I ordered my older son to get a paper bag while I joined the chase.

"Pup! Drop that!"

Pup's frisking days were long gone, but something about this adventure had set him off. There was a twinkle in his eye and a look of pure mischief as he easily avoided the little bodies that hurled themselves at him. He kept the long tail that bounced in his soft-mouthed jaw just out of their reach. Sticky, warm dog slobber drooled down the tip of the critter's tail and flung everywhere as Pup romped with his prize.

"Pup! Come here!" I yelled.

Tail wagging waves of happiness, Pup approached me coyly and sat, eyes rolling toward the kids, who for once obeyed my outstretched hand that told them to stay.

"Good dog," I said patting his head. I motioned to Aaron to bring the bag as one of the younger boys asked if the mouse was dead.

"It's wet and slobbery. Might be dead. Stay back," I said, eyeing our dog appreciatively as he looked proudly back. "Pup, you have to give it to me," I said holding the bag open just under his mouth. Then in my sternest command voice, I said, "Drop!"

To my surprise, he did. The wet little vermin plopped right into the bag where it lay very still for approximately 1.3 seconds, not long enough for me to close the bag, before leaping with great vigor onto my shoulder, causing me to do a crazy screaming wiggle-dance. The chase, along with the cries of encouragement from the kids, was on again.

"Run, Mousie! Get away!" screamed my daughter.

"Save yourself, Mouse!" urged my nephew.

"Poor little mouse!" wailed my younger son.

But it was Pup who stole the show. Jumping sideways, he followed the bounding leaps of the mouse until it settled near a bush. To further impress us, Pup lifted his forepaw, pushed his nose out and actually pointed!

Silence reigned as we took in the spectacle of our mellow old mutt behaving just like a spry hunting dog. The wretched rodent chose that moment to make good its escape.

Quick as lightning, Pup stuck out his head, opened his jaws, adjusted for the angle, and the hapless mouse went right back into his mouth as if pulled by an invisible cord. The kids whooped and praised Pup, who started his serpentine trail through the yard again, mouse tail flapping.

I retrieved the empty paper bag and once more issued the sit and drop commands. Pup obeyed, beaming, and as lively as I'd ever seen him. This time I closed the bag fast, mouse intact, dead or alive.

"Good dog! Okay kids, we got 'im!"

Pup's youthful glow remained as he basked in the praise of the kids, who lavished him with treats and superhero attributes, even fashioning a cape for him that he quickly gnawed off. This was clearly a crowning moment in his life we would remember forever.

It was at that moment my six-year-old son Sam asked the question that has led to the increase in our family by sixteen hamsters and two mice in the past several years.

"Mom, what are we going to name Pup's mouse?"

~Patti Zint

Size Matters

Things that upset a terrier may pass virtually unnoticed by a Great Dane.
~Smiley Blanton

"Let's just name him Dammit Dog," my husband Roy suggested. "It'll just save time later when those puppy teeth are chewing on our toes." Roy was talking about the new addition to our family, a registered Yorkshire Terrier, who was lying sleepily in my lap looking up at us with those adorable liquid brown puppy eyes as we drove home from the breeder's.

I wasn't in favor of the name, but when the registration papers went in, Dammit Dog was on them. True to Roy's prediction, Dammit did the puppy things that caused him to "earn" his name. He did the normal things—like chew on bare toes under the kitchen table at breakfast, and chew the leather off the heel of a new pair of patent leather high heels I had purchased for a company function.

Once, when I gave him a rawhide bone to chew on while I cooked dinner, I heard a strange crunching sound as he lay on the couch with his back to me. I always left my purse and keys on the end of the couch where Dammit was chewing the rawhide, so the strange crunchy sound made me stop cooking and go investigate. Dammit was chewing on the electronic key to my 4Runner. After I spent $250 for a new key, even I had to admit Dammit Dog was the perfect name for our boy.

But one time, Dammit Dog did something truly unbelievable to earn his name. We brought him to our weekend home on the river one Easter weekend. As soon as we opened the car door, he bounded out and ran over to introduce himself to our neighbor, Jack, and his German Shorthaired Pointer named Hunter. Dammit, or D-Dog, quickly won Jack's heart and began to visit often, especially when he discovered that Jack kept dog biscuits for Hunter. Jack enjoyed Dammit's visits and rewarded him with a biscuit every time he came socializing. D-Dog visited every chance he got—like every time our door was left open. If D-Dog was missing, invariably he was at Uncle Jack's.

Jack also got a kick out of Hunter playing with D-Dog. Hunter was a full grown, well-trained Pointer. His head was bigger than D-Dog's entire body. During playtime, though, Jack evened things out for the two by getting Hunter to lie down on the ground. As soon as Hunter was settled, D-Dog was on him—pulling on his floppy ears, jumping over him again and again, and grabbing Hunter's lower lip in grand Yorkie style, shaking his head and growling, "killing" it.

Hunter bore playtime with dignity. But when enough was enough, he would merely stand up—and playtime was over. Most of the time, that worked well for everyone. Once after a couple of dog biscuits, D-Dog was just getting started playing when Hunter had decided that playtime was over and he stood up, marking its end.

Not to be deterred, D-Dog looked around for something on Hunter's body he could grab hold of and give the "death" shake to. Then he saw it. With all the energy and enthusiasm of a puppy on dog biscuits, Dammit ran, jumped, and grabbed hold of Hunter's dangling manhood.

Hunter just stood there with a look of hurt indignation in his eyes as Dammit hung by his needle-like puppy teeth and shook his head trying to "kill" his new toy. Good thing Jack and Hunter had a sense of humor, because it took Roy, Jack and me a couple of minutes to stop laughing and rescue Hunter.

~Janice R. Edwards

The Naked Truth

Even if there is nothing to laugh about, laugh on credit.
~Author Unknown

Don't talk to me about dogs. I'll break out in a cold at. Don't misunderstand me. I love dogs; I really In fact, for most of my married life, I've had dogs, ch I spoiled rotten. Simply rotten. My son always said he wantecbe reincarnated as one of my dogs. I treat them that well.

We've owned Golden Retrievers, Boston Terriers, and a Pekise. But the dog of all dogs was a little white fur ball named Misour Cockapoo.

If you look up the word "adorable," you'll find Missy's pure in black and white. But if you look up "incorrigible," you'll firher picture in blazing color with the Boston Pops Orchestra playir the "1812 Overture" as a deafening background.

Missy held me hostage. She took complete charge of my lifrom the day she arrived. I was her willing slave and she knew it.

Before she was born, I honestly believe she chatted excitedlwith the rest of the litter in her mother's womb about how she wouldrive me out of what was left of my mind. And she came precariouslyclose to it several times.

Missy had two passions in life. One was to pull the end ofa roll of bathroom tissue down the hall, into the living room, through rearly every bedroom, ending back in the bathroom in one perfect loop.

And, without a single break in the tissue. An incredible feat. Unfely, I was the only one who thought so.

ther passion was my husband's underwear. She loved to chev shreds, placing the ragged fragments in front of John's closre he tripped over them and flew into a rage. She loved to bocus of a rage. It made her feel important and needed. Or som.

ne day Missy came perilously close to losing her beloved placay heart. She came even closer to permanent eviction from our .

s taking a leisurely bath one afternoon when I heard my husl close the kitchen screen door and drive off. The screen door offerery little in the way of protection and privacy, so I draped a towound me and headed for the kitchen to close the solid wood doo lock it before resuming my bath.

: as I reached across the open space to pull the kitchen door shutssy grabbed one end of the bath towel and ran with it, leaving me s you-know-what in front of the open door. To my horror, the UPSn stood on the outside step staring up at me.

both froze. Then I leaped back out of sight and stammered, "Do we you anything?" He dropped the package on the top step by the or and ran back to his truck, calling over his shoulder, "Lady, you n't owe me a thing!"

lever saw him again. Either he was transferred to another route, he di of cardiac arrest, or he suffered a total mental collapse.

; for what I did to Missy, I take the Fifth.

~Mariane Holbrook

Hungry Howdy

*The hunger for love is much more difficult to remove
than the hunger for bread.*
~Mother Teresa

Howdy wasn't my dog. He was a big Golden Lab from my mail route. Probably, his name wasn't even Howdy. That's just what I called him because it fit. The big wide-mouth grin on his buttercream-colored face and the brightly patterned bandana he wore around his neck made me think of the Howdy Doody marionette from my childhood.

Only service dogs are allowed in the post office, but Howdy didn't care about conforming to postal regulations. He was a dog with a free spirit. You could tell by the way he strutted up and down the streets that he believed each new day was created for his unique pleasure. Howdy made himself right at home one spring morning when he followed a group of mail carriers into the post office through the swinging orange double doors on the loading dock.

He sniffed his way around the workroom floor, from work station to station, tail wagging, tongue hanging out, eyes sparkling. At most stops, he was rewarded with a pat on the head for which he appeared most grateful. But at the supervisor's desk, he was shown the door. I thought I had seen the last of Howdy.

A couple of hours later, when I was delivering mail about three blocks from the post office and walking from house to house, always on the lookout for unrestrained dogs, I saw Howdy prancing gaily under the purple flowering Hawthorn trees at the end of the street. The jaunty gait gave him away. I watched him wander happily as I continued delivering the day's mail. I knew he was not a threat and something about him was compelling. Maybe a dog's life wasn't such a bad thing after all. It sure seemed to agree with Howdy.

Just before finishing this section of delivery, I had a registered letter to deliver. I stepped up on the customer's porch and rang the bell. While I waited for a response, I began filling out the Postal Service Form 3849 for the customer's signature.

I didn't notice that Howdy had joined me on the steps until the lady answered her door, swinging it back just far enough for Howdy to sashay in. Astonished, the customer's mouth gaped open.

"He's not mine," I said. "But, he's friendly."

I stood in the doorway and watched. Howdy wandered quickly over to the bookshelves, tilting his head back higher and higher as if looking for his favorite title. Then onto the hearth Howdy went, the pendulum motion of his tail never slowing and his nostrils flaring as he sniff-searched for canine treasure. Howdy was a dog on a mission.

Howdy squeezed his head and broad shoulders behind the gray tweed sofa, put his paws on the end table and finally, almost completely, disappeared behind the blue leather recliner. The constantly moving tail had begun to wag with such momentum that it now wagged Howdy's only visible part, his hindquarters.

"My breakfast!" screeched the lady. "That's it! Hold that screen door open."

I pushed my hips into the screen until it opened fully. My beleaguered customer disappeared into the kitchen and came out holding a hot dog. She shook the cold meat under Howdy's nose and, having his full attention, flung the wiener through the open door and onto the sidewalk. A flash of yellow fur blew past me, following the flying frankfurter, and I slammed the screen door shut.

"When you rang the bell, I was sitting in the recliner eating my breakfast. I sat my plate on the floor when I got up to answer. That dog ate my breakfast," she said, breathlessly.

"I'm so sorry," I said, trying to be sincere and hold back my laughter. "I need your signature for this registered piece of mail."

A few minutes later I drove past Howdy as I moved along my route in my mail truck. I'm not positive, but I'm pretty sure that Howdy had egg on his face.

~Karen R. Hessen

The Cookie Monster

A balanced diet is a cookie in each hand.
~Author Unknown

I stepped off the elevator, key in hand, ready to unlock the door to my one-bedroom apartment in New York City. Behind the door would be Winston, my seven-year-old Bichon Frise, ready to jump off his dog bed and give me oodles of tail-wagging love.

When I opened the door, I noticed that Winston had other things on his mind. Lying down and hunched over his front legs, he was chewing a cookie wrapper that he held between his paws. He was struggling with that package, but he had made quick work of the four other cookies whose wrappers lay empty nearby.

"Winston!" I said. He stopped and stood up, his head and tail drooping.

When I went over to pick up the wrappers I realized what they were. I couldn't believe it.

Each wrapper had contained a white-chocolate-dipped Oreo cookie. The cookies had been individually wrapped inside a cookie tin. The unopened cookie tin had one of those super-strong seals of super-sticky clear tape, double-wrapped around the top to keep the lid in place. Even I couldn't get that tape off easily, and I have opposable thumbs.

I had left the unopened tin in a zippered bag, under a heavy winter jacket—which is why I forgot the tin was there—on a chair in the living room.

"Winston," I said again in my disappointed, you're-a-bad-dog voice, still in disbelief.

How did he get into that tin? And where was the tape? I shook my head and grabbed the opened cookie tin and top. I counted eight cookies remaining. I threw away the wrapper and the cookie he was working on.

Naughty dog, I thought, as I put my purse away and went to my bedroom to change out of my work clothes. When I came back into the living room Winston was on the couch, another cookie wrapper between his paws.

"Winston!" I said again.

He looked up. I walked over to him and he wagged his tail. He looked at me as if to say, "You're not going to take this one away, too, are you?"

"Where did you get this?" I said, as I walked to the kitchen to throw it away.

As I cooked dinner I noticed that Winston wasn't standing by my feet like he usually did, in prime position for my droppings. I looked out of the kitchen and saw Winston prancing toward the couch with another wrapped cookie hanging from his mouth.

When I walked toward him, he ran.

"Winston!" I said. He stopped.

I grabbed it, threw it away, and marched over to the tin. How many cookies were supposed to be in that tin? Eighteen? Oh, boy.

Okay. There were eight cookies left in the tin, four empty wrappers on the floor, and three cookies that I had taken from Winston upon my return. Fifteen total. That meant that there were three missing.

I looked down at Winston. He looked back. I walked into my bedroom. Winston followed. As I walked around he watched me. I stopped in front of the laundry basket, one of his favorite hiding places.

As I reached into the dirty clothes he wagged his tail. As I dug deeper I heard a crinkle. I felt a wrapper and pulled it out.

"Hah!" I said. Winston barked and wagged his tail.

"One!" I announced.

I went to my closet and started searching again. No reaction from Winston.

I moved to my husband's closet. Winston wagged his tail.

I dug through the basket of clothes for the dry cleaner. No reaction again.

I bent down and starting putting my hands into my husband's size 13 shoes. Tail wag. I found a cookie in a brown loafer.

"Two!" I cheered. Winston barked and wagged his tail.

"Only one more, my little friend," I said, smirking.

Winston was having fun, and so was I.

Winston jumped onto our bed and walked over to my pillow. While wagging his tail, he looked at me and then looked down at my pillow. Again he looked up at me, and again at my pillow.

"You're making this too easy," I said, hands on my hips.

Under my pillow I found the last cookie.

"Three!" I said. "Sorry little buddy. No more cookies for you!"

I went back to the kitchen to stir my pasta again.

I marveled at how Winston, instead of eating all the cookies, took the time to hide them. Wouldn't most dogs simply gobble them all up? And he had hidden them in all his favorite places. It was so cute.

I began to feel a little bad. Winston was having fun until boring, no-fun mom came along. I sighed, took the pot of boiling water off the stove, and headed toward the sink.

I glanced out the kitchen doorway and saw Winston. He was wagging his tail and had another cookie packet hanging out of his mouth.

~Jennifer Quasha

Basset Mound

I named my dog Stay so I can say, "Come here, Stay. Come here, Stay."
~Steven Wright

Growing up in an apartment, I never had the opportunity to have my own dog. Other guys hunted and fished with great dogs, dogs that would point and heel, and lay quietly beside the campfire looking adoringly at their masters.

I often bemoaned the fact that I didn't own a dog, usually whining on the subject at least three or four times a day. I suggested to my parents that it bordered on child abuse to not allow a boy who loved to hunt and fish to own a dog, possibly leading to a life a desperation and crime.

Mom, who seemed to feel that a life of desperation and crime was a given, would with great sympathy tell me, "Enough already! How many times have I told you we can't afford a dog!"

Thus it was, with a sad heart, that I watched my friends train their own hounds to point pheasants, flush grouse, and do everything but pluck and cook their game for them.

I swore that when I was an adult, I would get myself a hunting hound, and that's exactly what I did.

The years passed and I found myself at last visiting kennels in search of my first dog. I convinced Vickie, who had only recently become my wife, that the best possible choice for a family dog was a hound pup.

"Bassett Hounds are great dogs to have around kids, you know,"

I said, "and look how cute they are, with their big paws and floppy ears."

As she cuddled a fuzzy little ball of fur that would soon become my hunting dog, I sensed that my subterfuge had worked. If so, this would prove to be the only time that my subterfuge ever worked on her, as she rapidly developed a near-psychic ability to sense it. Like in, "Enough already! How many time have I told you we can't afford a new truck!"

We paid for the pup, dubbed him Flash, and I gloated silently on the drive home. I was looking forward to bragging to the guys about finally getting a first-class hunting hound.

Unfortunately, I was soon to discover that Flash's ability for subterfuge outclassed even my own. Ten years later, and despite my expert training, Flash showed little interest in pheasant, quail, chukars, or any other species of bird that I hunt—yet he never passed up the opportunity to attack the neighbor's chickens. In fact, he always seemed perturbed that I failed to back up his threats with firepower.

"You drag me all over that mountain looking for stupid grouse, and here's a whole yard full of chickens right here. Shoot one already!"

He would also become enraged at the mere sight of geese, his general attitude toward them suggesting that they used to beat him up at recess and steal his milk money. Now, by golly, it was payback time.

The average goose could have taken Flash with one wing tied behind his back, yet Flash always seemed encouraged by the fact that they would scatter, complaining loudly, at his charge. I suspect that they feared he might be rabid, or perhaps criminally insane. Geese aren't as dumb as we think.

Flash wasn't much of a tracker either. He once got lost in a public campground, in full sight of the family, while tied to the car. My wife has commented that he must have inherited his sense of direction from his "daddy." As neither of us ever knew his sire, I don't know what she's talking about. Flash would amble through the woods, occasionally glancing about for an unsupervised picnic basket, and try to remember what side of a tree moss grows on.

His favorite items for retrieval were flies and lures, and he would launch himself into the water the instant one was cast. For this reason, he spent much of his time tied to a tree in camp. Often several yards up.

What he was most adept at retrieving was food from neighboring campsites, a hobby that often led to great embarrassment and the occasional life-threatening confrontation.

Flash wasn't much of a fishing dog either. One unseasonably warm afternoon, we happened along a stretch of river that teemed with huge, voracious rainbow trout, which were rising with abandon to mayflies.

After several back casts into a wall of blackberry brambles, I finally let go a long, graceful roll cast, gently dropped my fly directly into the path of a gargantuan trout. The fish had been rising steadily, yet the instant the fly touched the water, the bite stopped and the surface of the river became smooth as glass. As I considered what I could have done to spook the fish, I glanced up in time to see Flash grinning happily as he bobbed directly through the feeding lane and into the eddy below.

"Dude," I could almost hear him bark as he paddled by, "come on in, the water feels great!"

Luckily, Flash's favorite hobby was sleeping, which he would do for as much as twenty hours a day, waking only to sound of the electric can opener. He seldom got into serious trouble while asleep, so his laziness became one of his few redeeming features.

Any hike longer than a quick out-and-back to the Dumpster was a death march, and after a mile or so, he would flop on his side and demand to be carried back to the car. People who don't own a Basset Hound seldom understand why you're dragging a limp dog through the woods.

So, although I got my hound dog, I've never had much of a chance to brag about him to my hunting buddies, whose lunches he stole and vehicles he soiled without the slightest semblance of guilt. In fact, they all seemed to form their own opinions of him without any input from me.

"Enough already! How many times have I told you, you can't bring that dog!"

~Perry P. Perkins

Rozzie's Great White Snake

I never make stupid mistakes. Only very, very clever ones.
~John Peel

Ten years ago we brought home a beautiful little German Shepherd puppy we named Roswell, or Rozzie.

One night, when she was about a year old, I came home from work around 9 p.m. As usual I looked outside to make sure she was okay. As I stood by the back door, I noticed that it had gotten much colder—there was a cold draft on my bare feet.

Then I saw it. Roz was lying in the middle of the yard beside a large white snake with a gigantic head! I was puzzled because one, it was December, and two, we don't have large white snakes where we live no matter what the weather.

I grabbed slippers and ran out to save her from this freak of a snake. I carefully approached her only to discover this was no snake. She proudly looked up at me as if to say, "Look at this huge snake I killed all by myself!"

Quickly it became clear where the cold draft on the floor came from. She had removed the dryer vent from the side of the house and pulled out the hose through the wall, along with several pieces of insulation, before "killing" the snake in the back yard.

I tried to be firm and let her know she had done a bad thing but she looked so proud of herself I couldn't help but burst out laughing.

We played a game of "catch the dead snake" before I went inside to cover the hole in the side of the house.

Sometime before spring arrived Rozzie also managed to "kill" the air conditioner by removing the electric wiring—although we didn't find that out until June.

We recently lost Rozzie. I wouldn't trade those repair bills for anything if it meant giving up the love and laughter she brought into our lives.

We will probably get a new puppy when the weather gets warm. I'll set a lawn chair in front of the dryer vent just in case.

~Carol Witmer

The Seven-Year Itch

There is an itch in runners.
~Arnold Hano

Charlie Beagle had a mid-life crisis. He'd always been prone to wander, but when he reached seven years old he couldn't be confined. He was a Houdini hound, and his wanderlust caused a ruckus in our little river town.

Papo, my granddaddy, said that it wasn't Charlie's fault. "I told you not to make that dog into a house dog, baby girl," he said. That had been seven years earlier, when I'd first seen tri-colored Charlie at a breeder's. "He's a hunter. Born to run."

But I'd been sold on Charlie's sweet puppy face, and he was a good match for our family. My husband and I had a houseful of little boys, and we needed a sturdy, strong dog that could hold his own.

"Are you sure he's a Beagle?" my husband asked when Charlie grew.

Charlie's trunk had become broad and round, his soft ears hung low, and after a jaunt in the cornfield behind our house, his paws left mammoth prints on our hardwood floors. "He looks more like a Basset Hound to me."

"I don't know, Lonny," I said. "Doesn't matter. He's great with the boys."

And he was. Charlie was gentle and tolerant of our bevy of boys. He also kept them on their toes with his nose for adventure.

One day three of our sons had erected an army of plastic green soldiers in our living room bay window.

"Where's Charlie Beagle?" I asked when his deep, heavy snore was absent from under the dining table.

"He was right here," Logan said.

"Did anyone open the door?" I asked.

"I did," Logan said. "For a minute. To get the army truck from the porch."

I'd just slipped into my shoes to search the neighborhood when the garbage truck drove around the S-curve in front of our house. It stopped at the end of our drive. As I approached the mammoth truck, I peered up to see Charlie Beagle sitting in the passenger seat, happy as a lark.

"This your Beagle?" the driver shouted through the open window.

"Yes," I said.

"Well, I brought him home," he said. "Followed me all the way down Blackhawk Drive." Then the driver hopped out of the truck, walked to the passenger side, scooped seventy-pound Charlie up, and deposited him at my feet. I was still muttering thanks when the engine started and the truck disappeared.

Charlie licked my ankles. I squatted down and rubbed behind his warm, floppy ears.

"You've got to be careful, Charlie," I said. "You were lucky. It's not safe to chase trucks."

Charlie stood and headed for the house. He was tired and his spot under the table was calling.

We loved Charlie Beagle and gave him a good home. But he couldn't deny his nose, and when he got a good whiff of something interesting, he was off in a shot. It wasn't long before the phone calls started.

One day the call was from a stylist at the salon by the river. "Shawnelle, this is Pat. Charlie was here. He sat by the shampoo bowl and ate a cupcake, and then I sent him home."

Pat was none-too-pleased when Charlie showed up the next day, in pursuit of more cupcakes.

Another day, the barber called. "Charlie's been to the shop. It's closing time and I sent him on his way."

I was shocked. Charlie had just been lounging under the Norway maple in our side yard. How had he escaped the wrought iron fence to visit the barber? I'll never know.

The boys and I thought it was a good idea to help Charlie spend his energy in a positive way. One afternoon, we played fetch with Charlie while we waited for my friend, Nan, to visit. I was far along in pregnancy, and she wanted to check in on us.

We threw the sticky, wet rope toy across the yard and Charlie, lightning fast despite his bulk, retrieved it time and time again. But soon my young son lobbed the toy over the fence. When I creaked the gate open, Charlie bolted out and took off down the road.

When Nan drove past, we were a parade chugging down the street. Charlie was in the lead. I followed, baby belly swaying in front of me. Three little boys were next. Nan parked her car and pounded the pavement to join the procession.

"Charlie Beagle," she shouted. "You stop! You're going to send this girl into labor!"

Charlie's jaunts continued, and each time he returned home, I'd relish the sound of his content snores. More than once I crawled under the table, too, and prayed while I stroked the white fur on his tummy. "Keep him safe, Lord. And please, please keep him home."

I didn't understand Charlie's antics. He was an obedience school graduate, but we just couldn't curb the seven-year itch. We tried an underground fence. Didn't work. I looked deep into his chocolate-syrup eyes and kissed his warm nose and begged him to stay home. Didn't work. I hollered like a wild woman when he ran anyway. Didn't matter.

The most embarrassing Charlie Beagle episode occurred on a humid August afternoon. I listened to Charlie snore, loud enough to shake the walls of our old Victorian, while I tossed a salad for dinner. My boys splashed in our pool, and Lonny puttered in the garage.

The phone rang as I sliced tomatoes.

"Hello. Eliasens," I said.

"You got a dog?" the caller asked.

I was puzzled. "Yes," I said.

"Well, I'm at Dewey's and you'd better get down here. Your dog just ate my hamburger." Then the caller was gone. I stood there and listened to the loud buzz on the other end of the line.

Dewey's? The local bar? No way. Charlie was under the table. But the snoring had stopped. I hung up the phone and peered around the corner. No Charlie.

"Lonny," I called. "You'd better get in here."

Minutes later, Lonny and I walked down to Dewey's. We found a line-up of Harleys parked outside. We also found a large, angry lady dressed in black leather. Lonny apologized profusely, clipped a leash to Charlie's collar, and bought the woman another burger.

I suppose my Papo was right. But despite that darn born-to-be-wild streak, I loved that Beagle right though his mid-life crisis. Even if he did nearly send me headlong into my own.

~Shawnelle Eliasen

Reprinted by permission of Dan Reynolds
and Cartoon Resource © 2009

Ice Cream

Ice cream is happiness condensed.
~Jessi Lane Adams

My family is a Labrador family; we've had four over the years. Four who have all been well loved and spoiled. Out of the four, Dixie, a white-blond Yellow Lab was my best buddy and especially cherished. We got Dixie when I was in second grade, when my mom was dealing with breast cancer and our lives were changing dramatically.

Dixie was comic relief in a sense; she had her hyper moments and her "I want to snuggle" moments. She was always there, with some crazy antic about to happen.

One such afternoon that will always stand out in my memory was when my dad was watching TV in the front room, eating ice cream on the couch.

Dixie, like any good Lab, was sitting at his feet begging. My dad, thinking he was funny, laughed and told Dixie, "If you get your own spoon, you can have some."

My mother was working in the kitchen, unloading the dishwasher, when she heard my dad tell Dixie this. So mom called Dixie into the kitchen, where she placed a spoon in Dixie's mouth. She then told her to go get my dad. My mother stood in the doorway, between the kitchen and front room, watching as Dixie made her way over to my dad. Dixie, wagging her tail, walked over to my dad and sat down.

I am not sure who laughed harder, my mother or dad. Dad gave in as promised and gave Dixie her share of ice cream. She lapped it up, pleased with herself, as my dad continued to laugh.

We lost Dixie when she was thirteen, just after I had started my second year of university. She was a well-loved member of our family, and to this day when our family gets together, the ice cream story is told.

~A.R. Parliament

I Can't Believe My Dog Did That!

Chapter
3

Let's Play Ball

B-A-L-L

Properly trained, a man can be dog's best friend.
~Corey Ford

Rylee, our daughter Nicole's German Shepherd, dropped her soccer ball hopefully at our feet. My husband Doug and I had just gotten our first cups of morning coffee. We had not even made it to the kitchen table before she was begging to play ball.

"It's not even daylight out yet and that dog wants to play…." he said.

"Don't say that word," I interrupted. "You know how nuts it makes her."

Rylee, sensing that we were discussing her favorite activity, grabbed her ball and followed us to our chairs. She once again dropped it at our feet and stared at us with pleading eyes.

"It's the only thing that she wants to do," Doug said, and reached down and scratched Rylee behind her ears.

"Did you notice that Nicole spells it now?" I replied, "She never says that word."

"Wouldn't it be hilarious if Rylee could spell it," Doug said. "Can you imagine how much time Nicole would be spending outside, kicking that B-A-L-L?"

I sat contemplating what Doug had said as he continued to scratch Rylee's head. What if she could learn to recognize that word when it was spelled?

I grabbed the ball. Rylee promptly abandoned her head scratch and went to the door.

"Come here girl," I said. "Want to play B-A-L-L?" I rolled it across the floor. "Go get it." With each return of the ball, I repeated the spelling before sending it off again.

Throughout the day, after Doug had gone to work, I would head to the yard for Rylee's spelling lesson. By late afternoon I was still uncertain that she recognized the spelling, even though we had worked at it on and off for most of the day.

I was kicked back in my recliner when Nicole arrived home from her waitressing job. Rylee greeted her eagerly and then sat patiently beside the sofa while Nicole attempted to take a small nap.

"You look tired," I said. "But you need to go and play with Rylee. She's been bugging me all day to go outside and play with her...."

"Don't say it, Mom," said Nicole, with her arm over her eyes. "I just got home from work and I don't want to play B-A-L-L right now."

When Nicole spelled ball, Rylee went nuts. She searched the house for anything that resembled her favorite toy and came back with a squeaky ball. She nudged Nicole's arm with her nose.

Squeak, squeak, squeak went the ball in Rylee's mouth.

Nicole mumbled, "Not now." Rylee nudged Nicole's arm again. She worked her jaws faster and the squeaking sound of the ball got louder.

Delighted with what I was seeing, I tried hard to keep it out of my voice. "Awww. She wants you to play with her."

Nicole uncovered her eyes and rolled over on her side to face the dog. Rylee, thinking that she was going to get up, started to rush toward the door.

Nicole snapped her fingers. "I don't want to play B-A-L-L. Lie down."

I could not stop laughing. Rylee dropped the ball, pounced on it, then returned to Nicole. Prancing about, ball in mouth, she again nudged Nicole.

"What's gotten into you?" asked an exasperated Nicole.

I could not keep silent any more. "I taught her how to spell today."

"What do you mean you taught her to spell?"

"You know," I replied, gesturing to the ball in Rylee's mouth, "she recognizes what the four-letter word means. You spell it; she'll go and fetch it."

Nicole had a hard time believing me. It wasn't until later that night while the three of us were watching TV that she decided to see what the dog would do.

Rylee was asleep stretched out on the floor. Nicole said, "Rylee, B-A-L-L?"

Rylee got up and started searching the house. She soon found her ball and eagerly came back.

"Looks like I'll have to change the word to 'round thing'," Nicole said as she took the soccer ball from Rylee.

Early the next morning Rylee dropped her ball hopefully at our feet.

"It's not even daylight out yet and that dog wants to play…"

"Don't spell that word," I interrupted. "You know how nuts it makes her."

~Talia Haven

The Tentative Tent

Camping: nature's way of promoting the motel industry.
~Dave Barry, Only Travel Guide You'll Ever Need

Somewhere there has to be a child who doesn't love a tent. And somewhere there probably are albino crows and white elephants. I've never met any of these amazing creatures but I'm willing to keep an open mind.

As my three children were growing up, they were among that vast majority of children who believed a tent to be the ultimate toy. Books, toys, food, pillows, and blankets regularly vanished into these simulated shelters. The family dogs frequently disappeared into the melee as well, often with the only evidence of their presence being a protruding bit of wagging tail.

By the time Steve, Carol, and Joan had reached the ages of nine, ten, and eleven respectively, they'd become obsessed with the idea of actually tenting outdoors. Fortunately two conditions occurred simultaneously that summer that would make their dream a reality. Their end-of-the-year report cards had brought joy to our hearts and my husband Ron and I had managed to squirrel away a bit of money for a reward.

There was such delight when Ron carried the awkward oblong box into our back yard that beautiful July evening! Such scrambling to put it up immediately! Such heartfelt pleas to be allowed to sleep there that very night!

Finally we acquiesced. After all, they would be in our fenced back yard. Furthermore, what point had there been to buying them the tent if we weren't prepared to allow them to enjoy it?

The evening that followed was filled with a constant procession of goods and material (not to mention food and drink) from house to tent until I feared our home would be totally emptied.

At 10 p.m., as soft summer darkness descended over the canvas edifice in the centre of the yard, Ron and I were gently prodded out of our lawn chairs and herded inside. It was time for us to leave them alone.

I whistled to our two dogs, a black Lab named Jet and a Beagle named Brandy to come along. Instantly three indignant faces appeared in the tent's mesh doorway.

"Bran and Jet are sleeping with us!" came the chorus.

Here, a shadow of foreboding wafted over my mind but it was so nebulous, so apparently groundless, I forced myself to brush it aside like a cobweb. But, like a cobweb, bits of it persisted in clinging to my thoughts.

"Come on," Ron said, putting an arm about my shoulders and guiding me into the house. "They'll be fine. We'll leave the back door open, the screen unlatched. If anything goes wrong, they can be inside in a split second. But," he continued quickly catching my concerned glance. "Nothing will. There's not a cloud in the sky, it's a beautiful twenty-five degrees Celsius, and the gate is securely latched."

Try as I might, however, I could not quell those uneasy feelings. Straining to hear any hint of trouble from the yard through our open bedroom window, I lay awake for hours. All I heard were muted voices and giggles, the subdued (on strong parental suggestion) strains of rock music from a boom box, the rustle of snack bags, and the occasional admonition, "Bran, get your nose out of the chips!"

About 1:30 a.m., silence finally descended. I sighed, rolled over, and prepared to sleep.

Then, suddenly out on the lawn there arose such a clatter I sprang from my bed to see what was the matter. The moon on the crest of the birch tree beyond gave a luster of midday to objects on the lawn.

In its illumination I saw the tent pitching and rocking like a thing possessed. Brandy was howling as only a hound can. The screams and cries of my children made my blood run cold. Some horrible creature, human or otherwise, was attacking my darlings, all five of them! Like a tigress in a faded cotton nightgown, I raced out of the house, ready to fight to the death to save them.

I got into the yard just as, accompanied by terrible ripping sounds, Bran burst through a corner of the tent and bolted, baying at the top of his lungs, across the yard. Our neighbour's cat, the cause of the catastrophe, paused a moment on the top of our basket weave fence just long enough to hiss disparagingly down at the frustrated little dog howling and leaping up at her. Then, with a final triumphant yowl of pleasure, she vanished into the night.

Dismayed, I could only stand on the doorstep and watch as children and Lab extricated themselves from the crumpling structure. Beside the gaping hole Bran had made in pursuit of the cat as it had been casually crossing the lawn, the tent's pegs had been ripped from the ground with resultant tears in the cheap canvas to which they'd been attached. Now the entire structure, like a punctured hot air balloon, slowly collapsed until it was only a rumpled pile of weather-resistant cloth on the lawn.

Ron joined me as Carol burst into tears. Bran was still baying, front paws braced against the fence at the point where the cat had disappeared, Joan was desperately trying to find her boom box that, in the confusion, had been knocked into life at full volume, and Steve was spewing a volley of the new experimental swear words that he had just learned from his young friends. The only one that had remained calm throughout was Jet. He'd managed to crawl clear and now stood surveying the chaos, his tail slowly wagging in a confused but amiable manner.

Two hours later Jet and I sat alone in the dining room. His calm in the face of crisis had had a reassuring effect. It was 3 a.m. Bran, the instigator of our "wild party," was once more fast asleep, curled up and forgiven on the end of Steve's bed.

~Gail MacMillan

Operation Donut Binge

Be sweet and honest always, but for God's sake don't eat my doughnuts!
~Emma Bunton

When I graduated from university with my bachelor's degree in psychology, my husband wanted to make sure that my graduation gift was something that I would always cherish. After many years of apartment living, there was one thing that I missed more than anything: owning a dog. But since I was cursed with allergies, we had to look very carefully into what breed would work best in our household.

Every requirement was easily met when I laid eyes upon a sweet-natured Bichon Frise and Affenpinscher cross. When I picked her up for the first time, she tried to crawl into my purse as if to say she chose us as well.

Martini is the most brilliant dog in the world, but we might be more than a little biased. This has always been the best and worst trait in our puppy. If you have ever caught yourself wondering if maybe your dog is a little smarter than you, you know exactly what I am talking about.

Martini's downfall throughout her entire life has been her all-consuming love of food. While her appetite has eased a little since her puppy years, her brilliant brain combined with a constant desire for snacks has proven to be a bad mix.

When we first picked Martini up, we decided to take her to a nearby park to bond with us and have a snack. We were not sure exactly when she had last eaten, but we wanted to make sure that she had enough food in her little belly.

While at the local pet supply store, we were given a simulated sausage treat to feed her. As new pet owners, we asked the store employees just how much we should feed her, given her tiny size.

"No worries, she will stop when she is full. Just keep feeding her until she stops eating," the shopkeeper said. This is not exactly how things worked in reality.

Relaxing in the park, we sat in astonishment as we witnessed our three-pound puppy consume an entire one-pound simulated sausage, and proceed to go for the wrapper, licking her chops in pure bliss.

Before our little foodie turned one, we were met head-on with what happens when you mix a passion for food and scholarly brains in one dog. It started when my husband went to the local donut shop one Sunday afternoon to pick up a dozen of Canada's favourite calorie splurges. We each had one and saved the rest for later.

I woke up the next morning with images of donuts dancing in my head. I was craving the chocolate goodness only to be sorely disappointed as I opened the closed donut box on the counter. All that was left in the box was a single chocolate fondant smudge.

I figured that my husband had eaten every single donut before I woke up. That was weird because my husband does not have a sweet tooth, so I figured ten donuts was an oddly huge and sweet breakfast. I did not want to say anything and sound like a nagging wife. But I really wanted to get my donut fix, so I grumbled all the way back to the donut shop to pick up some replacements.

As I brought my new chocolate-covered prizes home, my husband greeted me at the door to pick out a donut of his own. How much food could he eat? I opened the bakery box for him and through clenched teeth said, "Just one donut for you!" My husband rolled his eyes and replied, "You should talk!"

After a little discussion we realized we both thought that the other had eaten the donuts in question, but we both swore up and down that we were not the culprits. Well this was quite the strange predicament. What happened to the donuts?

Right around this time we noticed that our tiny little dog was unusually quiet and sitting nervously in her kennel. As we crouched down and looked into Martini's castle, we noticed that she seemed to be sitting oddly on a large bulge in her blanket. Upon further inspection we found eight and a half of the missing ten donuts, hidden, mashed and smashed into the blanket. Martini's eyes darted from side to side, silently denying any involvement. There was cream filling and little fondant puppy footprints all over the floor within her kennel, but not a drop, crumb or morsel on the outside where we would have easily noticed.

Somehow my brilliant puppy had found a way to get ten donuts out of a closed container on the counter—with no steps of any sort to help her—transport them one by one into her kennel, and close the donut box to hide her tracks. She got us to blame each other, and her devious plan almost worked. I can imagine her doing this while we were sleeping, complete with suction cups on her little paws, a cape fashioned out of socks and a super-hero mask to conceal her identity.

I still am not sure how she managed this feat. My university degrees and street knowledge don't seem to equal my dog's innate brainpower. Martini is a constant reminder that even if our goals seem lofty and out of reach, with a little determination and cleverness that donut can be ours!

~Kristy Kehler

The Grandbaby March

O, she will sing the savageness out of a bear!
~William Shakespeare

I love my mom. I really do. She is bright, funny, talented, and always there when I need her. Nevertheless, she is not a dog person. It's not that she doesn't like dogs. She's just never lived with one. And most of what she knows about dog training comes from watching television, where any and all canine problems can be solved in half an hour. She doesn't know what it takes to really shape a dog into a well trained, well adjusted, and well exercised family member. And she certainly didn't know what it took in the case of Mythos, my purebred Border Collie.

I love my dog. He is beautiful, strong, spirited, and constantly inspiring. Nevertheless, he is also a one-year-old Border Collie—a breed known for its intelligence, but also for becoming very destructive if that intelligence isn't constantly challenged. In addition, he is a big Border Collie—nearly fifty pounds—who can easily jump six feet in the air and grows stronger and more leanly muscled every day. And while his training is coming along, he is still not 100 percent reliable when it comes to commands like "come" and "stay."

I had never really intended for the two to meet.

I take that back. I had always intended for my mother and my dog to meet. Just not until Mythos was a much older, flawlessly trained dog, with hopefully a few AKC Obedience titles after his name. But right after Mythos's first birthday, I learned that I needed to have a serious abdominal surgery. The doctors were very clear. For at least six weeks after the procedure, I would not be allowed to lift anything heavy, including stubborn, fifty-pound Border Collies. In addition, I would have to stay away from any "strenuous activities." Which left me in something of a fix. Life with a Border Collie is nothing but strenuous activity: training, going for runs, and playing endless games of chase-the-tennis-ball. I didn't want to contemplate what other "games" Mythos would invent to amuse himself if I couldn't keep him busy while I recovered.

My mother didn't understand the problem. Already committed to moving in with me to take care of me after the surgery, she didn't understand why she couldn't just take care of Mythos, too. "He's just a dog, dear," she said on the phone. "How much trouble can he be?"

I nibbled on my nails nervously. "I don't know, Mom," I said. "He's used to a lot of activity."

"Well, I can certainly walk him around the block a few times a day," Mom answered. "Don't worry, dear. It will all work out. You'll see."

I had my doubts—especially since Mythos was listening in on this conversation, wearing a suspicious-looking doggy grin. But I really didn't have a better option, so I agreed.

The first couple of days after my surgery, Mythos was too upset by the amount of pain I was in to leave my side. But as I started recovering, he started pacing and chasing his tail. I knew it was time for my mom to take her "furry grandbaby," as she called him, out for their very first walk together. I carefully demonstrated how to put his training collar on and how to give a leash correction should one be necessary, and sent the two off with a deep feeling of apprehension. This feeling increased to a downright foreboding when the very first thing I heard after the door closed was a sharp "Mythos Barney!" in exactly the same tone my mom used to use to shout my full name when I was little and misbehaving. But apart from a short bark from Mythos I heard nothing more, so I settled in to wait.

They came in about forty minutes later, Mythos trotting through the door with his leash trailing on the floor. He looked quite pleased with himself. My mother looked somewhat less pleased, pink-cheeked and rather strained. She flopped into a chair by the couch with a decidedly grumpy air.

"How did it go?" I asked.

Mom pursed her lips. "That depends on how you look at it," she said. "We made it all the way up the road to your neighbor's corral. We walked around it twice and came back."

"Wow." I was impressed. "That's a long walk, Mom. Are you sure you should have gone so far?"

"It wasn't my idea," Mom answered dryly. "Mythos pulled the leash out of my hand before we even left the front porch." She gave me a rueful smile. "Every time I bent down to pick it up, he'd just prance a little farther ahead, out of my reach. I was terribly worried at first, but he never got more than a few feet ahead of me. And he seemed to know where he was going, so I just followed him."

"Oh dear." It was one of those moments where it was impossible not to laugh. "And when you came back to the house?"

"I opened the front door and he walked right in." My mom looked at Mythos, who had flopped on the floor by my couch, panting happily. "I don't know whether to be mad at him or impressed."

"I often have that same feeling," I said, hiding a smile. "Next time, you'd better get a firmer grip on his leash before you leave."

"Hmmm," my mother said, and went off to get us all some supper.

Unfortunately, the next day's walk didn't go nearly as well. Mom did manage to hold onto Mythos's leash, but that was about the only thing that went right. The moment Mom and Mythos left the house, Mythos turned into a devil dog, pulling and jumping and nipping at Mom's ankles whenever she tried to make him heel.

This state of affairs went on for more than a week. By some great miracle, Mom managed to avoid any serious falls or other accidents, but I knew it would only be a matter of time. I worried myself sick over it, and authorized her to make stronger and stronger physical corrections, but nothing seemed to work. I was on the verge of suggesting she stop trying to walk him altogether.

But then one afternoon Mom came home from Mythos's walk glowing with happiness instead of exhaustion.

"Well!" she said. "Didn't we have a good time? Mythos didn't jump on me once!"

I frowned first at Mythos, then at Mom. It didn't look like aliens had come and taken over either of their bodies, but you could never be sure.

"What did you do?" I asked.

"I sang to him," Mom answered happily. "I started with 'The Stars and Stripes Forever.' Mythos gave me one strange look and then fell right into step. He didn't do very well with the waltzes I tried, but he seems to be a natural with marches. John Philip Sousa, Strauss... if it's got an inspiring 4/4 beat, he loves it." She looked at me anxiously. "You do think it's all right if I sing to him, don't you, dear? You don't think the neighbors will think I've gone crazy?"

I shook my head fondly. "No, Mom," I said. "I don't think they'll think you've gone crazy at all." And that was that.

For the rest of my recovery, Mom would march Mythos around the neighborhood, singing "The Stars and Stripes Forever" at the top of her voice. She gave me a demonstration as soon as I was well enough to leave the house, and I was astonished. Something about the sound and regular rhythm really did focus Mythos's attention, made him watch Mom's every move and move along in step. Mom reminded me that sometimes all it takes is one fresh, fun idea to get things back on track.

And a song in one's heart never hurts, either.

~Kerrie R. Barney

Anything Is Possible

H2O: two parts Heart and one part Obsession.
~Author Unknown

When I married my husband fifteen years ago, I was not a dog person—I was a cat person. I had not grown up with a dog and frankly wasn't terribly fond of dogs. However, my husband was a dog person and very much wanted a Brittany Spaniel like the ones he had grown up with.

So, we saved up all of our change to buy a purebred Brittany. We are now blessed with a fabulous, exuberant, nothing-is-impossible Brittany Spaniel named Sparky. She is seven years old and as energetic as the day she was born. We also have two children ages ten and thirteen.

A couple of summers ago we decided to get a small above-ground pool for the kids. Little did we know how much Sparky would enjoy it. Unfortunately, she spent a lot of time propping herself up on the side of the pool and all the water would drain out. We spent the entire summer refilling the pool. The results were a very high water bill and a really soggy yard.

So, the next summer we decided to get a bigger pool. We bought a pool that has structured walls, is four feet high and eighteen feet across—significantly larger than the previous pool. The pool had a ladder, which was essential for anyone to gain access to the pool. Or so we thought.

We could not have been more wrong. Sparky was determined to

get into that pool. She would take a running start and jump right over the side into the pool. Once in, she swam laps. She just knew she was supposed to be in that pool with the kids.

After our initial shock (and extreme laughter), we realized that she couldn't get herself out. Occasionally neighbors would call me to tell me that Sparky was in the pool and couldn't get out. I'd go out and lift her over the side. Not easy—and not a safe situation for our beloved and determined Sparky.

Our solution? The kids taught her to climb the ladder. With a small assist from them she learned how to climb out, onto the ladder top, and then jump down to the ground. Now, at any time she can get in, and out, of the pool on her own.

It seems that Sparky believes in her right to swim. It's as if it never crossed her mind that she should not swim like the rest of the family. Wouldn't it be great if we all possessed the same level of determination as Sparky? She has been a wonderful role model for the children.

~Diane Helbig

Daffy Dog

Praise the sea; on shore remain.
~John Florio

Gloria was a dog of nondescript origin. If one looked closely her spiky whiskers, one could say Terrier. Further study might reveal a bit of Shepherd. But in terms of body size, leg build, coat type, or any other normal canine species indicator, it was impossible to tell what kind of dog she was. One thing Gloria was not was a water dog. From the day we brought her home, it was clear she was not in any way related to any breed of dog that considered a body of water a wonderful topographical element for play, exercise, or work. Gloria's fear of water was especially unfortunate, and humorous, since we lived on a beautiful cove off the Chesapeake Bay.

We had eagerly taken our new pup out on her first boat ride, certain that she would love the smell of the salty air, the wind flowing through her coat, and the gentle rocking of a boat plowing through yielding waters. However, as soon as our boat pulled away from the pier, Gloria hid under a seat at the back of the boat. She shivered with such terror that we turned around and headed right back to the pier. We abandoned our dreams of owner/canine fishing trips.

In due course, Gloria adapted to her new home and she occasionally walked through the cove's shallow waters to reach our next-door neighbor, who enjoyed Gloria's company. But come time to fire up the boat motor, Gloria would head immediately up the sloped lot and far away from any human notion of a trip on the Bay that would include her.

One day was especially memorable and has gone down in family lore. It was the day Gloria had a run-in with some local waterfowl. Female ducks often laid their eggs on our waterfront lot, and incubated them for up to three weeks. Gloria suffered the ducks fitfully, but left the nesting mallards alone upon command from her human owners.

At some point the ducklings would hatch, large and ready to walk down to the water, and then launch themselves into a swim as directed by their mother. One day, when a new batch of ducklings was ready for its first swim, it was just too much for Gloria. She couldn't ignore the mama duck marching proudly down toward the water, her babies all following behind single file, loud and strong.

Despite our cries for the dog to stay, Gloria jumped up and chased the duck and her hatchlings down to the pier. The duck family quickly jumped into the water before the most amazing thing happened. Gloria jumped in right behind them.

Gloria could not swim a stroke. The ducks, on the other hand, were all quite handy in the art of the swim, even the freshly hatched ducklings.

It would have been sad had it not been so hilarious. For there was Gloria, flop-flopping some kind of variation of the doggie paddle that did little to keep her head above the water.

Mama Duck, meanwhile, did not try to push her youngsters to speed off in all disorganized directions.

Some of the ducklings found themselves close to the flopping dog, but the wise mama duck remained calm, spinning in the water to check her children by slow rotations of her wings in the water. The mother duck noted the dog and the dog's total inability to even stay afloat, much less be any danger to her or her youngsters.

Our entire family ran down to the pier to try to stop any damage to ducklings by an angry dog. As we watched the drama below, there wasn't even time to laugh. While Mama Duck treaded the water, her babies safety behind her wings, Gloria had to be saved. She was gasping and sputtering, her head disappearing frequently under the water.

Her rescue wasn't easy—it involved a net, a docked boat, and long arms, but we managed to rescue the gasping dog. All the while the duck and her family stayed close to watch.

It was only after Gloria lay splat upon the pier, wet and breathing hard, that Mama Duck checked her youngsters, all excited and in single file behind her, and turned to swim off—far away from the silly dog who dared to chase a duck into a duck's element.

Gloria never went into the water, or even near the water, after that. Ducks continued to lay and incubate their eggs on our lot, but they had nothing to fear from our dog.

Gloria watched with wary eye the many hatchlings that marched pass her through the years, content that soon they would be in the water and the insult of their intrusion on her territory would soon be but a distant memory.

~Pat Fish

Reprinted by permission of Dan Reynolds and
Cartoon Resource © 2007

Miss Congeniality

A dog will teach you unconditional love. If you can have that in your life, things won't be too bad.
~Robert Wagner

I had just sat down after a full day of cleaning when the phone rang. New Year's Eve was one night away and although we didn't have any big party plans, I thought it would be nice to start the year off with some semblance of order, no matter how superficial.

I looked at the phone ID. *Restricted.* I knew who would be calling.

"Hi. And who do we have tonight?" I said into the receiver without skipping a beat.

After ten minutes of taking notes, I hung up the phone. My husband Jack looked at me, not bothering to ask who it was. He already knew the answer.

"It's another rescue. I have to go to the shelter to pick her up."

"Okay. I'll get the crate ready just in case," Jack said, already en route to the garage. "What type this time?"

"Shih Tzu," I sighed. "Another little one—named Teeny."

I wasn't surprised to get the call so close to New Year's. The holidays are always stressful and that especially holds true for people already in a volatile situation. For the last year and a half my husband and I had been placing and/or fostering pets through a partnership between OPIN, a local pet rescue, and The Domestic Violence Crisis Center. The program was created to help abused women with pets enter into a safe environment while they work on creating a new, stable life away from their abuser.

Prior to this program, a woman with a pet who was in an abusive situation had to choose between leaving her beloved behind in order to enter the safe house, or stay in the abusive situation in order to protect her pet. Due to housing restrictions, pets are not allowed in the local safe houses.

The problem we had with fostering small dogs like a Bichon or Shih Tzu was Max, our 135-pound Lab-Mastiff. Don't get me wrong. Max was as sweet as can be. Not a mean bone in his body, but he was strong—very strong—and he could play rough. When he ran he sounded like a horse in full gallop.

Max played for hours in the back yard with his sister, Gracie Lou Freebush, our sixty-five-pound Heinz 57. We named Gracie Lou after Sandra Bullock's undercover FBI character in the movie *Miss Congeniality* because she is so good with everyone she meets, people and dogs alike. And like the movie character, she is very protective of any people (or any dogs) she feels cannot protect themselves.

Max and Gracie Lou were as thick as thieves from the day they met. They were always together, eating side by side, walking side by side in the woods with Jack, and sleeping side by side on their bed. I can't remember ever witnessing a moment of aggression between the two.

That was until the small rescues started coming into our home. After the usual introductory period, any dog weighing thirty-five pounds or more was fair game. They could fend for themselves. But, when one of the small ones came, it was as if Gracie Lou went into Mommy Mode. She was on guard at all times to protect the small, displaced and scared.

From the minute that tiny bundle of fur tiptoed into our home Gracie Lou would be the barrier between it and Max. If the tiny bundle got too close to Max, Gracie Lou would bark incessantly. Her back-off warnings were always directed at Max, never at the little one. She would physically place herself between them, protecting a dog that wasn't hers and was often her senior.

That particular winter when we were fostering Teeny was when Max had what we believed was a stroke. He fell and was unable to get up. After physically carrying him to the neurologist, we knew his time was short. We brought him home. When we returned, Gracie Lou somehow knew Max wasn't well and immediately snuggled next to him. Jack and I just watched as she showered him with kisses and groomed him as if to remove the smell of the vet and, along with the scent, any illness.

We were drained and trying to figure out how best to keep Max comfortable when all of a sudden out waltzed Teeny. We had totally forgotten about her. I was just about to run and grab her to prevent any conflict, when Gracie Lou looked up. Leaving Max's side, she moved toward Teeny and then brought her straight to where Max lay. Gracie Lou actually let that little dog lie down next to him. Teeny tucked herself right in between Max's front paws and stomach. Then, Gracie Lou strategically placed herself alongside Max and Teeny. Soon after, the three fell asleep.

This went on for two days. Except to eat and go outside for a stretch the three hunkered down in the living room, huddled together for dear life. The third day Max surprised us all as he lifted himself up and went to the door, signaling that he wanted out.

I ran over and quickly opened the door. We had had so much snow that winter that Jack had shoveled three different size paths for the dogs so we wouldn't lose that tiny white bundle of fur in the snow. This proved helpful for Max, who was still very weak. He was able to lean his way along the snow-lined path for his much needed walk.

When he returned inside, it seemed as if he had gotten a new, albeit temporary, strength and he ate ferociously. He turned from his bowl and started toward his bed for a much-earned rest when all of a sudden out popped Teeny. She was heading straight toward him until Gracie Lou, sensing Max's strength had partly returned, jumped right in between them, setting up a safe distance between the two once again. This time there was no barking, but her mothering status had returned as she placed herself as a buffer between the two during their naps.

When it was time for us to return Teeny to her mom, who had found a new home, Jack and I were sad to see her go. Teeny had proven monumental in the nursing process and she entertained the two of us while we worried about Max's health. Also, Gracie Lou seemed to have adopted a sister.

Teeny's mom was so happy to be getting her baby back. As difficult as it was to return her, we knew that Teeny added a loving stability to this woman's life, a real purpose. As I told her about the events that had unfolded over the past few weeks, she seemed proud that her tiny girl was a part of the nursing process. The expression on the woman's face as her immense bundle of joy ran toward her said it all.

~Jeanne Blandford

Screening Skills

Labradors [are] lousy watchdogs.
They usually bark when there is a stranger about,
but it is an expression of unmitigated joy at the chance to meet somebody new,
not a warning.
~Norman Strung

fter considerable family begging and discussion regarding the "D" word, we all came to the conclusion that our family could responsibly care for a canine. My husband and I chose a breed that would most closely suit our family's personality and decided that we'd start our search at the first of several animal shelters in the area.

At the third shelter, we successfully discovered a medium-sized male Chocolate Black Lab mix named "Duke." This regally named dog was approximately two years old and seemed to have the sweetest disposition. He looked at us through intelligent eyes and already knew how to fetch; he happily retrieved the tennis ball that our seven-year-old son tossed for him and delivered the drool-soaked ball to my son, dropping it at his feet, while my husband and I completed the adoption paperwork.

Just seeing how the two of them got along made me smile and I knew we had made the right choice. Duke seemed to think so too as he tagged along everywhere with our son and quickly fit into our family's busy lifestyle. He took his spot in the passenger seat next to my son on our Jeep/camping trips, and almost instantly became a member of the family. He worked his way quickly into our hearts with his intelligence and antics.

Immediately, as with most things outdoors related, the task of doggie obedience training fell upon my husband's shoulders. Duke took to it, well, like a Labrador to water. He quickly learned the more traditional training and tricks like "sit," "stay," and "come," as well as dog-related manners, and my husband had him housebroken within days.

But there was one skill that Duke could not seem to grasp — that of watchdog. My husband was trying to teach him to alert us when someone came into the yard. He did not want Duke barking at just anyone that walked by our house, but he figured he could teach Duke to "watch" for someone coming onto the property.

His goal was to teach Duke to notify us of company or intruders by giving a single warning bark. Duke would listen attentively to my husband's commands, but would cock his head to one side in confusion and frustration as if to tell his master that he just didn't understand what my husband was asking of him.

My husband would give his "watch" command, and Duke would stand up, muscles rippling in readiness, but would not have a clue as to what he was in readiness for.

One morning we heard the garbage truck stop at the house and the garbage collectors come up the gravel driveway to get our trash. My husband went to the open bedroom window and pulled the curtains back so Duke could hear and see the men through the screen as they took care of their business.

"Watch!" my husband commanded.

Duke rose up in readiness, looked at my husband as sudden doggie comprehension dawned, gave a quick tail wag, and promptly leapt through the window screen, prancing happily out to greet the garbage men, his tail wagging his whole body.

My hysterical gales of laughter did nothing for my husband's mood as he retrieved our Retriever and was then tasked with bedroom window screen repair. He ultimately had to put up with his wife's giggles each and every time I thought about how Duke learned that day to leap through windows in a single bound.

~Victoria Radford

Wake-up Call

I wonder what goes through his mind when he sees us peeing in his water bowl.
~Penny Ward Moser

It was early in the morning.
I was half asleep, no doubt.
I hadn't had my coffee.
The dog had not gone out.
At the bottom of the stairs,
I had left the gate undone.
Instead of staying with me,
Aspen sniffed out some new fun.
She dashed into our room,
and found her Daddy Dear,
saw him sleeping in his bed,
jumped high onto his rear,
grew more and more excited,
went rushing toward his head,
then peed upon his face
(won't repeat what Daddy said)
Aspen heard an earful,
but I bet that I heard more.
Now taking out that dog
is my most important chore!

~Kathleen Whitman Plucker

Touché

*If you think dogs can't count, try putting three dog biscuits in your pocket
and then giving Fido only two of them.*

~Phil Pastoret

n article on animal behavior sparked an argument with a
friend over how much—or even if—animals can think.
"Chimpanzees do," he conceded. "But dogs and cats?
Forget it."

"Yes, they can," I countered.

To which he replied, "Prove it."

That stopped me. I pointed out how quickly my two dogs—Inky,
a Heinz 57 variety Terrier, and Lucky, a Beagle and heaven-only-
knows-what mix—had learned to sit, speak, play catch and tug-of-
war with a rope. He said smugly, "That's just rote behavior. Any dog
can do that."

He had won the argument, but that didn't mean I'd changed my
mind. If only I had some way of proving it. But how could I do that?

I was still thinking about it a few days later when, as usual, I
settled down after breakfast to read my newspaper. Both dogs consider sitting on my lap their idea of heaven on earth. Since I have only
one lap, no sooner do I head for the couch or a chair than the race is
on to see which one claims the coveted spot. Inky's short legs versus
Lucky's longer ones mean she loses out more often than not.

"Atta girl," I said, delighted when she won by a nose this time.
Lucky watched her snuggle in my lap, then ran to the patio door and

began barking furiously. Inky's ears perked up. Seconds later, curiosity won over comfort. Down she jumped and raced over to check out the commotion, whereupon Lucky wheeled around and leaped onto my empty lap. From where I sat, I had a full view of the back yard. There'd been nothing out there to bark at.

I couldn't wait to tell my friend I was right. Dogs really are smarter than we give them credit for. He may not believe me, but I saw it with my own eyes.

~Marilyn Jensen

Rock Around the Clock

The first rule in successful dog training is to be smarter than the dog.
Which is why some breeds are easier to train than others.
~Author Unknown

Many of us pet parents accept the fact that our dogs are smarter than we are. It's just when our dogs rub our noses in it that it gets a tad irritating—and embarrassing. Such was the case for me one spring day when I learned how much smarter my dog was than I.

Buster von Baer was a very energetic and intelligent Boston Terrier—and spoiled. He had his own personal doggie door on the porch that allowed him to go outside to his fenced-in yard, where my husband and I, unfortunately, had used white rock for landscaping.

From the moment he arrived, Mr. Buster never found a rock that he couldn't chew. And he learned at a very young age, that, if he brought a rock into the house, Mama would chase him to retrieve it. It was especially fun for him to run in circles around the loveseat, which sits in the middle of our living room. Also, being the considerate dog that he was, Mr. Buster always made sure I saw the rock in his mouth—no hiding it from his mama. Suffice to say, I had lots of exercise on the "rock merry-go-round." Some days this was just so cute. Other days—well, this story is about one of those "other" days.

It was a beautiful spring afternoon and Mr. Buster was outside enjoying the sunshine. I was inside doing paperwork at the kitchen table. When I heard the familiar flap-flap of the doggie door and then the pitter-patter of little doggie feet on the linoleum porch floor, I knew Mr. Buster was ready to come into the kitchen. Being in the middle of something, I didn't rush to open the kitchen door for him. Then, I heard a tap-tap at the door. I knew that sound. Mr. Buster was knocking on the door with a rock in his mouth.

When I opened the kitchen door, there stood Mr. Buster. He looked up at me with a doggie grin and a white rock sticking out of his mouth. I was busy and in no mood to ride the rock merry-go-round, so I attempted to grab the rock before he could enter the room. But he quickly turned and hightailed it out the doggie door before I could grab him. I headed back toward the kitchen and had taken only a couple of steps when I heard flap-flap, pitter-patter.

I turned around and there he stood on the porch, grinning at me, again showing me the rock in his mouth. I tried to grab the rock, but he escaped one more time through the doggie door. No sooner had I turned around to go back to the kitchen than I heard—flap-flap, pitter-patter. We repeated this routine several times until my patience wore thin.

I decided to stand guard at the doggie door for several minutes, but he didn't come back in. I ventured a quick peek through the blinds on the window above the doggie door and saw Mr. Buster nose-deep in the rocks in his yard.

Peace at last. I thought he would be happy outside for a while.

I returned to the kitchen table and my paperwork. A few minutes later I heard flap-flap, pitter-patter, and then, silence. No tap-tap. I waited. Nothing. Tiring quickly of the waiting game, I went to the door. There he stood, looking up at me, grinning, and showing me the rock in his mouth. I gave him my sternest look and reached down to grab that rock. Mr. Buster just stood there like a perfect little gentleman and let me take the rock ever so easily from his mouth.

Wow! I needed to practice that look more often. He had given up his rock so easily!

I walked past him onto the porch and threw the rock out the

back door into the ever-growing rock pile on the other side of his fence. As I was doing that, I heard him peel off the porch linoleum like a car squealing its tires, entering the house at warp speed—exactly what he does when he takes something forbidden into the house.

What in the world? I could not imagine what was going on. After all, he had just given me his rock.

I found Mr. Buster stretched out by the loveseat. He gazed up at me with an adorable look on his face—and grinned. There in his mouth was another rock! The little scoundrel was smart enough to pick up two rocks, give me one and keep the other.

So, once again, I had to get on the rock merry-go-round and chase him to get the rock. Well, that was after I quit laughing and the tears had stopped rolling down my face.

~Linda Cox

I Can't Believe My Dog Did That!

Chapter 4

Barking Mad

My Boys' Choir

Some days there won't be a song in your heart.
Sing anyway.
~Emory Austin

I t was too lazy a day to do much. Even the birds were quiet. Trees whispered in the slow breeze from a cloudless summer sky. I strolled through my dining room, enjoying the gloriously quiet day. As I passed the arched window, I noticed my motley group of four male dogs lounging in the grass. They looked as lazy as I felt that day.

Sualty must have heard me in the house because he sauntered over to his wind chime and sat down, stuck his nose up in the middle of the chimes, and proceeded to knock them about. As they tinkled, he added his soul-filled song.

Like the Pied Piper, our Yellow Labrador Retriever, the only dog we truly owned, frequently played his wind chimes and sang in hopes that someone would come to the front door and let him inside.

However, that day I remained rooted in the shadows of my dining room.

Sualty ended his doleful stanza and checked to see if his plea had been heard. Nothing. He batted the chimes yet again and began a second verse.

Not more than ten feet away from Sualty lay Sir Thomas Brutus, a Labrador-Doberman Pinscher mix. Sir Tom belonged to the neighbors south of us. Some years ago, he decided to not only visit us but move in permanently.

Sir Tom rose up from the grass, lifted his regal black nose skyward. With eyes half closed, he released his own deep-throated mournful harmony to Sualty's ballad.

Barely three feet from Sir Tom lay Smiley, a longhaired, German Shepherd- Alaskan Malamute mix.

I will never forget the day he decided to join this group. I was out in the yard when Smiley came galumphing up the hill, tail wagging, eyes sparkling, ears perked, and greeting me as he does everyone, "snarling" every bit like Stephen King's Cugo.

That afternoon, Smiley simply lifted his furry head and added the haunting sounds of ancient wolves that once sat on Alaska's frozen tundra.

The day Smiley joined our family, he also brought along a young pup named Chico. Chico was a true Heinz 57 dog because he came with the purple tongue of a Chow, one blue eye, one brown eye, and the markings of a Siberian Husky with short hair. He still had the adolescence of youth because he was the neighborhood thief. He stole single tennis shoes, bowls of every kind, and gloves that never matched. He would leave them on our front porch so I would look like the guilty party. He was an imp.

Chico stood there gazing at this ongoing serenade with awe and wonder. In his young life, he had never sung. Could he? Should he? From the admiration in his eyes, I could see he wanted to. Oh, yes, he wanted to sing.

With a blink, Chico lifted his silverish nose to the heavens and added the crooning sound of… flat bagpipes. It was awful.

Three melodies and one tone-deaf bag of air.

Moments later, Sualty checked the front door one last time and finally gave up tinkling his chimes. Sir Tom and Smiley melted gloriously back to the grass as content as angels. Chico sat, triumphant and proud after assisting.

I wiped tears of laughter from my eyes, feeling ever blessed for this moment.

~J.F. Ridgley

Do Not
Machine Wash

Long live your laundry!
~Billy Mays

In most respects, Heidi, our first Shetland Sheepdog, was a great addition to our family. In a flash of tan-and-white fur, she would zigzag around the yard to demonstrate her herding abilities to us children. She was obedient and loyal, playful and loving. Never did I have a bad day without Heidi tottering over to stare up at me with sympathetic eyes.

But Heidi was far from perfect. New shoes, stuffed animals, plastic action figures, in her mind, were all chew toys. We couldn't even leave our school bags unzipped. My mother once had to write a note to my teacher explaining that our dog actually did eat my homework.

Heidi would dig through trashcans, eat bath soap, and rip open packaged foods. Once we left the dining room to answer the doorbell only to find a whole stick of butter missing from the table when we returned. So for her safety and our sanity, Heidi stayed in the laundry room when we left the house.

Our laundry room was a decent size—about twenty feet of hallway. There was ample room for a full-size washer and dryer next to the door leading out to the garage. Above the washer and dryer was a window, and beyond the cream-colored curtains and horizontal blinds was a view of our side yard. Because we lived in a humid climate, we always kept the washing machine's top-loading lid open when it wasn't in use.

I'll never forget the day my mother and I came home after an afternoon of running errands. I don't remember who entered first, but I know we both froze when the laundry room door opened.

Heidi greeted us from the washing machine. Her head, the only part of her visible above the top of the washer, popped up and gave us a pitiful look. The rest of her body was wrapped around the agitator.

"How the..." Mom's jaw dropped, and she quickly set her grocery bags down.

After determining that the only thing hurt was our dog's pride, laughter spilled out of both of us. Our dog was trapped in the washing machine. By the time we managed to free Heidi, tears streamed down our cheeks.

To this day, we're not sure how Heidi managed to leap so high. Maybe a squirrel dashed across the window screen or an insect crawled on the ceiling. Whatever the case, Heidi's collar needed to be updated with a new tag: Do not machine wash.

~Stephanie Winkelhake

Taking Care
of Business

You can avoid having ulcers by adapting to the situation:
If you fall in the mud puddle, check your pockets for fish.
~Author Unknown

Mornings are a busy time in our family. My husband and I wake up each morning and set about on our different tracks — his to shower and get ready for work, and mine to get the family up, fed and out the door to wherever they happen to be going.

We have two kids, a nine-year-old daughter and a six-year-old son. We also have two dogs, a fifteen-year old Bichon Frise named Scout and an adopted Beagle named Sugar, who is around three years old. I never set out to adopt a Beagle, but we fell in love with her when we fostered her, and we couldn't bear to give her up.

The problem with Beagles, I have learned since the adoption, is that they run away, especially if you border five acres of woods, which we do. Sugar needs to be walked on a leash, not simply let out. Despite our fenced-in back yard, Sugar can escape before you have time to blink, and coming back is not her forte.

Getting the dogs out the back door to do their business is often a production since the dogs are working at different speeds. Sugar is raring to go. When I grab her extendable leash, she wags her tail and dances around my ankles.

Scout, at fifteen, is a little different. We're not sure how blind and deaf he is, but it's not total. If you yell in his general direction he cocks his head like he might have heard something. His eyes are worse. They have gone from black to cloudy blue.

When it is time to go out and we are near the door, Scout always gets bonked by the irrepressible Sugar. However, it's calm once we get outside. Scout is off leash and has his usual spots where he routinely does his business. He's like a slow-motion boomerang. He goes out full and comes back empty. For all his old-age troubles, he's very consistent when he is let out.

This past summer was particularly crazy because, after four and a half years of trying to get our town to agree to let us connect to the town sewer that ran down our road, they were finally letting us.

Since having a sewer would let us add a bedroom onto our small three-bedroom ranch, this was very exciting news. But it also entailed digging a four-foot-deep trench from the road, down our driveway, and around the back of the house. And, it also meant workmen, kids playing in large piles of displaced dirt, a ruined backyard garden, a deep trench to bury pipes, and big machinery everywhere.

One day after "the sewer project" had just begun, the kids and I had arrived home from their first day at a new camp. We were later than usual, which meant the dogs really needed to go out—especially poor old Scout with his aging bladder.

It was the first time we had all seen our driveway completely torn up, with a digger and a mini-dozer going strong.

Since my normal access to the house was blocked, we had to leave our car on the street, walk up the driveway, and carry everything in. This led to complaints from the kids, of course. Hot, tired, and hungry, no one wanted to carry their own camp bags, not to mention the groceries.

When I walked into the house I noticed that the back yard also had a deep trench going through it. Wow, it sure didn't take long to destroy things.

As usual, my kids were grumbling, the dogs were barking in their cages, and my arms were laden. I dropped the bags in the mudroom, unlocked the dogs' cages, leashed Sugar up, and headed to the back door. I heard the kids rummaging through the fridge, and I yelled at them to wait for me to make them lunch.

"You're going to ruin your appetites," I yelled.

I opened the sliding back door and Sugar tore out after a chipmunk, only to be held back by the retractable leash.

"Sugar!" I yelled after her as she almost dislocated my shoulder.

Sugar had to wait for Scout to slowly, almost blindly, work his way out the door, and down our house's one step to the patio. Then I needed to close the heavy, sliding glass door behind us. Finally Scout made it, I closed the door, and followed Sugar.

I suddenly realized that it was a little stinky—they had had to dig the trench through our old septic system's leaching field to lay pipe for the sewer.

Lovely. I watched carefully where I stepped, finally getting to nice green grass away from our house.

Sugar and I completed our regular loop and started back toward the door. I scanned the yard for Scout but I didn't see him.

Where on earth could Scout have gone?

"Oh my God," I said out loud.

I ran to the sewer line trench, which I hadn't noticed had been cut right in front of where Scout usually did his business.

When I looked in, Scout was standing four feet below me, up to his belly in septic sludge, turning around and around, wondering how the heck to get out.

It took me a moment to process what was right there in front of me. I quickly went through the stages of grief: shock, denial, guilt, anger, bargaining, and finally acceptance.

"There's only one way out, Scout," I said from above. "And here I come."

~Jennifer Quasha

The Christmas Surprise

At Christmas, all roads lead home.
~Marjorie Holmes

hristmas day is always crazy at my in-laws' house. Gran and Pops McClanahan have four adult children: three sons and a daughter. All have married and together they have produced ten grandchildren—seven boys and three girls, ages twelve and below. I married their youngest son, Sam.

In the summers and at Christmas we all gather, driving from our various homes on the East Coast, to spend time together at Gran and Pops' nine-bedroom summer house in Narragansett, Rhode Island. Although it's a large house, twenty people make it feel smaller, create sporadic "sleeping" schedules, and usually offer grab-what-you-can eating arrangements. I am often reminded of the "Old Woman in the Shoe" nursery rhyme where "she had so many children she didn't know what to do."

But as unruly it is for the adults, it is a blast for all the little cousins, and at Christmastime it's double the fun. The cousins have often not seen each other since summer and Santa is coming too!

Unlike some families, the McClanahans don't draw a single name out of a hat so each person only has to buy a single holiday gift—no, each family buys gifts for every other person. Gran and Pops love the over-the-top merriment.

Surprisingly, despite our five families, the McClanahans as a group only acquired one dog, a large Yellow Lab with a square mug named Rumbo, a resident of New Canaan, Connecticut with Gran and Pops most of the time. Rumbo was once considered my husband Sam's dog, since Sam was the one who spent the summer raising and training him back when he was a pup; but with our growing brood Rumbo officially moved to Gran and Pops' place, with us remaining occasional dog-sitters since we live nearby.

Two years ago, Christmas in Narragansett was like the previous ones—the kids were another year older, they still had boundless energy, and the promise of Santa energized them even more. Rumbo also had gotten older. He was nine and arthritic. He would wander around wagging his tail looking for a pat, but he spent most of his time away from the chaos of fast-moving children, snuggled in his well-worn dog bed.

That Christmas Eve we, not Gran and Pops, had brought Rumbo up from Connecticut. When we arrived and started to unpack I tossed Rumbo's dog bed under the huge, beautifully decorated Christmas tree. He looked the picture of doggie adorableness under the twinkling lights and ornaments, his large mug resting on the edge of his dog bed looking out at us.

By that evening all the other families had arrived, one by one, unloading more bedlam into the house. As the presents were added under the tree, Rumbo's bed shifted, but we all lavished him with a tummy rub and a quick snuggle as we scooted him this way and that. Giving us his normal "smile" and wag, he didn't seem to mind.

That evening we had a festive dinner, and after the cleanup, Gran let Rumbo out. We all went to bed, knowing we'd be up again in a few hours.

Indeed, at 5:30 the first of the kids awoke. One by one, the eager children herded their parents downstairs. Over the next few hours, seemingly hundreds of presents were torn open. Long-desired toys magically appeared, somewhat useless household items were passed among the parents, and laughter could be heard sprinkled between

Christmas carols being played on someone's laptop. Paper and discarded wrappings were everywhere.

As I scanned the chaos I noticed Rumbo lying in his dog bed, wrapping paper scattered all around it. It was the first time I had focused on Rumbo since I had woken up, and I decided to give the guy a Christmas rub. As I walked toward him I wondered if anyone had remembered to feed him or let him out that morning. I didn't remember seeing him outside.

His eyes were open and I knelt down in front of him and pet his head.

"Merry Christmas, Rumbo!" I said, giving him a scratch.

Rumbo's eyes and mouth were open, and his long tongue was hanging out, but he didn't move. Suddenly I noticed that he felt sort of cold. As I looked into his unmoving eyes and held their vacant gaze, I realized that Rumbo… was dead.

"OMG!" I wanted to text somebody. What the heck was I supposed to do?

I knelt in front of him, blocking him from the rest of the room, as my brain went into panic mode. It was Christmas morning. I was in a room full of children and there was a dead dog under the Christmas tree. I touched his leg—yes, it was stiff, and rigor mortis had set in.

I actually laughed. I realized that it was a perfect McClanahan Christmas moment. Most people find squirming puppies under their tree, but here at the McClanahans… it's a little different. You always had to think on your feet around here.

I quickly deduced that this was a job for my husband—a "real" McClanahan. I stood up, casually pulled my husband aside, and gave him the facts. Word traveled fast through the adults. Each in turn looked over at the Christmas tree and saw Rumbo "asleep" underneath it.

I had recovered enough from the shock to ponder the details: Where does one take a deceased dog on Christmas? What happens when your vet lives three hours away? Who do you call? And then, how do you sneak a dead 120-pound dog out of a house full of ten children? If we chose to leave him where he was, when would one of the kids notice that Rumbo wasn't moving, or go over to pat him as I did?

Well, it turned out to be surprisingly easy. Each mom gathered her own brood to go do something "exciting" away from the family room, and the four dads got to work lifting the awkward, stiff dog, still in his dog bed, and placing him in the back of Pops' pickup truck. Someone grabbed a blanket and gently covered him.

And there Rumbo stayed on Christmas day, out in the fresh Rhode Island air.

It was a while before it occurred to one of the kids to wonder where Rumbo was. As a group we had decided not to tell them until Christmas was over. Our stock answer was to be "I don't know," which is normal since people never know where anyone else is in that house.

It certainly wasn't an easy decision to leave Rumbo outside, in the back of a pickup truck, on Christmas, of all days, but we told ourselves that our options were limited. We were sure that Rumbo—the kindest, and most gentle dog in the whole world—had joined Santa on his sleigh, and together they were finishing up the rest of Santa's Christmas deliveries.

~Claire Field

Picky, Picky, Picky

Research tells us fourteen out of any ten individuals likes chocolate.
~Sandra Boynton

"He prefers the 'yeh-yo' ones," said my mother, tossing another yellow M&M to our little black cocka-pomma-peeka-poo mix, Brudy.

"Yeh-yo?" I asked.

"Brudy can't say his ells berry well."

"Huh?"

Mom laughed. "When I talk to Brudy, I have to talk in Brudy-talk."

"So he can't say his 'Ls' very well?"

"Right," said Mom. "And he's not so good at 'Vs' either."

She tossed him a red M&M, and he left it right where it fell in the green shag carpeting, but he gobbled up the yellow one she followed with.

"See what I mean? He yikes yeh-yo the berry best, don't you?" she asked Brudy.

It was before we learned that chocolate was not good for dogs, and since our curly-tailed companion always wanted to eat whatever we were eating, we naturally shared our candy.

At the time, we also thought dogs were colorblind. Today, we know they have fewer cone cells in their retina and see only two primary colors—blue and yellow.

"Can I have some M&M's?" I asked.

"May I?" corrected Mom.

"Okay, fine," I said and sat down on the couch next to her. "May I have some M&M's?" and I held out my hand.

"You can have the ones he's missed," said Mom, clutching the bag tight to her chest.

"You want me to hunt around in the carpet looking for them?"

"Someone has to pick them up," she said, "so it might as well be you."

Brudy sat at her feet, wagging his tail and wriggling all over in anticipation. I got down on the floor on my hands and knees.

"Come on Bruds, let's use that nose of yours," I said.

Brudy tilted his head as if to say "Nose? What are you talking about?"

I started making sniffing sounds and crawled over to a green M&M. "Like this, see?"

He cocked his head in the other direction.

I handed him the green candy. He took it into his mouth, rolled it around a bit, and spat it back out.

Mother howled with delight. "See, I told you! He only likes the yeh-yo ones!"

I sat on the floor next to him and tried to figure out exactly why he'd done that, but he never told.

~Jan Bono

Under the Table

A dog desires more affection than his dinner. — Well, almost!
~Charlotte Gray

Oreo slunk into the house, trying her best to be inconspicuous. Not an easy feat for a full-grown Dalmatian. She seemed to have a stick or some other treasure in her mouth. I was in the kitchen making meat sauce for that night's dinner so I didn't pay much attention as I opened the door to let her in. The area surrounding our house was wooded, and Oreo often brought some of the outside inside.

I finished the sauce, did some laundry and finished a few other things in the house that I needed to do, then left to pick the girls up from school.

"Where's Oreo?" asked Andee, my younger daughter, as we walked into the house. Oreo always greeted everyone with abundant enthusiasm, especially the girls.

"I don't know," I said, realizing that I hadn't seen her since I'd let her in the house earlier that day. "Do you girls want a snack before soccer practice?"

I grabbed some cheese and milk from the fridge, and began opening a package of crackers. Still no Oreo. Food was always an incentive, as if our extremely social dog needed an incentive to be with our family.

"If you girls start eating, I'm sure Oreo will find you," I said.

Andee finished her snack, and still no Oreo. Andee left the kitchen to look for the dog, returning a few minutes later.

"I've looked everywhere, even my room, and I can't find her," Andee said.

She headed to the jar on the counter that held Oreo's treats.

"Oreo, come!" she called, shaking the jar and listening for the click of Oreo's paws on our wood floors. Silence. Andee continued her search. Suddenly, she came running into the kitchen.

"Oreo's under the dining room table. She won't come out, and she growled at me!"

Oreo had been part of our family longer than Andee, now six. Oreo devoured shoes, chewed heads off Fisher-Price little people, and shredded stuffed animals to bits, but she didn't growl.

As babies, the girls pulled her tail, sat on her like a pony, even took food out of her mouth. But Oreo did not growl.

We all went to the dining room. "Stay back," I warned the girls. "Don't get too close until I see what's going on."

Oreo was curled up, head raised, eyes on alert. As I bent down to get closer, she growled. A soft, gentle growl, but definitely a growl.

"Let's leave her alone for a while," I said, ushering them back into the kitchen to start homework before they got picked up for soccer practice.

"See you at 5:30. It's my turn to pick up," I reminded them as the carpool driver honked.

After the girls left, I went back to the dining room. Crouching down, just inside the doorway, I had a perfect view of Oreo. She seemed calmer, but was licking her front paws. I wondered if she was injured. That might explain the growling.

I stood up and moved towards her. I heard it again. That soft, gentle growl. She seemed to be saying, "I won't bite you. I'm just letting you know I don't want you to come any closer."

I retreated and left her to her paw licking. I set the table for dinner, filled a pot with water so I could boil the spaghetti when I got home and left to pick up the girls.

When we got home, the house was eerily quiet. No barking, yip-ping, jumping, delighted-you're-finally-home dog to greet us.

"Oreo's still under the dining room table and won't come out," Andee called.

I got out Oreo's bowl, and poured in her dog food. She didn't budge. Bowl of food in hand, I tried coaxing her out. She growled. The soft, gentle growl that now said, "I don't want to keep growling at you, so please leave me alone."

This was not our dog. I sent the girls upstairs to play. I went back to the dining room with a piece of hamburger left over from last night's dinner. I turned on the light to get a better look. Oreo was still licking. In the light, it looked more like she was licking a rock, or something similar, not her paws.

I held out the hamburger. The temptation was too much. Oreo stopped licking, put the object of her licking in her mouth gingerly, and slowly got up. Hamburger meat dangling in front of her nose, I led her to her bowl and dropped the hamburger into it. Then moved back to give her space.

She hesitated, not sure what to do. She wanted her food, but didn't want to let go of her treasure. Finally, very carefully, she placed the object she had been carrying in her mouth next to her dish, and began to eat.

Next to her dish, a terrified turtle remained tight in its shell.

I knew to stay away, but was also relieved to know Oreo wasn't hurt.

Oreo finished eating and gently picked up the turtle. Still holding it in her mouth, she scratched at the door to go out. She did what she needed to do, scratched to come in and returned to the dining room table.

By early evening, trusting us to stay our distance, she was ready to show off her new "pup." Turtle in her mouth, she paraded around the house, much to the girls' delight.

"Can we keep the turtle, too?" Andee asked.

The girls reluctantly went upstairs to get ready for bed. Oreo retreated to her spot under the dining room table.

After everyone had settled in for the night, I peeked into the dining room. Oreo was sound asleep, and must've been for some time, because the turtle had poked out its head and all four legs. I watched. Slowly, the turtle was able to make its way over Oreo's front paws. A few minutes longer and it would be far enough away for me to grab it without waking the dog.

Finally, success! Turtle in hand, I walked outside to my neighbor's pond and returned the turtle to its home, hoping that it would stay away from our yard and out of harm's way.

Time passed. Oreo passed. Our second Dalmatian, Dots, joined our family. A move took us from Georgia to Connecticut.

New state. New home. New dog.

Same dining room rug. Same dining room table.

New turtle!

It had been almost ten years since the first turtle escapade. I couldn't believe my eyes as Dots slunk into the house, trying her best to be inconspicuous, and headed straight for the dining room table.

But this time I knew to leave her be, let her enjoy her "pup," and rescue the terrified turtle at the first opportunity.

I couldn't believe both my dogs did that!

~Carol A. Boas

Passive Patch

The most important thing in communication is to hear what isn't being said.
~Peter F. Drucker

We bought our dog Patch from the county pound for fifteen dollars. He was the runt of the litter, and when we first saw him his siblings were chewing off his tail. Patch just stood there and let them, without a fight or even a bark.

His passivity grew. Dogs would venture into our yard and steal his food and water bowls, carrying them off to their own yards, and Patch sat there quietly, letting them rob him without a bark. Birds sat on his back and he didn't bark or even move. The mailman delivered mail to our home daily and found Patch to be the most lifeless dog he had ever known. I carried Patch to our vet, thinking he had a hormonal imbalance, or laryngitis. The vet said he was fine, just quiet natured.

One day I came home from work and two strange men were in our yard playing basketball while Patch lay on the driveway, watching them, without a bark. After the men left, I got on all fours and tried to teach him how to bark, barking at the cars passing by as any normal dog might do. My neighbors shut their blinds. The sight of a grown woman outside barking was not pleasant. They feared I might demonstrate proper fire hydrant etiquette next.

We guessed that Patch was just a shy dog, reserved and not given to much emotion, but he never caused us any problems and was loving and obedient. The fact that he never barked was just unusual, and we soon learned to accept his nature.

Then we moved to the beach. We had visions of playing catch with him in the waves that gently covered our feet. We longed for walks on the sandy shores with our beloved dog. But Patch had other visions.

When he was fifteen years old Patch saw the beach for the very first time. As soon as he saw the waves and the seagulls, and heard the sounds of the ocean, he barked. And barked and barked and barked and barked. We could not hush him. It was as if he had saved every bark of his entire life for the beach.

Barking at the ocean brought him to life. He stood tall and proud, strong and surreal, mustering up a deep voice of command, ordering the waves to stop their foaming, and demanding calm and stillness from the wind and birds that flocked above him. He barked as loudly as any dog could, even to the point of howling.

The first time I heard it I laughed. I was astonished. My dog barked. What a treat to hear him bark, to know he had the power to protect and defend.

I called my husband to let him hear Patch barking over the phone. It was as if our firstborn had uttered her first words. We laughed together and celebrated Patch's newfound voice.

Patch still doesn't want to walk on the ocean's shores or play catch in its waves, but he loves going to the beach to bark. It's like he is telling the waters his troubles and expressing his feelings, and showing us he knew how to bark all along.

~Malinda Dunlap Fillingim

Call of the Wild

The meeting of two personalities is like the contact of two chemical sub-stances: if there is any reaction, both are transformed.
~Carl Jung

The promise of spring filled the air as we parked our faded red truck in front of my friend's rustic cabin in Flagstaff, Arizona. The melted snow left patches of mucky earth.

My five-year-old daughter Kimberly dodged the mud and raced to the back yard to pick out the puppy she had been promised. There she found it in a large cardboard box squirming amongst its canine brothers and sisters. She was the best of the litter—frisky, sweet, and beautiful. The owner placed the puppy into Kimmie's arms. It was love at first sight. Kimmie enveloped her newfound friend and rocked her back and forth. Together, we stroked her soft coat. It was the color of vanilla ice cream. The reddish markings on her tail and ears accented her cream-colored fur. As I gazed into the pup's eyes, I noticed her eyelashes were extraordinarily long and reddish blond. Since I had been separated from Kimmie's dad, we needed to fill the void. A new member of the family was just the ticket for our recovery.

At the time, I was reading Shakespeare's *The Taming of the Shrew*, so I named the pup Katie after his character, Katherina, the shrew. I gave Kimmie the responsibility of raising this fluffy bundle of joy. Today, she tells me that this was the beginning of her desire to become a veterinarian. They spent every available minute playing together.

After a long day at work, I often found the inseparable duo fast asleep nestled together on the couch.

As a pup, Katie loved to chew on Kimmie's stuffed animals. From the living room, I could hear seams tearing and saw stuffing wafting through the air as Katie made short order of one of Kim's furry companions. She was a well-read dog; the corners of most of my books sported her teeth marks. Katie grew to be a fine specimen of canine perfection from all the nurturing we gave her.

When we moved south from Flagstaff to the warmer climate of Rimrock, we all had to adjust to the weather and location. Katie adapted quickly because she sensed a new freedom. She no longer needed to be strapped to a harness and leash every time she wanted to go outside. She no longer had to spend hours in a cramped apartment. She was truly free! We were truly free!

We took long morning hikes in the wilderness; the pungent smell of the creosote bushes and fragrant lupine filled the air as we strode into the open area behind our house. Avoiding the scratchy mesquite and prickly jumping cholla, we made our way through the high desert vegetation. Tail held high and swaying, Katie took the lead and ran far ahead, every once in a while returning to check on our progress. We figured that the ground she covered was probably twenty times the area we walked.

Off in the distance, we watched her bounce through the sparsely vegetated surroundings. Catching sight of a jackrabbit, she raced after it, zigzagging through the desert, and ultimately snatching the poor wriggling animal. Smiling with a mouth full of fur, she presented her trophy to us, laying it at our feet. On our return, much to our dismay, she pranced happily home with a tattered, rotting elk leg she had found in the wilderness dangling from her mouth.

Katie often spent hours exploring nature in the evenings. When she was outside, she felt the freedom of an animal unencumbered by the discipline of humans. I opened the door and she raced into the country, ready for adventure. After several hours, we wanted her home to the safety of our nest, so I shined a flashlight into the darkness. When the light reflected on her golden-colored eyes, she was mesmerized and hurried home. Her coat smelled musky. Leaves and mud clung to her sides.

Those long evenings outdoors eventually led to an introduction to a coyote clan. We imagined Katie joining the hunt with the scraggly gang, her wild spirit intertwining with nature. Yet, she always returned to give us affection and enjoy the rest of the evening in front of the fireplace. She was a member of the family, ready and willing to please, yet anxious to return to the wild.

It was obvious that Katie had developed a special relationship with the coyotes. She learned to yip and howl like her relatives. One warm summer's evening while we were all relaxing on the porch, Katie threw back her head and proceeded to sing. Melodic harmonies gurgled from her throat. Her song reminded me of a robin warbling as it prepared its nest. My daughter and I stared at each other, mouths agape, amazed at the beauty of the music she produced. Our void was filled and we were renewed.

~Dianne Marie Moen

The Battle of the Birds

Trouble is part of your life, and if you don't share it,
you don't give the person who loves you enough chance to love you enough.
~Dinah Shore

We weren't aware of the Beagle breed's regal history when we purchased our first one. All we saw was an adorable little black, white and tan creature with beautiful, long silky ears. We named him Brandy. Like the fortified wine that was his namesake, he proved to be a potent entity. By the time he was six months old, he'd raided barbecues, stolen pizzas, pursued local cats through beautifully tended vegetable gardens, and chased a neighbour's horses in carousel circles around a pasture with dizzying regularity.

He'd also gained a number of extra monikers that had nothing to do with wine, the most common of which cast dispersions on his parentage. Efforts to contain him proved useless. The Houdini of hounds, he viewed fences, collars, and any other restrictive devices simply as momentary challenges to his agile little brain.

As Brandy passed his first birthday, the school year ended. Our family—my husband Ron, our three children, Joan age nine, Carol eight, and Steven seven, the Beagle and myself—moved to our summer cottage near Miramichi Bay along the Tabusintac River. That spring Ron had purchased an ancient outboard motor boat. Proud of his purchase he'd often load the family aboard and we'd set off.

Occasionally the old boat churned decently along, but more frequently we ended our voyage wading home through the shallows — the "Undependable" in tow. Having sputtered to a stop, it (I refuse to use the nautical term "she" in reference to such a finicky creature) had refused to revive for the journey home. During these treks, Brandy would stretch out on the front of the craft, sunning himself while his galley slaves tugged and pulled.

One beautiful July morning we decided to take a trip out to one of the nearby islands at the river's mouth to dig clams. Shortly the entire always-optimistic family had clambered aboard, pails, shovels, and lunches carefully stowed away.

Undependable ran beautifully on the outgoing voyage. Ron manned the steering wheel and controls in the front, the children, myself, and supplies in the back. Bran stood with front paws braced against the dashboard head over the windscreen, ears streaming back in the breeze. His delight in our mini-adventure was contagious. Even old Undependable seemed to be humming along better than usual.

Once on the strip of sand and grass we called "an island," we discovered that the tide had cooperated, and gone out to allow us access to the clam beds. Since Brandy was penned in by water, we didn't bother to keep track of him. We paid no attention when he disappeared into the tall marsh grass that grew thick and rich along the island's elevated spine.

Suddenly screams erupted from the vegetation. Looking in the direction of the commotion, we saw a cloud of herring gulls rising out of the grass, their shrieks shattering the calm of the otherwise-perfect summer morning. A flash of black, white, and tan burst out of the three-foot tall grass, the furious flock in incensed pursuit.

"The little beggar must have gotten into their nesting site," Ron muttered.

Homing instincts in perfect order, Bran headed for his family at top speed, hoards of enraged gulls screaming and diving after him. Scenes from Alfred Hitchcock's classic *The Birds* came to mind and I was suffused with an urge to throw myself bodily over my children in a heroic effort to save them. Ron took a more practical approach.

"Run!" he yelled and we were off en masse. Two adults and three children hit the deck of old Undependable in a rush that all but capsized the thirteen-foot plywood craft.

Bringing his squawking, dive-bombing entourage, Bran leaped aboard behind us.

As Ron struggled to push and paddle us to water deep enough to employ the motor, the birds had time to reconnoiter, hover, and begin doing what herring gulls do best. We reached sufficient depth to lower the motor just as the first volley of guano hit us amidships.

True to form and uninspired either by the barrage of bird bombs or the cries of children, Undependable chose not to start. With Ron desperately trying to crank its twenty-five horsepower Johnson into life, we floated toward the bay. Bran alone seemed to be weathering the battle fairly well. He had dived under the front seat.

Later when Ron had finally managed to threaten Undependable's propulsion system into life with a combination of brute strength and his own special selection of expletives, and we were leaving the ballistic birds behind, Bran emerged from his bunker. He cast a disdainful eye over our splattered bodies and deck. He yawned, stretched, and then with a sigh (the Beagle equivalent of a shrug), he returned to his shelter to sleep out the remainder of the voyage.

~Gail MacMillan

A Collie Without a
Herd

*Women and cats will do as they please,
and men and dogs should relax and get used to the idea.*
~Robert A. Heinlein

Spicy, a black-and-white Border Collie puppy, came to live with us at the age of six weeks and immediately began searching for a herd. Although we raise cattle on our Central Texas farm, we've streamlined our cattle handling facilities so a pickup truck and a few bales of hay or buckets of Range Cubes do the work once required of cowboys on horses and working cow dogs. Believe me, it's much easier to lure the thousand-pound beasts into pens with treats than it is to chase them over hundreds of acres of land, a practice which works best in old Western movies.

At first, Spicy dedicated herself to herding our four grandchildren, the youngest of whom, a clumsy two-year-old, tripped over her and squashed her flat under his diaper-swathed backside many times before Spicy accepted the fact that grandchildren do not possess a herd mentality. Her brief contacts with the weanling heifers in the pen below the house were just as frustrating. Full of high-protein feed and rambunctiousness, they chased her gleefully across the pen with their tails in the air.

Border Collies are born with the instinct to herd other animals. The good ones have an inborn trait called the "collie eye"—they fix the target animals with an unwavering stare that communicates their dominance, and then move them wherever the handler (or the dog) wants them to go, ducking and dodging with agile grace to keep the unruly creatures together. Anyone who has watched a sheepherding demonstration at the fair has witnessed the Border Collie's uncanny ability to know which way the sheep are going to turn before they do.

We worked with Spicy on basic obedience lessons and she learned amazingly fast, but her life wasn't complete without something to herd, and we have no sheep or goats, not even a flock of ducks, which are sometimes used to train Border Collies. Although she loved people, she wasn't interested in fetching balls or sticks or any of the other favorite puppy pastimes. Finally, in desperation, she focused her attention on Pepper, a tortoiseshell cat. Pepper was a rescue cat, eternally grateful to be free of the shelter cage that had been her home before our daughter adopted her. As long as she didn't have to go back to the shelter, Pepper was cool with anything.

When I first noticed Spicy crouching in front of Pepper and giving her the "collie eye," I laughed. But I was a bit concerned that Pepper might run, encouraging Spicy to chase her. Pepper sized up the situation, arched her back, and rubbed under Spicy's chin, purring. She was happy to have attention—even from a dog. From that day forward, Pepper rarely went anywhere without Spicy at her side, glaring at her with an intensity that Pepper totally ignored. Tail in the air, she continued to her planned destination as though the black-and-white blur dancing around her didn't exist. Spicy raced from one side of the strolling cat to the other, pretending that Pepper was headed exactly where Spicy wanted her to go. Obviously, she didn't understand that "herding cats" is impossible.

As Spicy outgrew the playful puppy stage, I thought she might see the pointlessness of trying to herd a cat, but at the age of eight, her fascination with this pastime is just as strong. Pepper has a few carefully selected perches where she can escape when she's fed up with playing the part of the sheep, but mostly it's a symbiotic relationship. Pepper seems to view Spicy as her own personal escort and protector, a large, black-and-white lady-in-waiting, perhaps proving the truth of the old saying: "Thousands of years ago, cats were worshipped as Gods. Cats have never forgotten this."

~Martha Deeringer

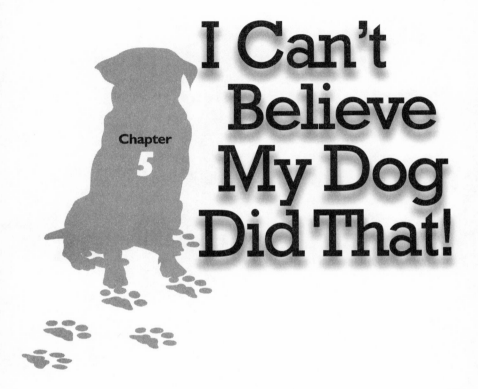

I Can't Believe My Dog Did That!

Chapter 5

For the Love of Dog

True Angel

It is not known precisely where angels dwell —
whether in the air, the void, or the planets.
It has not been God's pleasure that we should be informed of their abode.
~Voltaire

Two years ago I adopted a two-year-old Poodle/Terrier mix from our local shelter. I named her Angel. She had come from another shelter as a stray, had been abused, and was very skinny and extremely shy. I fell in love with her immediately.

With lots of love, patience, and socializing with other tenants and pets in my building, she was a totally different dog within a few weeks. We live in a high-rise building on Lake Superior with other seniors and/or disabled tenants. I live alone and have MS, and Angel is a perfect dog for me. We take care of each other. Fatigue and pain are my worst symptoms. On my bad days, if I'm up trying to do things around the apartment, she'll get on my bed and whine until I go and lie down. She then lies down right beside me.

Ever since I got her, she's been a wonderful dog. She seems to be grateful for everything and anything I do for her, even bringing me her favorite toy or treat when I'm feeling bad. She is the happiest and most popular dog in the building since she loves everybody. She's such a good dog—never misbehaves, never snaps or barks at anyone, and she loves to give kisses to everyone she sees in the building.

One night Angel became restless and woke me up at 1:30. I rarely go out late at night since Angel knows how to use a puppy pad when we stay in. But on that night, because of her behavior, I decided to go ahead and take her out since she was whining and seemed anxious. I got dressed and took her out.

I usually take her around to the parking lot side of our building, back by our garage. She was pulling me as hard as she could and whining, so I figured she had to really go and I unhooked her leash.

Instead of going to the grass like she usually does, she ran into the lot between two parked vehicles. When I got there, I found Angel sitting next to one of our tenants who was on the ground lying in a fetal position, his walker nearby. When I leaned down to ask what happened, he could only say he fell. He wasn't fully conscious, and he only had on shorts and a light jacket—although it was thirty-eight degrees outside.

He said he couldn't move, that he had recently had surgery on both knees and was in a lot of pain. I feared he might also have broken something. After calling 911, I asked him how long he had been lying on the cold pavement. "About an hour, I think," he said.

I took off my coat and laid it over the man's legs and placed my knees under his head to get it off the ground. We stayed like that, with Angel right by him, until the police and ambulance got there.

He was quickly transferred to the gurney, bundled in warm blankets, and was on the way to the hospital. When I told them Angel's name, they said it was the perfect name for her.

When we got back inside, I realized that Angel had never gone to the bathroom outside. Then I saw that she had gone on her puppy pad prior to us going out.

I have no idea how Angel knew about the man. We're on the eleventh floor, facing the lake—not the parking lot—with the windows closed and a small fan running.

The next day, I called the hospital and talked to the tenant. He told me that he had suffered a severe heart attack and had no idea why he had been outside by his van at that hour.

I went to see him at the hospital to take him his glasses, which had been found by another tenant, and I also took him a picture of

Angel. He kept thanking me, and I told him it was Angel he should thank.

She truly is an Angel.

~Jan Nash

Getting Lucky

Dogs never lie about love.
~*Jeffrey Moussaieff Masson*

There was a time when my Beagle was like any other dog. Lucky would somehow escape the confines of the yard, squeezing himself under the gate and disappearing into the wooded area surrounding the house. I would just wait for the inevitable. Noisy rustling of leaves would mark his trail and occasionally, the screeching of a cat, followed by a familiar bark. It was always the same. He would end up at the front gate, having gone full circle around the house, wagging his tail and looking up at me, happy to have returned from his afternoon exploration.

One day I was working in my garden, pulling out weeds, beginning to perspire a little. I heard the leaves on the other side of the fence give a little shake. I remember the afternoon breeze carried the scent of roses. It was teasing me, tempting me to stop, drink some water and perhaps take some photos of these fragrant gifts of nature. Once I began, it seemed I couldn't stop. Though I was paying careful attention to the angle of the sun in my photos, I was oblivious to the time.

The phone rang then. I heard a man's voice on the other end.

"Hello. This is Jake from Village Video downtown. Do you own a dog named Lucky?"

"Why, yes," I responded, afraid of what was coming next.

"He is here. Can you come and pick him up?"

I was incredulous.

"He is all the way downtown?"

I told him I'd be right there.

His long, lanky body leaning up against the doorway, Jake was waiting for me, but Lucky was nowhere in sight.

"Where is he?" I asked, my eyes darting around.

"Well, he's not here now," he responded rather coolly. "He's next door… in the bar," he said, head directing my attention to the left.

"What? What do you mean?"

"You'll see. He's in there," he said, motioning with his thumb. He half chuckled, shook his head and went back into the store.

I was really perplexed now. I approached the bar. It was called Hot Chili Saloon. Very slowly I peeked into the room. I could not believe what I was seeing.

There, perched high on one of those old barstools, was Lucky, sitting next to a very attractive woman who was feeding him tortilla chips, one by one. She had long black hair, red lips, golden earrings, a low-cut peasant blouse and a pair of tight blue jeans that rose above a pair of rust-colored cowboy boots. Oh, yes, and Lucky had a cowboy hat on.

He was in canine heaven.

Feeling like a mother coming to yank her underage son away from an experienced older woman in an off-limits drinking establishment, I stepped forward and said, "Hello. I am Lucky's… the dog's owner. I've come to get him."

The bartender and the two other "cowboys" sitting at the bar looked at me and let out a collective moan. One of them addressed me. "Aww, but he's having such a good time with Anita here."

Anita? Of course neither one of the lovebirds had ventured a look in my direction. Then Anita said, "He eez so sweet!" as she fed him another chip.

"Well, I am afraid he has to come home with me," I ventured, feeling rather guilty.

Stepping forward, I took his hat off, put it back on the bar and picked up Lucky, all while the others protested.

"Adios, mi amor, mi Looky," Anita cooed in her husky voice, kissing him on the nose. As I drove away, Lucky began howling and I could see Anita standing in the doorway.

Good heavens.

That's when everything changed. Lucky just wasn't Lucky anymore. He would mope around the yard or just lie there like a sack of potatoes. No exploring, no wagging his tail, definitely no barking. He wouldn't eat much either. He was obviously lovesick. He would whimper a lot of the time and I knew that in his little doggy brain he was thinking of Anita.

I began taking him for walks around the neighborhood or to the nearby park. I would also buy him little presents to bring him out of his brokenhearted daze.

Then, I would have the boy next door take him out to play with a ball, happy to give him some physical therapy. All these efforts were not wasted. It took a while for him to snap out of it, but little by little, he turned back into the Lucky I knew.

Now as I sit here listening to Lucky scratching at the gate to come in with his tail wagging, everything is back to normal. I never knew a dog could fall in love like that.

I didn't know Lucky had it in him. Sometimes I think I should change his name to Valentino or Romeo. Maybe Casanova? Then, when I really think about it, Lucky is the only name for him.

~Leah M. Cano

My Mother Made Me Do It

The apple doesn't fall far from the tree.
~German Proverb

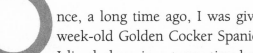

Once, a long time ago, I was given an adorable eight-week-old Golden Cocker Spaniel puppy. At that time I lived alone in a teeny tiny house with a teeny tiny living room, a teeny tiny bedroom and a teeny tiny kitchen, because I was a graduate student living on a teeny tiny budget. My childhood had been blessed with two wonderful Cocker Spaniels, and now I had another as a warm, soft furry companion.

I noticed right away that this little dog was a bit skittish. If I talked to her, she piddled. Or ran into a corner and pooped. I talked more gently. Same result. I figured training takes time, and love, and patience. I put out newspapers, hoped she would soon learn what they were for, and went off to my classes and research assignments.

Each time I returned home, I was amazed at the quantity and frequency of the doggy indiscretions. Yes, she did her business on the newspapers, covering the important events of the day with brown commentaries of her own. And when she finished editorializing on the newsprint she continued her dutiful discharge, overwhelming the limited real estate available in the tiny rooms of my home. I bought extra papers, and covered most of the open floor space. She proved up to the challenge. Puddles and piles, the yield per square foot was astounding, and she demonstrated the capacity to invade new terri-tory beyond the boundaries of the newspapers.

I cajoled, and corrected, and loved and encouraged. I bought scoopers and mops. Every night a suspicious tide of yellow water rolled in to cover my kitchen floor, waves lapping against the base-boards. Each morning, a freshly dropped pattern of landmines sur-rounded my bed. I scooped and mopped. I sanitized and deodorized. This loving and cuddly beast only improved how fast and efficiently she could cover my floors with doggy residue.

The vet said she was perfectly healthy, but I began to use scientific observations. Something did not add up. I measured. The magnitude of the output greatly exceeded that of the input. I know, because I provided the input, and I cleaned up the output. A cornucopia of inexplicable excess poured out of my beautiful Spaniel. There was only one thing a mature twenty-something young man could do. I called Mom.

"Mom, you know that cute little Spaniel I've had for a few months? Yeah Mom, she looks exactly like our first Spaniel you gave me when I was a little boy. Wasn't he a wonderful dog? Guess what, my mean old landlord won't have dogs in his house. (Well, he won't if Mom buys this story!) So maybe I'd better find a good home for her, so I was wondering if…?"

Thankfully, Mom came to my rescue and said she would take the dog.

The story I told Mom was less than honest, but I gave into the dark side out of desperation. Equally true, I did not divulge complete and accurate information, but I think that law only applies to selling a house, or maybe a horse.

I delivered the dog to Mom, and sped off to "an urgent appoint-ment" before the dog could reveal her unique talents. I did not call or visit for a few months. When I did visit, the icy stare and silent treatment that I got from my mom was enough to tell me that all had gone as I feared. When we were finally alone, she looked at me and, using her best mother's guilt-trip tone of voice and spacing her words out slowly, said: "How… could… you?"

Later on, noticing that the offending Spaniel was not present, I asked my dad what happened to her. He said, "Oh gosh, Bill, that dog piddled and pooped twice a minute. Fortunately, your mom remembered that Mary around the corner wanted a dog for a companion."

Mary was a spinster teacher who would invite the neighborhood ladies over on weekends for coffee and homemade pastries. Mom entered the room just as Dad finished with, "Yep, your mom took that dog right over and gave her to Mary."

Ah ha! So here I was, an apple that had clearly not fallen too far from the tree. Looking the tree in the eye, I spoke as sanctimoniously as I could, "Mom... how... could... you?"

The Spaniel lived a long and presumably happy life with the spinster teacher Mary—which we learned from reports by other neighbors. For some reason Mary never again invited my mother over for coffee and homemade pastries.

~William Halderson

Sam and the Buffalo

Spaniels by Nature are very loving, surpassing all other Creatures,
for in Heat and Cold, Wet and Dry, Day and Night,
they will not forsake their Master.
~Richard Blome

GRRRR! I tried to shush him. My seven-year-old Cocker Spaniel, his head raised from the bed, growled intently. I placed a hand on his blond body, attempting to lay his head back down. Instead, growling again, he raised his entire body into a sitting position, concentrating his stare on the patio doors off the bedroom.

I glanced at the clock—3 a.m. Groaning, I said, "Sam, it's not time to get up yet!"

He barked, not a Cocker Spaniel yip, but an intense woof! And he jumped off the bed. Wide awake now, I detected danger. A woman living alone eight miles from town in a sparsely populated region of Montana. I reached for the pepper spray I kept on my nightstand. I tiptoed to the curtained sliding glass doors. Standing to the left side, I began to pull the six-foot long swag from the glass. Sam's stare never wavered. He rushed toward the doorway, barking furiously, and causing me to jump further from the glass.

Then, I heard the moaning. Deep, bellowing sounds reverberated from the deck. Pepper can in hand, I poised, ready to spray the foe that waited outside. Sam's barking intensified and the hair on his blond shoulders stood erect. More moaning and groaning, but no body appeared.

I peered around the curtain. No person stood on the deck. Bright moonlight made the September night like day, so I surveyed the surroundings. Still no visible intruder. I stepped away from the safety of the curtain that covered the patio door. Smack! The wooden deck shook as if we were having an earthquake. The movement rippled to my bedroom floor, causing us to jump.

Then, I saw him. Dark brown hair rippled in the night breeze as he stepped from the shadows. Then another, smaller, most likely younger, fellow followed in his steps.

"Oh!" I exclaimed in astonishment.

Two bison stood in the light of an autumn moon, having sought a hideaway for a few hours slumber under my deck. Having recently moved to a small town outside the boundary of Yellowstone National Park, I had heard stories of bison leaving the park and traveling through the area where I now lived. And though I had visited Yellowstone numerous times and encountered the large, wooly animals while driving, never did I imagine any would come this close to my residence.

Fascinated that these bison were so close, I stepped onto the deck. And before I could reach backward to slide the glass door, Sam bounded through the opening, leaped down the deck steps and rushed the bison. Frantic, I commanded, "Sam, come!"

As usual, he ignored the summons. Within seconds canine and bovine were face to face, nearly nose to nose. Sam's barking persisted. With a combination of scolding and scaring, my fearless dog took on an animal nearly one hundred times his weight and three times his height.

The younger bison squalled and stepped back in surprise at the assault. The older, larger male, however, simply stared at Sam and grunted. As my dog rushed at the bull's face once again, my screaming for him to "get back here!" again ignored, the bull went from annoyed to angry. The great creature stomped his front foot and shook his massive head. I envisioned my dog pierced by one of the bull's black horns, caught in the air and shaken until dead.

Somehow, Sam sidestepped the bison's horns. He must have finally understood the danger he faced, for after one more deep growl and tough bark, Sam scampered back to the safety of the deck. He stuck his tan head between the rails and again railed against the wooly intruders.

Tiring of the incessant noise, the two bison lumbered away, heading for the quiet of those lots without houses. Sam and I watched as they moseyed several hundred yards away, snipping at dying grasses along the way. The two giants lay down near one another after leaving the area occupied by a crazy dog and his snooping human.

These would not be the last buffalo we'd encounter. About a month later, I came home late from work on a snowy night. As I entered the driveway, the car's headlights captured an unforgettable scene: about two dozen cow and calf bison taking refuge under my front porch. Several of the calves huddled like football players while their mothers surrounded them, protecting their offspring from the harsh elements. I sat in my car mesmerized by the incredible sight: snow, wind and very large mammals.

How was I going to get into my house with these huge creatures blocking the entrance? Female bison weigh nearly 1,000 pounds; the calves, about half-grown, easily weighed half of that, and these great creatures stood between my bug of a car and my front door. Then, I heard him, my protector, my rough and tough canine companion. At the living room window stood Sam, his Cocker Spaniel serenade braying from the house into the night air. Ten minutes later, the herd of mothers and their young wandered away, the lead female bison escorting the rest to the sanctuary of nearby forest lands.

~Gayle M. Irwin

The Gospel Truth

The world is hugged by the faithful arms of volunteers.
~Everett Mámor

Of all the dogs we'd known before—coming in and out our door—Rommel was the most unforgettable. One amazing, frightening night, he had saved us from a house fire by pulling on my pajama sleeve and then leading us all to safety. After that, we always expected our strong German Shepherd to be a hero, never a victim.

Until that one particular afternoon when the kids were outside playing in the apple orchard after the first snowfall of the season. I was gazing out the window, enjoying the beauty of the glistening snow, when the front door banged open.

"Mom, come quick! There's a funny sound out here."

I stuck my head out the door and heard a low keening from across the road and over the ridge. Rommel! Quickly, I grabbed my jacket and we all ran toward his mournful echo.

When we crested the hill, we looked down the ravine and gasped. He was stuck in the middle of the pond. Submerged up to his chest, Rommel had scrabbled to grasp the edge of the ice. His eyes were frantic but hopeful as we all gathered at the pond's edge.

"Oh Mom. What are we going to do?"

"Look for sturdy sticks," I said. Stepping onto the ice, I felt it sink a bit, then heard a soft crack. Rommel was more than fifteen feet from me.

Soon, we had a pile of sticks and dead saplings. I grabbed the longest, sturdiest one and pushed it over the ice as far as possible.

"Come on, fella. Grab hold. Good boy, you can do it."

Rommel grabbed the wood with his teeth and pulled mightily. I held fast and he inched forward, the soft ice sludging away in a coarse wave. Then the deadwood broke. Rommel sank out of sight.

The children screamed and my heart began to rip in half. A moment later, Rommel surfaced again and looked for purchase somewhere, anywhere. "Larry, run. Call the fire department. Quickly."

The others stifled their sobs and called out encouragement to their companion.

"Hang on, Rommie, hold on. Help is coming. We love you."

I couldn't let this happen. Emboldened with desperation, I tore off my jacket and prepared to take the icy plunge.

"Wait, Mom. Here come the firemen!"

Sliding down the slope came four huge men dressed in rubber.

They quickly unleashed a coil of rope, attached a sling contraption to one end, and then tossed it behind Rommel. Two of the firemen pulled fast on the rope and Rommel's body, inside the sling, ripped through the ice and toward shore. Then one fireman lifted Rommel out of the sling and laid him on a blanket.

Everyone stood silent for a frozen moment. Then Rommel wagged his tail.

"He's alive!"

The kids hovered around the firemen as they wrapped Rommel in blankets and carried him home. Alive, but how damaged?

A crowd had gathered at the roadside, attracted by the sight of the fire truck.

"Make way, please," said one fireman, "we have to get this fellow warmed up."

Out of the crowd stepped our town veterinarian.

"Dr. Garrity, what are you doing here?"

"I heard about all this on my scanner. Let's get him inside."

The kids set Rommel in a cocoon of blankets before the fireplace and Dr. Garrity examined him.

"He might be a bit stiff for a while. But, with lots of love and some of this, he'll be fine."

The doctor handed me a prescription slip. Now, what do you suppose was prescribed? Why chicken soup, of course. And that's the gospel truth.

~Lynne Layton Zielinski

Canada or Bust

There is no hope unmingled with fear, and no fear unmingled with hope.
~Baruch Spinoza

Nestled along the shores of Lake Ontario, my grandparents' camp in upstate New York provided a recreational paradise for my rambunctious one-year-old Labrador Retriever, Plinko. It was a perfect September morning as the leaves on the oak trees overhead began their transformation into autumn. The wind was whipping off the lake, churning four-foot waves in its path. Plinko was lying on the grass, chewing on a stick, while I was gathering my belongings in preparation for the drive back into the city.

I should have known better than to leave a Labrador Retriever unsupervised for more than five minutes.

Once the car was packed, I called for Plinko. He didn't come running, which was not too worrisome since he rarely obeyed that command. I checked the side of the house, where I had last seen him contently chewing the stick. There was no sign of him.

"Plinko! Plinko!" I shouted, my voice shaking with worry. Still nothing.

I went toward the water and found Plinko was paddling about 100 feet out. His head was like a buoy, bobbing with each wave, then disappearing until the waves briefly subsided. I called his name, but the wind threw my voice back to land without Plinko even acknowledging me.

Plinko couldn't see or hear me, and he wasn't making any effort to turn around.

I began throwing rocks as far as I could, hoping that he would see or hear them splash in the water and turn around. Rock after rock sank to the bottom of the lake without Plinko even changing direction. He seemed to be on a mission: Canada or bust.

Fearing he would drown or become disoriented, I jumped into the water, sweatpants and all, and began my swim to Plinko. I got about 100 feet out, screaming for Plinko with each stroke. My sweatpants were becoming an anchor, and Plinko was almost 500 feet from shore. I knew I couldn't reach him, so I reluctantly retreated.

As I got out of the water, neighbors who heard my screams had called 911, thinking that I was drowning. "No, I'm fine," I told one of the neighbors who had come to see what all the commotion was about. "It's my dog. He's too far out, I don't think he's coming back," I said as I looked for any sign of him in the water.

I stood along the shoreline, scanning for any indication that Plinko was still afloat. It had been almost forty-five minutes since he initially went into the lake, and I couldn't see him anywhere.

Believing that my dog had drowned, I went into the camp to call 911. "What's your emergency?" the operator asked. "I am calling from Shore Oaks Drive, I am the person who was in the water. There is no need to send the Coast Guard," I said.

Although the operator seemed to be thrilled that a human crisis was averted, I was sick with grief over the dog crisis. With water dripping off my trembling hand, I hung up the phone, dried off, and went outside to get my car keys, fully preparing to go home without Plinko.

A neighbor and fellow dog owner approached me as I was gathering my car keys and the rest of my belongings. "I don't think he's coming back," I said to the neighbor, as I took one last glance at the water.

"Wait, wait," the neighbor said. "What's that? Is that him?"

We were shocked at what we saw. A little cream-colored head was bobbing up and down, coughing and panting about 75 feet out.

In disbelief, I began shouting for Plinko, who had been swimming for more than an hour. He continued to dog paddle toward the sound of my voice, spitting up water with each breath.

When he reached shore, I ran to him, wrapping my arms around his cold, wet body. I was covered in fur and I smelled like a wet dog. I didn't care. I didn't want to let him go.

~Sarah McCrobie

One Good Roll

Anybody who doesn't know what soap tastes like never washed a dog.
~Franklin P. Jones

Our Nova Scotia Duck Tolling Retriever, Ceilidh, like many gun dogs, had a penchant for attempting to disguise her scent by covering herself in another. Usually these alternatives are incredibly stinky and repulsive, at least to humans. I once read that dogs respect the smelliest among their numbers most. If this is true, then I'm sure that at times Ceil must have rivaled royalty in doggy terms. She had a gift for ferreting out decaying matter and fresh feces with astounding regularity and rolling in the disgusting stuff.

Ceilidh's penchant for stinkiness reached an all time high one summer's evening when we took her for a run a few miles up the road from our cottage. There had been Old Home Week celebrations in our little community during the previous seven days. Visitors had been camping in the vicinity and we'd kept Ceilidh close to home during the seven-day period so that she wouldn't bother anyone who didn't fancy canines. Now that the festivities were over, we felt it was a good time to let her have a run.

We stopped the truck on the edge of a wide meadow and let her free. She ran only a few yards before stopping short, sniffing, and then heading into a little thicket. A moment later we heard the unmistakable sounds of her rolling in… something.

"Not again!" Ron leaned wearily against the side of the truck. "This time she definitely rides home in the back!"

Prepared for such a problem, I'd put our travel crate into the truck's box before we'd left the cottage. There had been too many occasions already that summer when Ceil had rolled in unacceptable materials, leaped into the black mud of marshes, or gotten tangled in burdocks.

This, however, would prove to be her crowning achievement. When she emerged from the trees, the stench was incredible. She'd apparently found the place where some careless travel trailer owner had emptied his septic system. As she trotted proudly back toward us, the stench took our breaths away.

"She's your dog." Ron clambered into the truck. "You load her."

Mentally muttering Yuk! Yuk! and trying to close my senses to the reality of the situation, I boosted the little stinker into the back of the truck and pushed her into the crate. Then I dropped to my knees and rubbed my hands on the grass with all the vehemence of Lady Macbeth as she cried out, "Out, damned spot! Out, I say!"

"Don't worry, Ceil," I couldn't help pausing to reassure the reeking little critter peering at me from behind the bars of her kennel. "We'll have you clean in no time."

Ceilidh looked benignly at me with those gorgeous teddy bear eyes. She didn't appear in the least concerned.

As fast as the speed limit would allow, we drove to the nearest accessible bit of shoreline. Ron leaped out and headed for the beach. I was left behind to release my odoriferous little friend.

I snapped the cage open. Water-loving Ceilidh didn't wait to be assisted from the back of the truck. Instead she made a flying leap and headed for the river. But after going only a few yards she skidded to a stop. Her head swiveled around, her nose lifted as she sniffed the air (although how she was capable of smelling anything beyond her stinky self I don't know). An instant later she was off again, but this time away from the water, back toward a grove of trees to our left.

As I turned to see where she was headed, I glimpsed, through a small stand of birches, a blue pickup with its tailgate lowered. Seated on folding chairs beside it, a middle-aged couple was enjoying a leisurely lunch.

Oh, Lord, no!

I started to run toward the unsuspecting pair but I was already too late. The man had spotted Ceilidh. Apparently a dog fancier (although not astute at gender recognition), he called, "Hey, boy. Come here, boy!"

Ceilidh, seemingly in response, was instantly galloping toward him. I wasn't deceived. I knew the truth. It was the sandwich in his hand that had garnered her attention.

"Nice dog!" As Ceilidh arrived at the man's side (downwind), he reached out and stroked her.

"Oh, sh...!" He jumped to his feet, holding up the hand that touched her fur as if it had been burned. Ceilidh, taking advantage of his surprise, snatched the sandwich, whirled, and raced away.

"I'm so sorry!" I tried to explain as I arrived, breathless, at the picnic site. "Ceilidh got into something...."

"I've told you not to play with strange dogs!" The woman ignored me as her companion grabbed a sheaf of napkins and began scrubbing at his hand. "Maybe next time you'll listen!"

"How could I possibly know...?"

"Sorry," I murmured again, then hurried away from what seemed well on the way to becoming an all-out recrimination session.

Shortly I caught up with Ceilidh as she was finishing her sandwich on the bank above the beach. With my stomach heaving, I managed to get a leash on her.

Totally unperturbed, she licked her lips, then agreeably, perhaps even a trifle proudly, trotted along at my side as we headed for the river. And why shouldn't she? After all, not only was she the stinkiest dog in the universe, but she'd also gotten that lovely ham sandwich to boot.

~Gail MacMillan

Swinger

To swing or not to swing? Swing.
~*Brendan Fraser,* George of the Jungle

W atching our eleven-year-old, mostly Spaniel dog, Peggy, follow me from room to room, my husband Gord said, "What are you going to do when anything happens to old Peg?

"I don't want to think about it," I said.

"Maybe we should get another dog now, so you won't feel so devastated."

"Maybe," I said, without much enthusiasm.

Fate has a way of stepping in sometimes. That very afternoon our neighbour Linda asked us if we knew of anyone who wanted a two-year-old purebred Basset Hound.

"I've always wanted a Basset Hound," Gord said. That was a surprise to me, but I didn't argue. Two dogs had to be twice as nice as one dog.

Before you could say Jack Russell, our new Basset Hound Milford took up residence and established his top dog status to all the humans, but not to Peggy, who wasn't going to accept any nonsense from the upstart. The rest of us were enamoured of this canine aristocrat. So much so that I wrote to the Marquis of Milford Haven, a cousin to Queen Elizabeth II, to ask permission to use his illustrious name when I registered him. The Marquis replied in his own hand that he would be delighted, but I was to use the alternate spelling of Marquess when I registered him.

Milford was the perfect dog for the first few weeks. When he felt he had wheedled his way into our affections enough, he showed his true colours. He did everything we asked him to do, just as long as he wanted to do it too. Otherwise he disobeyed and if pressed to conform, he bit.

In the house, with just the dogs for companionship, I was startled by a noise that took me a few seconds to identify. Then I recognized the sound of the rocking chair, rocking. Suspecting an unwanted intruder, I tiptoed into the living room to find long-bodied Milford positioned in the rocking chair so that he could rock.

Milford had an adventurous spirit. He liked to go on unsupervised walks, but generally returned before mealtime. Once, he was gone overnight. We worried about him, so we placed an advertisement in the local paper. A lady phoned to say that she didn't know what Basset Hounds looked like, but there was a dog on her swing seat. She paused for a moment and added with surprise in her voice, "And now he's swinging himself."

We went and claimed our swinging dog.

~Pamela Kent

Chew Bone Chicanery

You can't teach an old dog new tricks.
~Proverb

Kirby came to us several years ago, when he was little more than a pup. Weighing in at just over twenty pounds, he'd grown larger than his apartment-dwelling owner had expected. He was also a high-energy dog that needed a yard to run around in.

Next, Dakota joined us. She was five at the time, a white fluff ball of a Spitz who'd lived her entire life with an elderly couple, my husband Grover's godparents. When Grover's godfather passed away, his godmother Ruth, who at eighty-five was nearly blind, moved into a nursing home. We told Ruth we'd make Dakota a part of our family.

Then, about a year ago, my daughter's little Yorkie, Bella, needed a home. Toni had moved into an apartment that didn't allow pets. She asked if we'd take Bella.

Bella is a nine-pound bundle of energy with an attitude. And, having been an only dog all of her life, it didn't take long for her to show us how determined she could be. She's jealous. She's dominating. She is the yappiest little thing I've ever been around. She's also very smart. This I learned quickly, as Bella maneuvered to get what she wants despite two older, bigger dogs who had been there longer than she had.

We never intended to have three dogs. It had been easy, petting two dogs. After all, I have a hand for each. With three it's trickier, and Bella does not tolerate being left out. She barks and growls for attention if I'm petting the other two, her expression furious. If I don't get to her right away she climbs onto my lap, then works her way up until she's nearly in my face, growling and casting sidelong, I-dare-you-to-do anything-about-it glares at the other dogs.

Dakota, gentle and even-tempered, will sigh in resignation and walk away. Kirby doesn't give up quite so easily, but eventually he too gets tired of Bella's noise and wanders off. Once she has me to herself, Bella is, at last, happy and blessedly quiet.

There are the occasional scraps over toys, even though there's more than enough for everyone. Sweet Dakota usually lets Bella have her way, but once in a while even she gets tired of being bullied. Kirby doesn't fight. If he has a toy and Bella approaches, all he has to do is emit a low growl and she backs off. She knows that he's not quite the pushover Dakota is.

The chew bones, however, are another matter. I buy extra large rawhide bones, which give the dogs many hours of contented chewing. The bones are nearly as big as Bella, making her a comical sight when she carries one in her mouth. It's even funnier when she tries to jump on the sofa with one of them.

I buy several at a time, and there are always at least three of them in circulation. Somewhere. I don't know how it happens, but it seems that the extras are always getting lost under a sofa or behind drapes, leaving one bone for three dogs.

Of course, Bella wants that one bone. And so it was not that long ago I witnessed an act of cunning on her part that surprised even me.

Kirby was on the sofa, contentedly gnawing on the only visible rawhide bone. Bella stood a few feet away with a covetous expression on her furry little face. Being busy, I wasn't paying much attention.

Suddenly Bella ran to the sliding patio doors on the far side of the room, yapping energetically. When one dog barks, they all have to bark, even if they don't know exactly what it is they're barking at. So of course Kirby and Dakota both sprang into action. Also woofing at the tops of their lungs, they ran to the patio doors to look out at the back yard, where there surely had to be something to warrant all this attention. There they were, all three of them, sounding like an army of frenzied canines.

"Oh, my God, what is going on here?" I yelled over the noise. I opened the patio doors and three dogs exploded forward, like a herd of elephants stampeding across the deck.

At least Kirby and Dakota stampeded. They were already halfway down the steps when Bella stopped, made a quick U-turn, and came back into the house.

No longer barking, she trotted over to the sofa, hopped up and took over possession of the chew bone. When the other dogs came back into the house a short while later, Kirby spotted Bella with his former chew bone. But he looked so puzzled as to how this had come about that he didn't even attempt to take it from her.

I might have believed this to be a one-time trickery, but a few days later Grover said, "Have you seen what Bella does? She lures the other dogs outside, then doubles back in and gets the chew bone."

We let her have it. We figured anyone who works that hard to get what she wants, deserves to keep it.

~Jean Tennant

"Finally, something to howl about."

Sadi On Duty

One of the most enduring friendships in history —
dogs and their people, people and their dogs.
~Terry Kay

"**D**oug, I don't think I can drive anymore," I said to my husband. He was driving the moving van in front of us. The cell phone crackled. I wasn't sure if he could hear me. I waited a few seconds.

"The baby's crying, and the others are so tired they can't see straight, and I can't either," I said.

More static.

"If you can hear me, please stop at the next exit. Okay?"

The phone hissed and spat like an angry cat.

"I'm going to hang up now. Love you."

I tossed the phone on the passenger seat. Its screen light faded and with it my hope that Doug had heard anything I'd said.

I scanned the highway. In the dead of night, it was impossible to know where we were. No lights or signs to distinguish one stretch of road from another. I would have been utterly disoriented, except that I was following Doug and trusted he knew the way from Fort Campbell, Kentucky to Quantico Marine Corps Base in Virginia. However, I also knew that even if I couldn't contact him, I had to take the next exit. Soon, my fatigue would make driving dangerous, and I'd rather be hopelessly lost than dead.

Baby Elena was well past her normal feeding time, and her cries kept me alert for the next mile and a half. Unexpectedly, Doug's blinker flashed in the darkness like a friendly wave. He'd seen an exit and was stopping!

Our caravan of three—the U-Haul, my van, and my mother's truck—pulled into the gas station. All of us were relieved to stretch and eat after hours of driving.

Doug took me aside while my mom watched our six kids and Lab-Chow mix. "Honey, it's after midnight. It's not practical for you, your mom and the kids to keep driving. We still have five hours until we get to the new house."

"Five hours! I thought we just had a couple more."

"The construction in Knoxville and that heavy rain really set us back."

"But five hours…" My disbelief morphed into discouragement. Moving was my least favorite part of military life. "I don't think I can manage five more hours."

"That's why I want you and your mom and the kids to stay here tonight. There's a decent hotel and you guys can start fresh in the morning."

"Mom and the kids and I? But what about you?"

"I've got to go on. The unloading crew we booked will be at the new house at 7 a.m. I have to be there with the U-Haul."

"But aren't you tired?"

"Sleep—it's a crutch, like air and water." He gave me a wry smile. "I'll be okay. Really. This is nothing compared to two combat tours. Besides, I have Sadi with me. She's great company. Never complains about my radio stations and sings good harmony, too." He kissed my forehead. The matter was decided.

I kissed my husband goodbye and scratched Sadi's ears. Watching the taillights shrink in the darkness made me suddenly lonely. I remembered the comfort of friends we left behind, the familiarity of our favorite kids-eat-free buffet. I thought about the littlest things I'd miss, like the flagpole on our porch. I remembered Doug teaching our kindergartner how to post and retire the Colors before he left for Iraq. I remembered Sadi sleeping right against the front door every night while Doug was away on back-to-back tours to the Middle East. I slept more easily knowing intruders would have to make it past her to get to us. Thankfully, no one tried.

The taillights were gone and I let the memories fade. I hoped Doug wasn't as tired as I was.

The next morning, Mom and I followed Doug's map to our new home. I couldn't help checking ditches and ravines for signs of a crash. As a combat pilot, Doug was trained in risk mitigation. I knew he'd stop to nap when he needed to, but the "what ifs" plagued me anyway.

Five hours and fifteen minutes after we checked out of the hotel, Mom and I pulled into my new driveway. The first one to greet us was Sadi. She bounded down the porch to lick each of the children, and then Doug showed them to the back yard, which was a dream come true for child and dog—two acres of fenced paradise with trees and swing sets and forts.

Then, he brought me a cup of coffee, and we sat on the front porch. "That dog really earned her kibble last night."

"Oh?" I sipped my coffee.

"It was like she could sense when I'd get tired. Most of the time she kept her head on my lap and enjoyed the ride. But about the time I started to feel even the slightest bit drowsy, that little lady would sit up and lick my face."

I smiled. The whole time Doug was deployed, Sadi protected us while we slept. Last night she protected our soldier by making sure he didn't. We might have just moved halfway across the country, but I for one was thankful that some things hadn't changed.

~Mary C. Chace

Chapter
6

I Can't Believe My Dog Did That!

Treat, Play, Love

Bringing Up the Rear

When it comes to skiing, there's a difference between what you think it's going to be like, what it's really like, and what you tell your friends it was like.

~Author Unknown

For sixteen years my family and I shared our lives with an amazing Beagle named Brandy. I say amazing because although he astonished us, horrified us, humbled us, delighted us, inspired us, and at times downright exasperated us, he never once ceased to be a little devil-may-care rake. His was the spirit of the swashbuckler, never to be bowed or broken. We could not help admire it. His escapades became legend both in our city neighborhood and in the fields and streams around our cottage. One of Brandy's adventures the second winter he was part of our family is indelibly etched in my mind.

It began one beautiful day in early March, that time of year when the snow crust was as hard as pavement and sun-glazed to the slipperiness of an eel's back. Skiing conditions, both downhill and cross-country, were in the treacherous to suicidal range. Undaunted by the precarious footing, my friend Christiana and I set out to walk our dogs—Brandy and Christiana's Boxer named Ross.

We headed through the woods and across a meadow glistening with snow diamonds and framed by spruce and pines iced in ivory under a perfect sapphire sky. The sun warmed our faces, awakening pleasant thoughts of spring, but also glazing the snow's hard surface with a treacherous liquid sheen. Several times Christiana and I caught each other's sleeves to prevent falling. Even the dogs were finding it difficult to remain on their four paws.

At the far end of the meadow the land dipped downward into a long, sweeping slope of virginal white that terminated in a cluster of alders and dogwood. When we reached a vantage point, all four of us paused to view the panorama.

Suddenly I saw Bran's ears prick into that alarming stance that indicated "the game" as Dr. Watson would say, "was afoot." Following his line of vision, I saw a rotund lady in a pink ski suit perched atop the hill about fifty yards away. On her feet was a pair of cross-country skis.

"What can she be thinking?" Christiana, a veteran skier of the Austrian Alps said as she, too, caught the object of Bran's interest. "Cross-country skis… on this slippery crust… on a hill?"

As we watched, the lady plunged her poles into the crust and then squatted to adjust her boots. Her pink bottom hung between her widely spread skis.

And then disaster struck. A howl went up from the smallest member of our company. Before I realized what was happening, Brandy was off, charging toward that pastel bundle as if someone had just yelled, "charge!" or he'd discovered the Energizer Bunny slowing down within his reach.

There was a scream, a frantic scratching. The lady, still in squat position, plunged down the slope, pink rear end bouncing over each natural mogul with an accompanying shriek.

Christiana, Ross, and I half-slid, half-staggered down the slope toward the crumpled mound that had finally come to an abrupt halt in the thicket at the bottom. Brandy had vanished into the bush.

"Are you all right?" Christiana, a nurse, was instantly at her side.

"Yes, yes… I think so." Slipping and sliding on the skis still miraculously attached to her boots, the woman hung suspended between my friend and a dogwood like the personification of that well-rounded cartoon creation in Michelin tire commercials. "But who owns that miserable little dog?"

Christiana and I exchanged glances. "We have no idea. He's been following my Boxer through the woods all morning," my quick-thinking friend replied.

We helped the woman unclamp her skis and assisted her to her car parked on the road below the meadow. That was that... we could but hope... as Brandy stuck his head out between two small pines.

But it wasn't. Not by a long shot. The following morning when Christiana returned to work in the hospital, a colleague told her of an unusual case she'd treated the previous day.

"This lady had bruises and lacerations all over her bottom," she reported. "She tried to tell me it was the result of some kind of weird skiing accident involving a dog. Now I ask you, do I look gullible enough to swallow a crazy story like that!"

~Gail MacMillan

The Visitor

Guests always give pleasure—if not their arrival, their departure.

~Portuguese Proverb

There was no doubt about it. Jazzy was the highlight of my sing-along sessions at a local long-term care center. My eight-pound ball of fluff took center stage and stole the show each week.

"Over here," cajoled Ida from her wheelchair. Jazzy sprinted across the room and, with the litheness common to Toy Poodles, leapt into her welcoming lap.

"Lookie what I saved for you," wheedled Harlan, who sat behind the chrome cage of his walker. Never one to forego a treat, Jazzy jumped back to the floor and darted to the limp slice of cheese dangling from his fingers.

While I opened the grand piano and arranged my short stack of music, Jazzy made her rounds. Residents felt slighted if she didn't pay them a personal visit. As beloved as a favorite grandchild, she'd grown up with them—readily accepting each new addition who came to replace one whose sojourn had ended. Like a kindergartner who expected to be liked, she made friends easily and openly. And it seemed no one could resist her.

Jazzy had already moved on, taking attendance, checking to make certain each of her friends had arrived. She knew who sat where and, if someone was missing, often darted down the hallway of the west wing to encourage him or her to join in.

Today's attendance was sparse.

I approached an aide. "Where is everyone?"

"Oh, it's been a tough week. Stomach flu," she sighed. "And we lost Helen."

Helen? Bright, alert Helen? Helen with her gracious ways, quick wit, and riveting stories? She'd lived at the center for several years and was a favorite.

We let the silence of mutual grief envelop us. Even in a place where death was a frequent visitor, it was never easy on staff members who engaged in daily acts of intimate caregiving. Bonds ran deep; we all cared.

Jazzy sniffed at the vacancies in the lounge before prancing past our feet and through the double doorway. We watched as she tap-danced down the hall—straight to Helen's room.

The aide stiffened. "Uh-oh. There's a brand new resident in there…." She raced after Jazzy and I was hot on her heels.

But we weren't quick enough. A scream pierced the air.

"Eeeek! A rat! A rat! Help me someone, there's a rat in my room!"

By the time I arrived, the aide had lifted Jazzy from the bed where she'd jumped to pay a visit. I held out my arms for the bundle of wriggling fur while the aide tried valiantly to calm the distraught woman who cowered in the bed once occupied by Helen.

Back in the lounge, a confused Jazzy slunk to safety beneath the piano bench. I turned to the stunned residents, but before I could explain or apologize for the disruption, Gerald slapped his thigh.

"By golly, this'll be a first," he guffawed. "Hers will be the only certificate this place ever issues that says 'Death by eight-pound Poodle!'"

~Carol McAdoo Rehme

54

The Bilingual Dog

It is good to have friends everywhere.
~French Proverb

Sammy is a mutt. He is also a rescue dog. My daughter was eight years old when she saw him at the Blessing of the Animals at the Cathedral Church of St. John the Divine in New York, which takes place every year on the first Sunday in October. His owner was looking for someone to adopt him.

Sammy is primarily my daughter's dog, but as is often the case when you live in New York City and your eight-year-old has a dog, who ends up taking it out for walk? Mom or Dad.

You should also know that I am French, and my other half, Jill, speaks the language fluently, as does our daughter. At home we usually speak French.

Sammy is cute but weird looking, and weird is putting it mildly. He's some sort of small, skinny Terrier, mixed with some other kind of animal, like one of those wading birds that stands on one leg.

Sammy has four very skinny long legs and a spider-monkey face. Almost everyone who looked at him when we first got him asked in astonishment, "Excuse me, but what kind of dog is that?"

I got so tired of answering the same question that I said, "He is a German Shepherd who had a sex change."

Not long after our family adopted this strange creature and poured love on him, he became another kind of dog. Love works miracles. Now strangers would stop us and say, "I love your dog. He is beautiful. What kind is it?"

But my answer remains the same because I love to watch people's reactions.

Apart from being really cuddly and very smart, one of Sammy's unique characteristics is his speed. In spite of being small, with his long legs and slight frame he can outrun any dog in Central Park. And every morning I take Sammy to Central Park. Jill walks him in the afternoon, and at night it's yours truly back on the street, rain or snow, with Sammy.

When I am with Sammy I always enter Central Park on 79th Street and Fifth Avenue, and as soon as we hit the park, I take off his leash. Our route is always the same. We cross over to the west side, walk inside the park to 110th Street, head back to the east side, and back down again to 79th Street and Fifth Avenue. Then we walk home. Most of the time, while we're in the park, I have no idea where Sammy is; he simply appears, disappears and reappears.

But one morning, disaster struck. At around 9:00, as we reached 110th Street on the west side, a huge, scary dog—I think it was a Doberman Pinscher—also off the leash, went for Sammy.

Although I tried to block the Doberman's way by standing in front of Sammy, who was behind me, the Doberman went around me at full speed. When I turned around to find Sammy, there was no Sammy. He had bolted so fast that all I saw was the end of his tail disappearing into thin air. Sammy was gone; the big dog had stopped in its tracks. Its owner apologized and left.

I was left with a leash and no dog.

I alerted the park rangers and the police. Fortunately Sammy had on a collar with a tag that had our telephone number on it and the inscription: "If I am lost, please call this number."

On my way home, I told every doorman from Fifth Avenue to Third Avenue about Sammy's disappearance. They all knew us, and I learned quickly that among the doormen Sammy was a favorite dog.

Short of broadcasting Sammy's disappearance on TV, every effort was made to try to find him—and before my daughter got out of school at 3:30 that afternoon.

Pressure, stress, fear, frustration... all of these emotions grew with the passing of time. At 2:00, Sammy was still nowhere to be found. The adult world was searching. The child would soon be out of school. At 3:00, still nothing.

Jill and I were on the lookout in the park, believing that at any moment we would see the familiar face or the familiar tail. Nothing. A friend of ours stayed home just in case someone called to report that they had found the dog.

Which fortunately is exactly what happened, and not a minute too soon. Sammy had been found, and by 3:15 our friend had returned home with both Sammy and the telephone number of the person who had found our dog.

At 3:30, Jill went to pick up our daughter while I called the number to thank the Good Samaritan who had found our beloved Sammy.

I dialed the number and the person who answered said, "Ambassade de France, bonjour!"

Why had I dialed the French Embassy? Obviously I had made a mistake. I hung up and dialed again.

"Ambassade de France, bonjour!" I heard again. It was not a mistake.

Had someone at the French Embassy found our dog? I spoke to a man in French and, yes, he had found Sammy. Where had he been found, I asked? The man found Sammy sitting in the garden of the French Cultural Embassy on 79th Street and Fifth Avenue.

It appeared that Sammy had taken off, had followed the equivalent of a thirty-block route with which he was familiar, and ended up at the 79th Street entrance to Central Park. There he must have heard someone speaking French, a language he recognized, and followed that person across the street to the Embassy where he sat and waited to be rescued.

From that day on, Sammy the bilingual dog, Sammy the best of dogs, was considered worthy of becoming a French citizen.

~Richard Temtchine

55

Park

To think creatively, we must be able to look afresh at what we
normally take for granted.
~George Kneller

Princess, the Great Dane-Boxer-German Shepherd mutt, was a loveable though often exasperating dog who joined our family at the age of three years. She was the eternal puppy, and kept us all entertained on a regular basis.

Say the word "park" to her, and she would go nuts. Jumping high into the air, she would do a little semi-spin and touch down on her hind feet. Enthusiastic could not begin to describe the utter joy she felt at the prospect of going to the park. It was actually an open field we took her to, but what did she know? To Princess, the word meant going for a ride in the car, which she loved, and being able to run freely through the field when she got there. In short, it meant good times.

Before we even pulled up in front of the sacred ground, Princess would begin to hyperventilate, running wildly back and forth on the back seat in anticipation of her freedom. Once her eager paws hit the dirt, she was gone. The last thing we would see is her streaking toward the deep brush located at the far end of the field, her tail wagging triumphantly; there, she would disappear from sight.

The real problem always came when it was time to leave. If we called her name she would come, maybe. More often than not, we would have to go in search of her while calling out another key word in her vocabulary: treat.

Many well-trained dogs respond to the command "come." Ours only responded to "treat." I carried a supply of her favorites in my pocket for departure time, knowing that by whipping one out at the necessary moment, I could coax her into the car.

One day, on one of our customary outings, we were having an especially difficult time getting Princess into the car to go home. For whatever reason, I had forgotten to bring along the essential bait, which not only left me "treatless" but powerless as well.

Without the treats, I had nothing as valuable to Princess as the park. All of the pleading and coaxing could not get her into that car. Suddenly, in the midst of my frustration, an idea struck me. I shouted with all the enthusiasm I could muster, "Do you want to go to the PARK?" The fool jumped right in.

Although we still chuckle over that one, Princess has never fallen for that trick again.

~Nancy Ilk

Signs of Endearment

A dog can express more with his tail in seconds than his owner can express with his tongue in hours.

~Author Unknown

Entering the mailroom at work, I saw a new card on the bulletin board. "Deaf Dalmatian puppy needs a good home." Just that week my new husband and I had decided to get a dog, and this one had to be a perfect match. I worked at a school for deaf children, and Charlie was an American Sign Language interpreter.

The people at the shelter told us Brenda's life had begun in a Kansas puppy mill and she'd been shipped across the country in a cage. Because the first owner had hit her when she failed to obey his spoken commands, his girlfriend took Brenda with her when she fled from the abusive man.

We brought the cute dog home to our San Francisco apartment and, being inexperienced with dogs, treated her just like a child. Because dogs naturally use body language to communicate, Brenda easily learned to understand more than 300 signs.

A year later we became foster parents to a young, deaf boy, and Brenda loved having her own human kid.

During the week Julian lived in the dormitory at the School for the Deaf, and one weekend a month he visited his birth family. The rest of the weekends, school vacations, and holidays he spent with us. Whenever he carried his suitcase out the door we'd tell Brenda how long he'd be gone by signing "bed, finish, one; bed, finish, two" etc. up to the number of nights he'd be away. If we didn't stop at "bed, finish, five" she'd turn her head away and refuse to look at us.

Brenda was not the only animal in our family for long. We gave Julian a mouse, the first pet of his very own he'd ever had. He named the mouse "Skunk" because it was black with a white stripe down its back. The boy would often hold and pet the little creature, feed it, and clean the cage responsibly.

Whenever Julian or other people Skunk liked held him, the mouse would show affection by wrapping his tail around one of their fingers. But he never did that with a stranger. When Brenda sniffed the mouse gently, he would touch his tiny nose to her large, damp one.

The friendly little creature hated to be alone. Sometimes at night he would squeeze between the bars of his cage and climb into Julian's bed. We'd find him the next morning sleeping on the pillow, snuggled next to his favorite human. But once in a while Skunk would get out of the cage and simply disappear.

Whenever that happened, we would sign, "Mouse. Where?" to Brenda, and she would lead us to the tiny animal, who was cowering behind a bookcase or cabinet, apparently lost and frightened. He always seemed grateful when we returned him to the safe familiarity of his own cage.

One summer afternoon I found Julian sobbing. He had discovered Skunk's cold body lying in the cage. I hugged the boy and tried to calm him.

"I'm sorry," I signed. "I know you loved Skunk. We all did. But mice only live a few years and it was time for him to go."

None of my efforts to calm Julian stemmed the flow of tears. His beloved pet was dead and he was overwhelmed with grief. Brenda also tried to comfort him, rubbing her face against his leg and licking his hand. She kept looking at me inquisitively as if to ask, "Why is he crying?"

"Julian wants mouse," I signed to her.

Immediately the dog ran out the open back door. She returned less than a minute later carrying a young field mouse. Brenda gently laid the mouse on Julian's shoe. Julian's tears turned to laughter as we watched the frightened little creature run, jump, and somersault down the back steps to escape into the yard. The dog had cheered him up when I couldn't.

Some people think dogs can't really understand humans and insist owners only imagine they can communicate with their pets. Too bad those people never met Brenda.

~Janet Ann Collins

Someone's
at the Door!

Charles and I could spot the differences at first sight. George, our black Labrador/German Shepherd cross, with a few other breeds thrown in for variety, had a very high, dome-shaped skull, a squared-off muzzle, and a wide range of facial expressions.

By contrast, Ashley's Siberian Husky heritage gave her a flat-skulled, wolf-like appearance.

Where George was intelligent, Ashley was instinctive. There were vast discrepancies in their intellects. George understood and responded to perhaps a hundred different words and phrases—at times we had to speak in code, or spell, to keep him ignorant of our plans.

Ashley had trouble with "come," "sit," and "stay," but she was a gifted natural predator and kept the property free of rodents.

George loved playing games. He delighted in swimming, and even enjoyed diving off a diving board. He was quick and agile, and could catch a ball, stick, or Frisbee in mid-air; it was his greatest pleasure to chase and retrieve anything we could be persuaded to throw for him. He had a sense of humor, and was clearly amused when Charles would pretend to throw invisible objects for him to run after.

Ashley had no concept of play. Toys and games were meaningless to her. "Catch!" was incomprehensible. Toss a ball — or even a piece of steak — toward her and, time and again, it would hit her squarely between the eyes.

George had been an only dog for years when Ashley came to live with us.

Though he appreciated being Top Dog in her company, he did have some issues with jealousy. We rarely had to reprimand him for anything, but we made it clear we didn't like his growling at her or pushing her out of the way when she approached us for affection.

Keeping his temper was most taxing during meal preparation. Formerly, George had been the lone snout under my elbow while I chopped ingredients or stirred a pot, and he had trouble tolerating a competing presence. Worse, he had to share. If he got a morsel, she also got one. This was the limit! He curled his lip, bared his teeth, and growled a warning.

"No!" I said. He looked up at me, surprised. It was clear he disagreed with my rules.

As part of their self-appointed jobs as our guardians and protectors, the dogs habitually announced visitors. They heard cars turning into our driveway well before we did, and bounded clamorously to the front door. As the door opened, they would leap outside and down the steps to confront whatever might be out there, the loud barking continuing nonstop until the "intruders" were given our approval and admitted into the sanctuary.

One evening, the dogs were snoozing on the floor after dinner. We were relaxing in front of the TV, when Charles got the idea to play a joke on George. He leaped up and ran to the front door hollering, "Someone's at the door!"

George woke instantly and scrambled into the foyer with Ashley close behind. Charles threw open the door, and both dogs bounded outside and down the steps, barking. They screeched to a halt at the top of the driveway — but there were no intruders! George looked back to see Charles laughing. Oh! It was a new game!

The next evening I stood over the kitchen counter, preparing a beef roast for the oven, with a canine muzzle at each elbow. The scent of meat was strong, and George was becoming agitated. He insinuated his body between Ashley and me, and started pushing her away. His lip began to curl, a growl started low in his throat.

"No," I warned. His shoulders slumped; his head drooped. Oh, the shame....

Suddenly, he straightened up. He started barking wildly, and ran to the front door with Ashley at his heels. I followed, wiping my hands. When I opened the door, Ashley rushed outside and down the steps, barking.

Standing next to me in the doorway, George silently watched her run down the driveway. Then he turned and trotted back to the kitchen.

~Penny Orloff

Snack Attack

Food should be fun.
~Thomas Keller

Wishbone is quite fussy and also a bit of a drama queen. He prefers dog food of the highest quality—and price—and has a particular gentlemanly way about him. He likes routine, and he prefers his bowl to always be in the same spot in the kitchen—although when the weather is nice he doesn't mind dining al fresco.

Wishbone won't take a treat from you unless you ask him to sit first. He likes to demonstrate how well behaved he is. For him, the chance to show off is as much of a treat as any dog snack could ever be.

A few months ago, Wishbone went off anything that was cube shaped. He would eat all of his dinner; the round, crunchy beef-flavoured bits, the odd-shaped, green vegetable bits, but he wouldn't touch the cubes.

Not only that, but he would pick them up through gritted teeth, one tiny cube at a time, and place them in a neat, symmetrical row alongside his bowl for everyone to see. Almost like a military line-up of kibble. He'd eaten cubes for six years previously, but now, for some reason, they were off limits.

His brother Nibbles, or Nobs as he's been nicknamed, is not quite as fussy. In fact, he's not fussy at all. Nobs has developed a particular liking for carrots recently, but his snack selection hasn't always been so healthy.

The first few months of Nobs' life coincided with a period that became commonly known in our household as The Great Disappearance. It began with the first big food shop. I was certain I had bought a packet of fresh salmon. In fact, I was certain that I had taken it out of the shopping bag and placed it on the side, but when I turned to get it to put in the fridge, it was gone.

Where had it gone? Straight into Nobs' belly.

Wishbone on the other hand was once offered fresh prawns, but turned his nose up. I guess they weren't organic or something. As I said, he has very high standards.

Over the next few weeks the salmon was joined by an entire loaf of bread — which poor Nobs couldn't hide very well, as it swelled up inside him like a big, yeasty balloon. He didn't keep it down for very long. Shortly after, Nobs stole a cream-cheese-stuffed jalapeno from the barbeque. And that too didn't stay down. Until then, I had never seen a dog physically cry.

Wishbone simply looked at his gluttonous brother in disgust. How could he be so uncouth?

This was just the tip of the iceberg though. These at least were all food stuffs.

During the first year of their lives, Wishbone snacked on dog food, dog treats and the occasional tin of sardines. All things that he was allowed to have, and that were perfectly acceptable.

Nobs, meanwhile, ate his way through shoes, socks, and hats before slowly progressing to more expensive items such as mobile phones, television remotes, the chargers for both, DVDs, books and even a computer mouse.

Then he began to tackle bigger items — kitchen cupboards, the sofa, my bed, the guest bed, his own bed even. He ate inconvenient things, like my passport, and money. He ate messy things, including a blue pen, which he chomped while sitting on my crisp white bed sheets (where he was not allowed to be I hasten to add). Then he got more adventurous and injected some danger into things by snacking on a serrated bread knife, some kitchen scissors, and a lighter.

The ultimate in his culinary expedition, though, was the venomous green snake that I caught him sampling when I came home one day. He wasn't sure what to do with it at first. Should he eat it? Should he play with it?

What he should have done was leave it alone, but there was no telling him that.

There was a good ten minutes of Nobs throwing the snake up in the air while it swung at him viciously. I frantically tried to call him away from the snake before he was bitten. In the end the snake didn't make it, but not before poor Nobs got a nip on the tongue, causing him to spend two days under close observation, receiving medication to counter the effects of the bite. However, he was given lots of treats during this time so it wasn't all bad.

Wishbone and Nobs are middle aged now. They are coming up to their seventh birthday and, if anything, Wishbone has gotten even fussier. Cubes are back on the menu this week, but anything chicken flavoured is off.

As for Nobs, he still eats anything. Including cubes.

~Lauren Smith

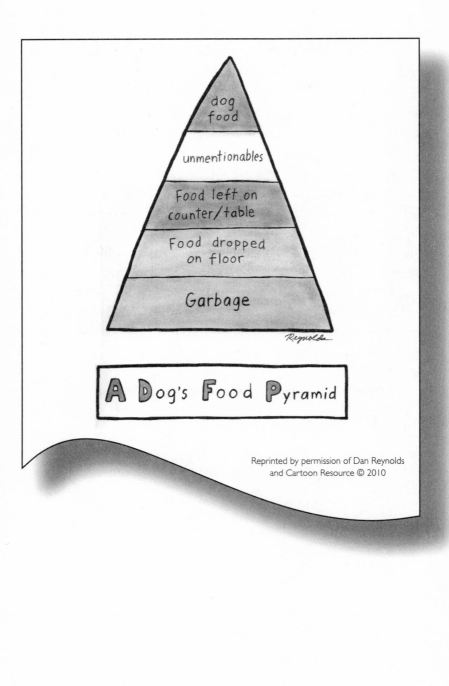

The Odd Couple

The purpose of a liberal arts education is to learn
that a person can like both cats and dogs!
~Author Unknown

nce I thought pet adoptions were only done by people. Never would I have dreamed that a pet might adopt another pet until our shaggy Collie-Shepherd, Chandu, chose a cat to be his very own.

Over summer, while walking Chandu the length of the alley that ran behind our block, we saw a large orange Persian cat in a back yard. She was exceptionally beautiful, that first time standing stiff-legged with fur fluffed up when she saw us. Chandu did not bark at her or strain at his leash. He merely muttered a soft sound of acknowledgment, and we continued walking. Later on when we walked down the alley, the cat hopped onto a gate to watch us and once followed us from a distance. It was most curious.

On an autumn afternoon when I came home from school, there sat the big orange cat on our front steps. Chandu was sprawled on the porch in his usual waiting-for-Marcia place. The cat jumped up and skittered away when she saw me approaching. Ears cocked, Chandu gave me a look that said, "Hey, I was just getting acquainted with her and you scared her off!"

A few days later my mother reported that she saw the cat drinking from Chandu's outdoor water bowl and that the feline appeared to have lost weight. That evening when Dad and I walked Chandu down the alley to the vacant lot where all the neighborhood dogs were walked, we saw that the grass had not been cut at the house where we thought the cat lived and the curtains were gone from the windows.

"I think that orange cat's people have moved away," I said. "The house looks empty."

Dad agreed and we saw no sign of the cat.

But the next day when I came home, Chandu was waiting on the porch to greet me and the big orange cat was sitting on the top step near him. This time she did not run away as I came up the steps. I noted that her thick coat was matted and she was definitely thinner. She meowed and I stooped to pet her. Chandu stood up proprietarily near the cat, his plumed tail wagging fast and friendly. When I opened the front door, he did not rush forward as usual but stood to one side watching the cat. He made a soft sound, as if urging the cat to go inside first. And she did, Chandu and I following. She warily circled the living room, one eye on us all the time.

Chandu proceeded to the kitchen, gave a small whuffle and nudged his food bowl. I opened a can of his dog food, filled his bowl, and expected him to rush forward and scarf down his food as he usually did. Instead, again he stood by as the cat, smelling food, came into the kitchen and attacked the dog food as if she had not eaten in days.

When she was full, Chandu advanced slowly and finished off what remained of his supper. The cat retreated to a corner under the table and washed her face, then walked to the front door to be let out. For a week we never knew where she spent her nights, but she appeared on our front porch each afternoon and the pattern was repeated.

Could such a beautiful cat have been abandoned? It would seem so, according to the neighbors we questioned. It was wartime and the huge army camp outside town had brought vast changes, including sudden moves by hundreds of people as troops were transferred. Wives and families followed, often with little notice. Others simply moved away from our small town to take high-paying defense factory jobs. It was not unknown for an occasional pet to be left behind.

There came an evening when both animals had filled their bellies, and after the meal the cat went close to Chandu and rubbed against his legs. The dog stood still, giving a sigh, obviously enamored with the attention. When he lay down on his regular evening spot on the living room rug, the cat came and curled up next to him.

From that moment Chandu had his pet and companion. The two became inseparable. Chandu frequently gave the cat, whom we named Fluffy, a bath with his long tongue. Fluffy tried to return the favor but her small cat tongue was no match for a big Collie-Shepherd with a thick coat of fur.

In those days in small towns like ours, most dogs and cats ran loose during the day. Chandu watched over Fluffy as one might a small child, flicking her gently across the face with his tail if she ventured too near the street or followed where he did not want her to go. He shared his favorite ball with her, the two of them bouncing and chasing it around the back yard. She accompanied us on the bedtime walks down the alley, often running ahead and then pouncing out from a bush in front of Chandu, who pretended great surprise. Although Fluffy now had her own food bowl, the two animals liked to have their meals side by side. In cold weather, when Chandu bedded down for the night beside my bed, Fluffy arranged herself in the warm middle of his curled body. When he chose to spend time in his doghouse in the back yard, Fluffy joined him. And in afternoons, she joined him on the porch to wait for me to come home from school, the two sitting side by side.

One Sunday afternoon when the two were playing in the back yard, two dogs strange to the neighborhood jumped over our fence and barked ferociously as they chased Fluffy. She leaped on top of Chandu's doghouse and Chandu rushed to attack. Hearing the racket, I ran outside screaming at the intruders. Terrified, I watched the fight—which was over quickly—as the dogs were no match for Chandu, who moved like lightning. The strays were routed and sent howling back over the fence. Chandu chased them a short distance, gave a few parting barks, and returned to leap gracefully over the fence. He strolled across the lawn with all the dignity and pride of a conquering knight. He stood on his hind legs at the doghouse to check on his friend, who rubbed her face against his as he smoothed her fur with a slobbery tongue. In turn, Fluffy purred the loudest purr I ever heard from a cat.

All was well once more with our beloved dog and his cherished feline pet and pal, the odd couple.

~Marcia E. Brown

Sight Comes in Many Forms

Any glimpse into the life of an animal quickens our own and makes it so much the larger and better in every way.
~John Muir

She sat looking up at me intently, waiting for our conversation to begin. Yet she had no eyes.

Skye, a Norwegian Elkhound, was six years old when her caretaker Janis called me for a consultation. As an animal intuitive I talk with animals, provide healing energies to them, and consult regularly with a variety of animals regarding emotional, health, and behavioural issues. Janis had heard about my gifts from a friend and called because Skye had digestive issues that were compromising her health.

During my initial talk with Janis, I had the impression that Skye was grey in colour. I had never seen a Norwegian Elkhound. So when my conversation with Janis ended, I went to my dog book, opening it at random, right at the page for Norwegian Elkhounds. They were indeed grey.

When I prepare to work with an animal I meditate at my home, calling its energy to me and talk with it that way first. I will then either complete my consultation long distance, talking to the caretaker with the information I collected from the animal, or arrange for a site visit.

It is the animal, not the human, who tells me if I need to arrange a physical visit.

If an animal hurts somewhere, I will generally feel that pain in my body in a corresponding spot. In Skye's case, her digestive system was somewhat tender. But Janis had recently adopted a diet more compatible with Skye's system, so that no longer appeared to be a major issue. My sense was a few tweaks were still needed.

In meditation I asked Skye to come into my inner awareness and she did. Most often, an animal will show itself to me in some manner. In my inner vision I will see an eye, face, tail, or nose. In Skye's case I felt her presence in a strong way, but did not see any part of her body. I asked her about her sight, how she was coping with not having eyes, and she told me she could see. From speaking to Janis I knew Skye had her eyes removed, yet she insisted she could see. I asked her to show me what that looked like. I immediately saw darkness, but when I rested in that darkness I began to see outlines of the furniture in my meditation room. Skye could see outlines of furniture, walls, people, other animals, and so on. I was amazed.

That strong sense of her presence, and that she could see but visually couldn't, intrigued me and I wanted to meet her. She told me that she wanted to see me in person, so I arranged a visit when next in Winnipeg, a city two hours away.

Skye lived with her sister Ginger, their human Janis, and Pita, the younger dog who lived with Maya, Janis' daughter.

Everyone was at the door to greet me when I arrived. Greetings were vigorous and a great deal of milling around occurred for a few minutes with Skye right in there with the other dogs.

When I visit multi-animal homes, the animals tend to sort out who goes first to visit with me. This time was no different. Once everyone settled down from the greeting and the humans were busy trying to figure out the appropriate protocol, Skye quietly presented herself in front of me, looking very intently, waiting for our chat.

This action in itself is not unusual when an animal speaks with me — we maintain direct eye contact while the messages are shared.

If I couldn't see with my own eyes that her eyelids were sewn shut, I would have said she was looking at me with a piercing gaze.

The other two dogs took themselves off to different areas of the home, one right around the corner so she could listen in (for she also wanted to talk with me), and the other further away because she did not want to talk with me.

Skye's eyesight had begun to fail two years ago, leading to removal of one eye six months later with the diagnosis of primary glaucoma. The veterinarians who were involved at different times with her care informed Janis that the probability of the other eye going was extremely high.

Janis treated Skye's remaining eye with medicines that helped prolong the sight, until a year and a half later when her other eye was removed. Throughout her medical care Skye was stoic and coopera-tive. Janis informed me that the glaucoma issue tended to be inherent in that particular breed. Although Skye's sister Ginger had the same genetic background, her sight was fine. It was just the luck of the draw for Skye. The reason the eyes had to be removed had to do with the pressure building up and not dissipating, even though her sight had failed.

Skye moved around the home like she was sighted. When she sat in front of me and looked up at me, she could see me. I have visited with other dogs who had lost their sight, and they tend to navigate with their heads lowered toward the ground at a bit of an angle, almost like they were hearing an echo from the earth as they moved. They also walked slowly with care, sometimes stumbling if the terrain was new. Skye moved like any sighted dog without any hesitation.

I observed that Skye is clearly the Alpha in the house, and so the others deferred to her. I watched her movement and was amazed at how smoothly she carried herself. Her head was up and she moved with confidence around furniture, around moving people, around the other moving dogs and navigated to a sit stance right in front of me. She impressed me with her calmness. She was well mannered and a gentle dog, and I felt her strong presence—her soul if you like. She had a sense of humour and a certain regal feel. As we chatted and got her diet balanced out for her, she told me that sight was not an issue. Janis dittoed that! Janis said the only thing that throws Skye is a loud, unexpected noise when she is outside walking.

Skye said that she did not like the new house (she and Janis had moved into it just a month before she lost her sight) as much as she had the other house, because she had favourite spots to visit in the old neighbourhood and friends to greet on her walks.

Skye controls her pack, including Janis, with a serene and gentle presence that calms the other occupants of the house. She claims her space without the need to boss any dog around and provides a peaceful energy to the house. She is unique — a dog without eyes who can see. She senses your emotion and relaxes into it, providing comfort to those around her. Janis affirmed that Skye tapped into her emotions quickly and spread her love to everyone, humans and dogs alike.

~Camille Hill

My Roadie

Yesterday I was a dog. Today I'm a dog. Tomorrow I'll probably still be a dog.
Sigh! There's so little hope for advancement.
~Charles M. Schulz

Years ago when I toured numerous schools with my one-woman mime, clown, and circus children's shows, I would take my Golden Retriever along with me for companionship. Kane wasn't a great conversationalist, but he was always a great listener, giving me his undivided attention.

When my performances were over for the day, though tired, I would pack up my van and we would drive to our next destination. After finding a local motel and checking in for the night, Kane and I would set out on a long walk to discover our new surroundings. Sometimes by chance we'd find a park and occasionally some waterfront for Kane's enjoyment. Accompanied by my portable security system, my one-hundred-plus-pound canine, I felt safe exploring new areas.

With my best friend by my side I never felt alone despite being the outsider in each community we visited. My furry buddy taught me how to project a positive first impression, giving strangers the benefit of the doubt with his friendly disposition.

After we finished exploring the area, I'd buy a few groceries and we'd return to our motel room. I'd carry in my belongings and necessities from the van and then place a few personal items around the room to help me feel more at home. Unlike me Kane, who had no materialistic ties, had minimal needs. With some food, water, and me for company, he'd settle in for the night and be snoring away in no time.

Early the next morning, we'd head off to another school and begin the process of preparing and performing my show once again. Kane would escort me into the gym and hang around while I organized my props, sound system, and other equipment. He was the ultimate theater ambassador who knew how to manipulate the school officials into allowing him to stay in the building, despite the health codes.

"You know you're not supposed to have dogs in the..." a school official's comment would always begin. Then Kane would approach him or her and turn on the charm.

"He's so beautiful..." the official would continue, while petting Kane. "What's his name?"

Then I would hear "If you need anything please let me know."

"Thanks, I will," I'd respond politely.

Before the show would start, Kane and I could be found in the locker room. As I smeared on my stage make-up and donned my costume, he would calmly loll around or sleep close by. Nothing seemed to faze him, not even the sound of the gym filling up with hundreds of excited children awaiting my show. It always thrilled me to hear the students' energized pre-show chatter, no matter how many times I performed. This steadfast dog would continue lying there peacefully and usually not even wake up.

When the time was right, a staff member would knock on the door and inform me that the audience was ready. As planned, I would start my sound system with my remote control and listen for the taped sports broadcaster announcing the start of a race.

Once I heard "... and they're off..." that was my cue to open the door and enter the gym as a clown riding on my unicycle. While I pedaled around the audience, the taped announcer would comment on the race between me and other imaginary contestants. As the race progressed I would pretend to interact and pass the other supposed athletes, resulting in my first place finish.

One time, unlike any other, right after I rode into the gym, I heard the crowd go wild. I assumed that this was just an overly enthusiastic audience. The cheering crowd, to my delight, added to the fun of this mimed race. It wasn't until I rode around the audience for a whole lap that I realized Kane had joined in the race too. He must have followed me as I was leaving the changing room, but I didn't notice him behind me. No doubt it appeared planned and well choreographed, which carried a huge amount of audience appeal. Since I couldn't stop my show to remove him, we both kept circling the spectators. My heart was beating in my mouth. I didn't know what to expect. All I could do was to continue and hope for the best.

As the race neared its end Kane was closing in on me, but luckily I was still in the lead. I was able to break through the crepe paper finish line when Kane stopped just after me. I managed my big finale, with lots of bows and confetti throwing as he sat panting with tail wagging. To show my good sportsmanship, I applauded this second place contestant. The sound of the audience clapping was monumental.

I calmly walked my dog off to the side, quickly gave him to a teacher to escort back into the locker room and continued with my performance. The spectators booed at the sight of this star being taken out of the show. Who could blame them? As the music changed, the students soon became engrossed in my next act and didn't take long to settle down.

After the show, hugging Kane and chuckling, I told him "You were great! I didn't know you were such a good actor. What a good dog!" I could hardly say anything other than praise his performing debut. He gave me a proud gaze as if to let me know that he understood his accomplishment.

Undoubtedly, Kane's performance was the highlight of that school tour. Tempted as I was to use my favourite canine again in my show, I just couldn't take the chance. Kane, I guess, was satisfied with his few minutes of fame and never tried to jump into the act again.

It will always remain a mystery to me why Kane decided to join in that show. If he could speak, no doubt he would have an interesting version of the event to share.

~Dalia Gesser

Chapter 7

I Can't Believe My Dog Did That!

Throw Me a Bone

Country Life

I have no relish for the country; it is a kind of healthy grave.
~Sydney Smith

Buster couldn't understand why he wasn't invited to accompany my husband George on his trip to the woods that cold January afternoon. Though George and I, born and raised in the suburbs, were struggling to adjust to our new life in the country, our high-energy Yellow Lab loved everything about living on a farm. A pond for swimming. Barn cats to chase. Manure to roll in. Not a care in the world. Buster wasn't the least bit concerned about what to do with the old billy goat we'd found dead in the pasture that morning. But we were.

Most of the options we could think of for disposing the carcass seemed downright barbaric. Tie a concrete block to the goat and sink him in the pond. Throw him on top of the brush pile and set it ablaze. Leave him for the buzzards. We decided that there was no choice but to bury the goat.

Which was problematic for one big reason. The ground in Middle Tennessee, though not frozen solid, was rock hard.

No matter. George took the shovel and pickax from the tool shed and hauled them and the goat, already cold and stiff, up a steep hill to the wooded area at the back of the pasture. Then he began to dig. Deciding that narrow and deep was preferable to shallow and wide so that wild animals wouldn't scavenge the remains, he painstakingly carved out a hole that looked to be the perfect size. Covered with sweat despite the frigid temperatures, he picked the goat up by its feet and gently lowered it into the grave.

The legs and hooves protruded almost a foot above the ground. George tried bending them. He tried twisting them. He tried folding them. It was no use.

He pulled out the goat and dug some more. The wind picked up and the weak winter sun began to dip behind the mountain, but at least the heinous task was almost done.

Well, no. The grave was still too shallow. Again George heaved the goat out of the hole and kept on digging.

"This grave is deep enough to hold a camel," he muttered to himself half an hour later.

For the third time, he picked up the goat and unceremoniously dropped him, upside down, into the hole. Six inches of legs still stuck up above the ground.

"That'll have to do," George said, picking up the shovel and beginning to fill in the hole. Enough dirt was left over that he was able to form a small mound over the entire grave. The mound covered everything but the goat's hooves, which somewhat resembled four eerily colored mushrooms. He kicked some leaves and sticks over them and bent to pick up the tools.

"Rest in peace, old fellow," he said and left.

By the time he made it back to the shed, snow and sleet were falling like crazy. Buster was overjoyed when George finally returned to the house. He'd been pacing the floor for almost an hour, begging to be let out. Now, without even pausing for a scratch behind his ears, he charged out the back door into the darkness.

"You don't suppose…?" I began.

"Nah. He probably just needs a bathroom break. No way will he travel clear to the back of the pasture in this weather. And even if he does, he won't be able to find the grave. I buried that goat but good."

I could only hope he was right.

A few minutes after Buster bolted outside, we heard a scratching at the back door. And there he was—wet, muddy, and out of breath—with a full six inches of gnawed-off goat leg clenched firmly between his teeth.

Country life definitely agreed with Buster.

~Jennie Ivey

A Dog on a Bender

Strength is the ability to break a chocolate bar into four pieces
with your bare hands — and then eat just one of those pieces.
~Judith Viorst

Quimby is our stately, black Labrador, tall, beautifully proportioned, calm, and a deep thinker. The trouble is that he is addicted to chocolate. He prefers at least seventy-six percent dark, organic, expensive chocolate, but he'll eat any kind in a pinch.

We are Quimby's family only because he was too cautious to continue in the Guide Dog Program. His trainer called it "fear response," and she was right, but we like to think of him as too wise to put himself in harm's way. Still, he couldn't be a guide dog if he was going to hide under a table every time he saw his reflection in a skylight at night.

At first Quimby would just steal a double chocolate chip cookie that fell to the floor, or a piece of Halloween candy forgotten on the bottom of a plastic jack-o'-lantern — nothing that would hurt a ninety-pound dog.

Once he ate most of a large Hershey's Special Dark Chocolate bar, so we called our vet. She calculated the amount of chocolate versus his weight and said he'd be okay, but that we needed to be very careful. Quimby was clearly in need of a doggie intervention.

To tell the truth, I share Quimby's addiction. As a human, however, all I have to worry about is weight gain and a caffeine rush if I eat too much chocolate. Therefore I am very careful to have small amounts of the very darkest, most satisfying chocolate I can find, and only indulge when I need it most, a surprisingly frequent event.

Before small packages of chocolate were readily available, I would take great pains at Christmas, Easter and Halloween to buy several packages of Hershey's bite-sized candy bars in the assorted multi-packs. I pulled out all the Special Dark Miniatures and stashed them in Ziploc bags in a drawer in the kitchen.

If my family ever noticed that they never got Special Dark in their stockings or baskets, they never said anything. Smart family. They know they are better off when Mom has plenty of her Special Dark.

One Easter I'd just finished packaging my stash. It had to last me until miniatures would be available again at Halloween. I keep my Special Darks in a drawer low enough that Quimby could reach, but it's very hard to open, so I was stunned when I came home from errands to find Quimby surrounded by shredded Ziploc bags and tiny bits of pink, yellow and silver aluminum foil wrappers.

Wrappers stuck to his nose as he shook his head and flicked his tongue in and out, trying to dislodge more wrappers from his teeth, all the while offering that "who me?" look Labs are known for. I laughed, then panicked, as I realized how much chocolate he had actually eaten.

My six-month stash was not a trivial amount of chocolate.

It was after-hours for our regular vet. How long did I have to get it out of him? How would I manage that? Would that save him? I called the ASPCA's animal poison control line. I waded through the recorded voices until I reach a real person who told me I needed to force-feed him hydrogen peroxide to make him vomit right away.

Ten minutes later, I found a bottle of peroxide in the back of a cabinet in the bathroom. Was time running out? I took him outside and squirted a dose down the back of his throat with a turkey baster.

Nothing came up, and he tried desperately to escape. He was a big dog determined to be wherever I, and the turkey baster, were not. Still no action.

I called back the ASPCA to see if I could give him another dose. More time was lost with more recordings, and then the live person wasn't sure what to do. Supervisors were consulted and finally I was told I could give him more peroxide.

But Quimby was onto me now, so I had to wrestle a ninety-pound Labrador while holding a turkey baster full of peroxide, which was flailing around my head. (The bright side was that the "highlights" in my hair had never been so inexpensive, or so orange.)

Having no success with the second dose, my husband and I opted for the emergency vet clinic on the other side of town. I wished ambulances would carry doggies as we careened down our mountain road, bumped onto Highway 99W and hoped for more green than red lights on our way past town.

A vet tech took Quimby to a back room immediately upon hearing our story. We tried to laugh at the comedy of the situation instead of thinking about the possible dire consequences. We picked up, then put down, one slobber-coated, torn-up magazine after another, unable to concentrate on any of them.

Another vet tech came out to say they were having trouble getting him to vomit and wanted more clarification on the timing of his chocolate bender. We weren't exactly sure how long before we got home he actually got to my stash. After a few minutes, yet another tech rushed from the back room and ran out to the parking lot. Before we could get out the door and catch her to see what was wrong, she returned with a camera in her hand, smiling.

"Oh, he finally vomited. He should be okay. I'm a student at the vet school, so I just want to get a picture." She stopped to shake her head and laugh a little. "None of us has ever seen that much chocolate come out of one dog. Some of the pieces were still whole and in their wrappers!" She hurried off, still chuckling.

Quimby survived his chocolate bender and became famous in the process. A picture of him standing next to his astonishing pile of chocolate is still on a wall at Oregon State University's College of Veterinary Medicine.

Quimby, however, is still a chocoholic.

~Sallie Wagner Brown

"Tell me this isn't celery."

She Knew

Intuition is a spiritual faculty and does not explain,
but simply points the way.
~Florence Scovel Shinn

I knew she wasn't an ordinary dog the moment I saw her. She had a presence, a dignity, and a calmness, which no other dog that I have ever seen possessed. Our eyes met in a kind of surreal moment and those gentle eyes seemed to be pleading, "Why am I here?" which, amazingly, was exactly what I was thinking.

The card on her cage stated "Becka — two years old, owner surrendered," and my faith in the goodness of human nature diminished.

I grabbed the first attendant I saw and asked to see Becka. A German Shorthaired Pointer mix, the color of honey, Becka's eyes never left me as she was being leashed. We were led to a visiting area where Becka and I could spend some time together. To say it was love at first sight is an understatement, and I didn't need to know anything else; I didn't need any more time. Becka was mine.

Becka eased right into the routine of my home as if she had lived with me forever. She lay next to me while I watched television; she "helped" me in my garden chores; went with me almost everywhere I went; tried to eat from my dinner plate; and slept with me every night. I had a close companion to help fill the lonely hours of living alone. I tended to Becka's needs as if she were a queen.

About a year after Becka came to live with me a very noticeable change came over her. She had always been a close companion, but now she stuck to me closer than ever. Whenever she could, Becka would lick my abdomen. There seemed to be a sense of urgency in her eyes every time she looked at me, and she began looking at me constantly. It felt like she was trying to tell me something, but of course, I didn't know what it was. I made an appointment with the vet and took Becka in for a complete examination. All tests came back clear. The vet told me I had nothing to worry about and to stop imagining things.

So Becka and I carried on with our lives with some unanswered questions about her new attentiveness and sense of urgency—until my next physical examination, that is, when the doctors discovered that I had colon cancer.

I had surgery, and since the cancer was in its early stages, the surgeons were able to get all of the cancer out. I did not need chemotherapy.

When I returned home from the hospital, Becka was as ecstatic to see me as I was to see her. And my old Becka was back. There was no more licking of my abdomen; the look of concern that had been in her eyes for weeks was gone; and she stopped clinging to me.

Then it dawned on me that Becka must have known about my cancer all along. I couldn't believe it. How she could have known? But there was no other explanation for her behavior.

Now I trust Becka with all of my heart, and I just know that she will let me know if anything else goes wrong.

~LaVerne Otis

Trick or Treat

Shadows of a thousand years rise again unseen,
Voices whisper in the trees, "Tonight is Halloween!"
~Dexter Kozen

"Trick or treat!"

A sea of cherubic-faced princesses, ghosts and goblins raised their jack-o'-lanterns in the hopes of obtaining candy. Marley sat to our right, wagging his tail incessantly. He loved little people. And despite his imposing size, most of them felt likewise. Many times, Marley found himself surrounded by neighborhood children—especially giggly girls.

"May I hug him?" they would say squealing, burying their faces into his clumpy, white dreadlocks.

But that night, after the third or fourth Halloween salutation, Marley grew agitated. Our Komondor watched anxiously as brightly wrapped candy clunked into buckets and bags, then issued a whimper.

"What's wrong with him?" I asked.

My husband shrugged, mystified. We didn't know what to make of it. Marley's whines escalated and eventually coincided with cramming his dinosaur-like head into bags for candy retrieval. We replaced the candy, of course, and then reprimanded our large companion for his outburst. Marley plopped to the ground.

"Maybe we should put him inside," I suggested.

"Let's give him another chance," my husband answered.

"Trick or treat!" a child cried, his feet creating a chorus of crunching and crackling over the carpet of red, yellow, orange and brown leaves.

Marley sat up straight and tall, leaves clinging to his Velcro-like hair. His expressive eyebrows moved up and down and enormous, pink tongue remained frozen. Marley's eyes shifted from us to the child, until... plunk, the candy dropped into the bag. Marley pawed the sack.

While my husband took care of the matter, I went inside to grab more candy. Upon returning, he had a peculiar smile on his face and suggested putting our overwrought assistant inside. Marley assumed a seat near the window. I went back outside.

"I know what the problem is," said my husband.

"What?"

"Trick or treat," he said.

"I don't understand," I replied.

My husband smiled and repeated the phrase, with emphasis on "treat." Then it hit me. Marley connected the word with doggy biscuits. The entire evening he must have felt the victim of a cruel prank, hearing the word over and over and watching youngsters run off with booty. His booty.

I turned toward the house. Marley's face pressed against the glass. I went inside, grabbed some biscuits, asked Marley to sit and presented the coveted reward. Outside, skeletons and pirates paraded across the yard. They yelled the magic phrase and Marley's ears lifted.

So every crisp, Midwest October, our former, overzealous Halloween helper spent the evening indoors on his doggy bed, waiting like Scrooge at Christmas, for the unjust holiday to pass him by.

~Lisa Mackinder

Class Picture

The true gift of friendship is the gift of yourself.
~Author Unknown

I walked to South School every day with Glen, who lived in a broken-down house—more of a shack really—down the street from me. We'd join up on our way to school, kicking rocks down the sidewalk in the fall, throwing the odd snowball in the winter, floating little matchstick boats down the gutter rivulets in the spring.

We never said much to each other. Glen wasn't much for words. He had been held back a grade or two in school, and he was much taller and bigger than the rest of the kids in our third grade class.

He always seemed to be a bit embarrassed, scrunching to fit into the little desk in Mrs. Lougheed's class. Or sad. Maybe he was just sad. All I know is sometimes when I'd look at him across the room, struggling with his reading or his arithmetic, my heart would hurt a bit.

Glen loved one thing more than anything else—his dog, Blackie. A big old black Lab, as quiet and gentle as Glen himself. Outside of school the two were never apart. Maybe that's why Glen seemed sad in school. He missed Blackie.

Often Blackie would walk Glen and me to school and then make his way back home by himself, and often Blackie would be there all by himself at the end of the school day, waiting to walk us home again. Those were Glen's favorite days. And mine too.

Blackie wasn't supposed to be at the school though. Glen's mom had been told that dogs weren't allowed on the school grounds, and Blackie didn't have a license or even a collar for that matter. I don't think Glen's mom could afford stuff like that, or if she could, she wasn't the kind of person who would worry about dog licenses and such.

One perfect spring Wednesday I looked out the classroom window to the playground when the school bell rang and saw Blackie sitting in the schoolyard, in the shade by the baseball diamond, thumping his tail in the cool grass. Like only elementary school children at recess can, we rode a wave of excitement out the classroom, floating through the boot room, a torrent of goofiness gushing out the school doors, barely touching the ground.

Glen made a beeline for Blackie, me right behind him. We were both instantly rewarded with a woof and a lick, but Glen was worried. He told Blackie to go home, that he wasn't supposed to be there, that he would get in trouble. But the big old black Lab wasn't going anywhere, and when he decided on something, there was no budging him.

By this time, most of our class had gravitated over to see Blackie, to pet him and rub his big old square head, kneeling down for a hug, hoping for a lick on the cheek. The most popular girl in the grade, Penny Bond, was on the receiving end of a mighty slurp when we heard it.

The gravel crunched as a van pulled up right beside us, near the baseball diamond on a narrow driveway behind the old school building. Nobody ever drove on that gravel—except the dogcatcher. He had a bright orange van, and pretty well every single kid at South School hated that van. To this day I don't like that shade of orange.

"I have to take the dog," said the dogcatcher as he got out of the van. "Move away now kids, go play over there."

He gestured with a big pole toward the playground equipment. The pole had a loop of rope on it. It looked like a noose to me.

"Come on now kids, I gotta take the dog. Go play now." He was still keeping his distance, but nobody moved. Blackie woofed. Glen kneeled beside Blackie, hugging him, blinking back tears.

"He's my dog," said Glen. "It's okay, he's my dog, Blackie."

But the dogcatcher just took a step toward us, slowly swinging the pole with the noose on the end. "I don't see a license on this animal. He doesn't even have a collar. I have to take him to the pound, kid. If he's your dog, you can claim him there and pay the fee. He ain't allowed on the school grounds."

"But, we don't even have a car," said Glen, trying really hard now not to cry in front of all of his friends. He didn't want to say that his mom didn't have the money to get Blackie out of the pound. He didn't want to say it, but we all knew what happened to dogs that nobody claimed from the pound.

The dogcatcher wasn't listening. He took another step toward Blackie, and Glen started to cry and suddenly, somehow, we all stood in front of Glen and Blackie. We stood between them and the dogcatcher.

And then Penny Bond grabbed my hand, and I grabbed someone else's hand, and somehow we all linked together, and we were forming a circle — a huge circle of gritty third grade kids, arms outstretched, building a human fence around our friend and his dog.

It was one of those moments. One of those moments you know you'll always remember, even when you're old. Especially when you're old.

We stood there in our circle, Glen and Blackie in the middle of that circle, the dogcatcher outside of the circle, not exactly sure what to do. Nobody said a word. All you could hear was that Glen had stopped crying.

We would have stood there forever if it weren't for Mrs. Lougheed. Somehow she was out the back door of the school and calling to the dogcatcher. They stood over by his ugly orange dogcatcher van, Mrs. Lougheed doing most of the talking.

We hung onto our circle even harder now, and then something amazing happened. The dogcatcher got into his van and drove off. He didn't say anything to us at all; he didn't even look over at us. He just drove away.

When all the cheering and hugging and crying died down, Mrs. Lougheed got us settled down back in our own classroom, Blackie sprawled in the corner at the back of the room, snoozing away contentedly for the rest of the afternoon. I think it was Glen's happiest time in school ever.

Glen and his dog and his mom moved away that summer, and I never saw them again. But if you look at our old black-and-white class picture, beyond all the silly smiles and goofy hairdos of proud and shiny eight-year-olds, if you could look beyond the frame, you'd see what I can see: an old black dog curled up just outside of the class picture not very far from the biggest kid in the class.

~Harley Hay

MasterCard

Dogs are animals that poop in public and you're supposed to pick it up.
After a week of doing this, you've got to ask yourself,
"Who's the real master in this relationship?"
~Anthony Griffin

rowing up in a sleepy New England town in the 1950s meant long, slow summers. We made our own fun by jumping in the creek, coloring sidewalks with chalk, and playing tag. Still, some summer days we complained of boredom. Our Wire Haired Terrier, Tara, seemed to feel the same way.

My father, pastor of a well-known Episcopal church in the center of town, noticed that Tara slipped away from time to time. She would return hours later, exhausted, with her tongue lolling to the side. Where had she been?

The mystery might never have been solved except for the phone call we received from the manager of a popular five-and-ten-cent store. He had observed a certain four-legged shoplifter entering his store on a regular basis. He had also identified the perpetrator as the good reverend's pet.

The next day, my father followed Tara as she trotted down the sidewalk to the town commons. He watched as she stopped in front of the five-and-ten and waited for a customer to approach the entrance. As soon as the door opened, Tara slipped inside. Moments later another customer exited, and Tara emerged with a bright rubber ball in her mouth.

Carrying the ball across the street, Tara walked up to a park bench where an elderly man was seated. She dropped the ball at his feet, sat down in front of him and wagged her tail.

"Isn't she cute!" the man exclaimed.

He picked up the ball and tossed it for the dog to chase. Tara delightedly retrieved the ball and dropped it once again at his feet. If he didn't pick it up, she nudged the ball with her nose and yipped with excitement. Soon the rules of the game became clear, and the man found himself in an endless cycle of throwing and receiving the ball.

At last the man sighed, "That's enough, old girl."

Tara refused to be discouraged. When her aged acquaintance became tired and neglected to pick up the ball, Tara simply approached another bench and found a new playmate. Eagerly she moved from bench to bench, making friends all around the green and delighting each one with her antics.

An hour later Tara returned home panting and exhausted. She slurped great gulps of water from her bowl and then sprawled on the cool linoleum floor of the kitchen.

Where was the ball? No one knew. We had to assume that Tara left it under a bush somewhere on the commons. The balls never came home. Each day she helped herself to a new one.

Dad called the store manager and confirmed that Tara was indeed the guilty party.

"Reverend, I keep the balls in a bin right near the door. I don't mind so much about her taking one ball now and then, but this has become a habit."

My father apologized profusely and promised to pay for the missing toys. But what could be done to prevent problems in the future?

On the one hand, Dad's reputation was at stake — our dog was stealing merchandise. On the other hand, she was bringing much joy to the older residents of the park benches. They obviously looked forward to these visits from the friendly canine.

At last my father proposed a simple solution. Would the store manager keep an inventory of the balls and let my father know how many went missing each month? Tara would continue to entertain her friends in the park while my father would settle the credit account on a regular basis.

Our dog Tara gave new meaning to the term "master-card."

~Emily Parke Chase

68

Happy Holi-dog

It is Christmas in the heart that puts Christmas in the air.
~W.T. Ellis

My dog's personality didn't fully develop until he was about seven. By eight, Buddy was so smart that we began to suspect he'd been a genius all along, but was merely hiding it under the theory that stupid dogs get away with more fun stuff.

With dogs, old age really is a cherished gift worth celebrating, and at no time has that become more clear to me than during our family holidays.

My two children and I don't have much extended family, so we've always included the pets in our celebrations, giving them their own gifts and stockings and Easter baskets. Dogs are some of the most satisfying gift recipients in the world because they are so easy to please. Their happiness is contagious, and they never seem to notice much beyond the excitement of the moment.

Except Buddy, who had an epiphany at age eight. It happened the year Easter came right after his birthday. I started a tradition of putting refillable Easter baskets on the fireplace mantle ahead of time—like Christmas stockings—in order to prevent being stuck with cheap baskets that seem to breed faster than the bunnies that bring them.

When Buddy discovered the baskets, a look of recognition spread across his fuzzy face. He had become aware not only of our symbols of holidays, but also the pattern: we gather, we give presents and attention, and we eat. In dog world, that's pretty much the definition of heaven.

From then on, our dog learned to anticipate those wondrous occasions. He spent the following spring and summer checking the fireplace for the containers that would hold gifts. When winter rolled around and the stockings finally went up, our Christmas season took on new life. Just as parents of young children become infused with the little ones' excitement, my family's Christmas spirit was renewed by our dog.

Better yet, all of this happened just at the time when the children were getting too old to maintain the thrill of their younger years. The Budster brought it back. We took to gathering in the family room more often just to watch the Daily Stocking Check. The furry pet stockings are traditionally hung on the far ends of the fireplace at our house. Buddy began by giving his own stocking a thorough sniffing, and then strolled to the other side of the mantle to check out the competition—to make sure it wasn't just that Santa liked hamsters better.

At some point Buddy realized that cameras are often involved in these events. From then on, the appearance of a camera became cause for excitement, even if the purpose of the picture was to, say, show a new piece of furniture to a relative. It is no accident that a dog figures prominently in all of our pictures, posing importantly. He is always waiting for the celebrating to begin.

This year Buddy is fifteen, and our last Christmas was one of the most exciting we've seen since the children were toddlers. Although Santa was very quiet while making his delivery, the dog discovered his gifts shortly thereafter and getting any sleep the remainder of the night was a struggle. In the morning it was Buddy who was up bright and early and overwhelmed with excitement, and the teenaged children had to be roused from their beds in order to allow the festivities to commence.

Recently I had my own epiphany, and I have our wise and beloved dog to thank for it. We really do create our own holidays with the anticipation, enthusiasm, and the magic we put into them. And we don't have to get more subdued as we age, either. The joys of life and family are timeless and ageless—and without regard to species.

~T'Mara Goodsell

69

Unearthing the Meaning of Life

I have a simple philosophy:
Fill what's empty. Empty what's full. Scratch where it itches.
~Alice Roosevelt Longworth

It all started a few weeks ago when my ancient Beagle, Buddy, picked up a stale dinner roll while on one of our walks around the neighborhood. Buddy is famous for the things he finds on his walks. I'll be strolling along, lost in thought, and then I'll look down and somehow, Buddy will have an entire cooked pot roast in his mouth. He has found, at various times, a frozen baked ziti, a toy reindeer, and a turkey carcass. You don't know humiliation until you've trotted around the neighborhood with a purple satin bra dangling from your dog's mouth.

And woe to the person who tries to get any of his treasures away from him. He may only weigh twenty-two pounds, but I doubt that Ali and Foreman, together and in their prime, could pry Buddy's finds out of that mouth. Which is why, when I had to deal with the dinner roll, I didn't get too worked up over it. At least it wasn't desiccated animal remains. After a few feeble stabs at getting it away from him, I let him bring it into the house. I figured he'd eat it and we'd be done with it.

Wrong. With much deliberation and effort, I watched Buddy bury the roll in our couch cushion, a snack for a rainy day. I decided to let him have his fun. I could move it later when he wasn't looking. As if he could read my mind, a few minutes later, he dug it up and moved it under the dining room rug. Shortly after that, he dug it up again and reburied it elsewhere.

It was quickly becoming clear that Buddy was obsessed with this dinner roll. My sweet little puppy was responding to something older and stronger than he, something dating back to the primordial ooze days. In other words, my sweet little puppy was losing his sweet little puppy mind.

Over the next week or so, Buddy spent most of his time worrying about his roll. My husband and I would be sitting and reading contentedly on our couch. Buddy would be wedged behind my back like a pillow or snoozing on my husband's chest. Then, for no reason, the dog would snap to attention and stare at us. It was obvious what he was thinking: "What am I, insane? Lying here and sleeping, when these people are undoubtedly scheming to get my dinner roll!" And then he'd storm off, with that determined look that said "Not while I'm alive, suckers."

Once again he'd dig it up and rehide it. I pulled down my bedcovers one night to find it sitting on the mattress. It turned up in the linen closet, mixed in the dirty laundry, in shoes, in the kitchen pots and pans drawers. (How did he open the drawers? How did he get it into the hamper?)

He started to resemble Ingrid Bergman being driven insane in *Gaslight*. The darting, scared eyes. Not knowing whom he could trust. His burials became more frantic, less meticulous. One day the roll was pathetically sticking out from underneath the bath mat where just anyone could find it.

I, on the other hand, was starting to worry about ants and mice. The roll was taking on a slightly greenish hue and was now hard enough to break glass. Why didn't I just throw the thing out? Because there was something about Buddy's desperation that deserved respect.

Finally, it had to end, as these things do. One morning, Buddy moved the roll around a few times, but you could tell his heart wasn't in it. With a great sigh, he eventually picked up the dinner roll, walked to the front door and scratched to be let out. He went to the maple tree in our front yard where he dropped it without any ceremony. The responsibility of being Keeper of the Roll had just become too much. He sprinted back to our house as frisky as a puppy.

"Good boy!" I cried, as proud and weepy as any mother at her child's first piano recital.

You never know when universal truths are going to turn up by the side of the road. Buddy and his roll taught me this: that sometimes there is victory in defeat. That it can be liberating to walk away from the object of your desire when you realize that you no longer own it—it owns you. But that takes strength, wisdom and dogged determination.

~Beth Levine

70

The Other Woman

The art of love... is largely the art of persistence.
~Albert Ellis

When it comes to couples, there are a variety of hurdles that can obstruct an otherwise clear path to coupledom. For my husband and me, our relationship felt like second nature the instant we met. It was like I was catching up with an old friend. I secretly entertained thoughts of him by a campfire, telling our grandchildren stories about how he won my heart. I was on cloud nine, but I could not have anticipated that there was already another lady at the core of Lee's heart.

The leading lady in his life came in the form of a forty-five-pound black Labrador mix named Nyko. Based on what I pieced together from Lee, she was a rescued stray with an untamed heart who possessed the unique ability to stare into one's soul with her distinctly wise, golden eyes.

It was on our third date that I got to meet Nyko, and I was eager to gain her approval. Unfortunately for me, my enthusiasm to make new friends was not reciprocated. Nyko suspiciously sniffed at my ankles while I gushed about how happy I was to meet her. Once she satisfied her curiosity and determined that I didn't have any food to offer, Nyko gave me a skeptical glance as though to say, "Who are you and what do you want with my dad?" With a shake of her comically crooked ears, she coolly turned away from me and strutted over to the couch where she stretched herself across the cushions like a lioness inspecting her kingdom. With a lurch in my stomach, I realized I was the "other woman" in Lee's life.

Before I came into the picture, Lee and Nyko had their routine. They hiked together, he gave her belly rubs, and he let her lick the bottom of his TV dinner containers. Nyko even had a designated spot on the bed. I was a deviation from their unspoken contract, and she was set on establishing herself at the top of the pecking order.

Nyko often exhibited her superiority by wedging herself between us when we were snuggled on the couch watching a movie. Plopping down right on top of our laps, she wiggled her way between us and stretched her legs as far as she could, pushing me away with her paws as her tail thumped triumphantly. She then rolled onto her back with an exaggerated sigh, beckoning Lee to rub her belly. Her greatest pleasure was rummaging through my overnight bag and scattering the contents all around the house.

Two months into our relationship, I still didn't feel like I had broken through to Nyko. Her usual habits continued, and Lee and I were hardly permitted to sit within two feet of each other. She started racing us to bed, defiantly claiming her spot next to Lee's pillow. One night, as we gently tried to coax her from her spot, Nyko rooted herself like a tree, refusing to move a single inch. I knew that it was absolutely necessary for me to win Nyko over if we wanted the relationship to progress.

One crisp morning after Lee left for the day, I crept out of bed and roused Nyko. I slipped on her leash and we stepped out the front door into the glowing atmosphere created by the blazing fall leaves. Nyko and I frolicked in the refreshing air, relishing the morning sunlight, until our legs were tired. We explored the train tracks, and I laughed as she explored empty gopher holes. She twitched her ears like antennas trying to pick up any sounds muffled underground.

As we meandered back home I talked to Nyko. I told her that she was a good girl for looking out for her guy, and that I wanted us to be a family. Using her nose to sniff out hidden treasures beneath the tangled undergrowth that lined the narrow road, she seemed to be in her own world far away from me. Discouraged, I walked in complete silence until we reached the creaky staircase that marked our return home. As I bent over to unclip her leash, I felt her damp tongue glide across my cheek and she shifted her weight so she could lean into me. I patted her on the belly, and looked into her bright eyes. An invisible thread connected my heart to hers. From that moment on, little by little, I grew on Nyko. Within a short time, we all fit on the couch comfortably, me in Lee's arms, and Nyko next to me with her head on my lap.

~Rachel Rosenthal

71

Our Vegetarian

You've got about as much chance as finding a vegetarian pit bull terrier.
~Author Unknown

Canines are generally known as carnivores, and their teeth are appropriately designed for shredding and ripping prey. Little did I know our pet dog had an alter ego, and would use those pointy teeth on harmless vegetables.

The fetish was first discovered when we decided to plant a garden one summer, not long after we added Brandy, a beautiful copper brown Golden Retriever, to our family.

Rows of corn, potatoes, lettuce and carrots were carefully planted in the freshly tilled soil, as well as mounds of cucumber, squash and zucchini plants. For our collective sweet tooth, we added enough watermelon and cantaloupe plants to satisfy a small army.

After weeks of watering and fertilizing, sprouts, and then produce, appeared and we were excited. Soon we would enjoy, literally, the fruits of our labor... fresh, tasty, homegrown produce.

Brandy was an outdoor dog by choice, and we kept her kenneled most of the time. However, she was able to exercise frequently, and daily, and enjoyed energetically running around. She never strayed far, and unless there was a cat or squirrel nearby to chase down (but only to sniff, never to harm), she faithfully stayed on our half-acre property.

We checked the garden daily. It was exciting to see nature at work, our own personal food supply growing in the back yard near the end of our property line. Then one day we noticed paw prints in the dirt between the fertile, rich growth. My wife suspected raccoons or some other form of wildlife, maybe even possums, probably visiting our garden while we slept.

I was never a hunter, but I was tempted to purchase a rifle. This was our garden and no hungry animal was going to reap the delicious dividends of weeks of our dedicated, hard work.

Later that week I let Brandy out and she sprinted straight to the garden. I assumed that she smelled the scent of whatever creature had been visiting our land during the nighttime hours. And then my eyes widened as I witnessed her seek out a large, oblong cucumber, rip it from the vine, locate a patch of comfortable grass to lie down on, and proceed to eat the vegetable as if it were a large, juicy bone.

"Brandy!" I yelled. "What on earth are you doing?"

She grabbed her prize and ran off, continuing to eat the cucumber until it was all but gone.

I told my wife that it was an inside job, the culprit being our own beloved, trustworthy best friend.

Over the next few weeks we discovered her penchant for all produce, including tomatoes, squash and especially corn. She particularly enjoyed jumping onto her hind legs and selecting an ear of corn, skillfully twisting it off the stalk, then shucking the husk off with her jaws before devouring the kernels from the cob. We learned she had no preference between white sweet corn and yellow—she relished both.

She also enjoyed digging up potatoes, like a pirate exploring for treasure. Only she didn't need a map to locate the bounty.

Eventually we gave up the fight to protect the garden and allowed her to enjoy herself, at times even playing with her and her produce. One of her favorite games was chasing down small watermelons or tomatoes that we bowled across the lawn. She would scamper after them, pounce, and then devour her captured prey. Some dogs chase balls; ours chased fruit.

Another game we played was to hold out an ear of corn, verifying that we had her full attention, then like a quarterback on a football team, cock our arms and toss it across the yard, spiraling through the August air.

But her favorite activity, being a bird dog retriever, was to go to the pond near our home and leap with reckless abandon into the water to swim after a cucumber or zucchini that we tossed. She played a game with herself after retrieving it that included pushing the vegetable beneath the surface and then pursuing it while underwater. The dog was skilled at swimming while holding her breath. Finally she would return to shore with the remnants of the vegetable, excited and proud.

Years later when Brandy died, we buried her. We lovingly wrapped her in a blanket and placed her inside a large box, then included many of her favorite toys and bones. Of course, one of them was a red squeaky tomato.

~David Michael Smith

I Can't Believe My Dog Did That!

Chapter 8

Love Me, Love My Dog

Destiny

The purpose of life is a life of purpose.
~Robert Byrne

For many years I had been privileged to take in old abused dogs that were rescued from a life of cruelty and misery. This was no great self-sacrifice on my part. It was as gratifying for me as for the victims. The dogs came from many sources and were just as likely to be a Great Dane as a Toy Poodle or a mixed breed of unknown parentage. I loved them all.

I grew up in England in the 1920s and always had a variety of pets, from horses to white mice, so I was well accustomed to caring for animals. Our home was on the edge of the Yorkshire Moors, not far from veterinarians Alf Wight and Donald Sinclair, better known as James Herriot and Siegfried Farnon of *All Creatures Great and Small*. Alf Wight and I were friends long before he wrote his beloved books, and I greatly admired the work he did.

From early childhood I loved the herding dogs who lived and worked all around us. One of the highlights of my life was to watch the fleet Border Collies as they competed against each other in sheep-dog trials that were held each year at the county fair. A farmer's life in the "old days" was one of drudgery and hard work from dawn to dusk, and the sheepdog's life was often no better. When they became too old or sick to work, they were more than likely to be shot by their masters. This distressed me, and no doubt formed the basis of my rescue efforts in later years.

The Second World War came and went. England changed, and life as I had known it changed forever. Eventually I emigrated to America, married, and became involved in the rescue of abused animals, especially elderly dogs that had suffered wretched lives. But I couldn't forget the faithful, hardworking sheepdogs of my childhood, many of which suffered harsh treatment at the hands of their masters. Each time I returned to England on vacation, I tried to find one that had toiled all its life and bring it back with me to America so I could give it love and comfort for the rest of its life. I searched diligently in the farming communities, contacting old farmers I had known many years before. I phoned British rescue groups and, at one point, even advertised in the paper. The only offers I received were not what I had in mind. Puppies, young dogs in training, and dogs that had never worked were available for money. I finally gave up.

Years later, when I decided I was getting too old to take any more needy dogs. Max, an Old English Sheepdog, and Meg, an Australian Cattle Dog, were the only canine survivors in the household.

"Absolutely no more rescues!" I told myself, meaning every word.

It's strange how things you wish for sometimes happen in the most unexpected ways. When you have already accepted the inevitability of failure, a different—and sometimes even better—solution presents itself.

One day the phone rang. The call was from a local animal shelter and I knew at once what was coming.

"We have a case of extreme cruelty," began the supervisor at the other end, after the initial pleasantries. "We have just taken in more than twenty breeding dogs from a puppy mill, all of them in terrible condition. They were in little cages, living on top of wire, with no food or water. The whole place has been shut down. We have a dog I think you would like to work with. She is about eight years old and must have been badly abused. She is so terrified of everybody and everything that she is not eligible for adoption. If you won't take her, she will have to be destroyed."

"What breed is she?" I asked, curious now, even though I knew I would take her anyway. The next words were the culmination of my half-forgotten dream.

"A Border Collie," the woman replied.

The next day my son and I went to the shelter to bring Jess to her forever home. She was a wispy little creature that crept into the waiting room at the heels of the supervisor, crouching close to the floor. When she was led across the room to where we were sitting, she immediately rolled onto her back in humble submission. There were many signs of deprivation in her bony frame, which clearly indicated neglect to the point of starvation. She had been given an early morning bath at the shelter, but the pungent odor of urine and feces clung to her body, a silent reminder that she had been forced to live in a cage, perhaps for years, in filth and misery.

When I gently stroked her, she sat up and put her head on my knee, her whole body shaking. She was terrified and confused, but ready to follow anyone who had a kind word for her. It was easy to recognize a sweet, gentle disposition in spite of her overwhelming terror.

By the end of three months her emaciated body had filled out, her previously sparse coat was thick and shiny, and she no longer cowered fearfully at the sight of a stranger. Jess was on the road to health and happiness.

As she recovered her strength and became one of the family, I noticed how closely she watched Max and Meg—sometimes lying with her chin on the ground and her eyes following every move they made. Occasionally, a reluctant Meg was herded around the lawn or a surprised Max was guided over to me, with Jess running back and forth at his heels, urging him on. It seemed to me that this behavior was far more advanced than the natural instinct ingrained into every Border Collie, so I began searching for a farmer who had a flock of sheep. I finally found one forty miles away and arranged to have him try her out. After I explained that she had been a breeding female in a puppy mill he was very skeptical.

"Don't expect much," he said. "She will probably follow the

sheep, because that is her natural instinct. But to be a herding dog she'd have to be trained."

He demonstrated this with one of his own trained Australian Shepherds.

But as soon as Jess saw the sheep her whole demeanor changed. She was alert, focused, and ready for action. To my utter astonishment, as well as that of the farmer, she followed his instructions flawlessly, responding to verbal commands, whistles, and his hand signals. She guided the sheep effortlessly in whichever direction he indicated, finally assisting him in penning the flock.

"You've got yourself a top working dog," he said with admiration. "Probably worth three thousand dollars."

I looked at Jess, lying contentedly by my side. "I wouldn't part with her for a million," I said.

~Monica Agnew-Kinnaman

Pug Therapy

Courage is resistance to fear, mastery of fear—not the absence of fear.
~Mark Twain

I was making dinner when I heard our Pug Lollipop's frantic barking, punctuated by loud splashes coming from the pool. I dropped my tomatoes and ran as fast as I could to the deck, my heart in my throat. I had told my husband Mark we should put a fence around the pool. The poor dog sounded terrified. Pugs can't swim. At that moment, I forgot that neither could I.

When I reached the pool, I saw Lollipop racing in circles around the edge—her usual routine when our nine-year-old daughter Jenny practiced laps. But where was Jenny?

Kablam! Another loud splash shattered the pool's clean surface. I turned and saw Jenny, perched on the diving board, chucking one swim trophy after another into the water. Tears rolled down her cheeks.

"Jenny, what is it?" I approached the diving board and stood next to my daughter. She stared down at the water, where several of her blue ribbons floated. At the bottom of the deep end, her trophies gleamed.

"I quit the team, Mom," she said. "I'm never swimming again." She stepped off the springboard, scooped up Lollipop, and carried her inside, crying into the dog's fur.

I'd always been so proud of Jenny. I joked that her real mother must have been a mermaid, because I sure couldn't swim. I was so grateful that my athletic daughter hadn't inherited my fear of water.

Thanks to my husband, Jenny learned to swim before she could walk. She'd been swimming competitively since first grade, and talked about competing in the Olympics someday. She'd just started learning to dive that year when her beloved swim coach and mentor, a competitive diver, took a bad dive and was badly injured. Jenny and her teammates learned that Coach Forster would probably never walk, much less dive, again. I thought Jenny had been handling it well. She visited her coach in the hospital, sent cards and letters, even went to practice and seemed to work well with the new coach. What had changed?

I went up to Jenny's room. She curled herself around the Pug, who snuggled with her patiently.

"Well, Lollipop," I said, "for a dog who's supposed to be mine, you sure seem to belong to Jenny."

Jenny hugged her tighter. "She can't swim either, Mom, so she can keep me company."

We got Lollipop about four years ago, when I joked to my husband that I felt left out of the family swim club, and wanted another member who hated the water. Mark showed up with a Pug puppy the next day. And sure enough, that dog would not go into the pool. But she always stayed outside when Jenny swam, racing alongside her and barking.

"Remember how I tried to teach Lollipop to swim?" asked Jenny. "Coach Forster said anyone could learn." She burst into fresh tears.

"Coach came to practice today," said Jenny, "in a wheelchair. She looked so different. She told us we had to keep swimming, that her getting hurt didn't mean we should stop, but Mom, if the coach could get hurt that bad, what about me? I can't go back. I'm too scared."

For months Jenny proved as stubborn as Lollipop. She refused to swim, to even go near the swimming pool. Every afternoon at 4 p.m., Jenny's usual home practice time, Lollipop ran out to the pool, barking, but Jenny never followed. The Pug would come back inside and sit on Jenny's lap in front of the TV, looking up at Jenny.

Jenny didn't respond to anyone. Not to my husband, her teammates, her coach, or me. We were so worried we considered sending her to a therapist. People said to give it time, but I was scared. What had happened to my brave little girl? Where was her spirit?

I know she missed swimming. How could she not? Every morning I set out her practice suit and swim cap, offered to drive her to swim practice, but she turned over, hugged the dog, and went back to sleep. I was beside myself. If Jenny learned to give up this early, how would she handle life's real setbacks?

One afternoon, I was preparing dinner as usual when I heard Lollipop barking. Then I heard a splash. Then, silence. I just knew. I ran out to the pool. Lollipop had fallen — or jumped — in. She paddled frantically, but her dense body and little paws weren't made for the water. She sank, came up snorting, sank again. I couldn't reach her with the pool net. Every second counted. Mark wasn't home. I couldn't wade in — she had fallen in the deep end. I watched her sink and surface, sink and surface, and I could see she was getting nowhere.

"Jenny!" I screamed. "Get out here!"

Jenny came running out and without thinking took the most beautiful dive I've ever seen straight into the pool. She struck with clean strokes for that little dog, grabbed her just as she was sinking, and swam her to the edge. Jenny tried to get out, but when she did, Lollipop jumped straight back into the water. Again and again, the girl fished out the dog, and the dog jumped back in. Finally, Jenny gave up, and stayed in the water, floating the Pug in a lazy circle.

"Look Mom," she said, "Lollipop's trying to swim!"

Never let anyone tell you that Pugs can't swim. Ours can. I still don't know for sure if that Pug fell in the pool or jumped. But she got my daughter back in the water.

Jenny went back to swimming, and Lollipop swims, too. Not well, and mostly in the shallow end. But she swims. Looks like I might have to overcome my fears and take some lessons, too.

~Helen Rucker

A Holiday Romance

If you can look at a dog and not feel vicarious excitement and affection,
you must be a cat.

~Author Unknown

"I'm watching Olive while India's in Costa Rica," announced my daughter, Dana, home on summer break from college. The news alarmed me because Olive is a dog.

"Where are you watching her?" I asked, hoping Dana was moving into India's apartment for the duration of the caretaking assignment.

"Here. I'm getting her tomorrow. She'll be here for nine days."

I smiled the "that's great!" smile moms conjure when they need to show support for something their kids are doing that moms wish wasn't happening, while I wondered how I'd survive what I was sure would be the longest nine days of my life.

I'd had a dog, Licorice, when I was a kid, and I loved him. But my good dog feelings had been gnawed away by years in a town where dogs roamed unleashed in the green spaces where I run. Owners would invariably say, "Don't worry, he doesn't bite," as Rover nipped at my Nikes. And where a half-dozen dogs on my street bark early, late, often, and for prolonged periods, making sleep difficult and life less enjoyable. I'm not shy about letting my neighbors know I don't appreciate the auditory assaults. Once I sent a morning e-mail that read: "It's 6:23 and your dog is killing me."

When Dana pulled up with Olive, a Pyrenean Shepherd puppy, I admit to feeling an odd joy at seeing her round-eyed, hairy face. And when Olive strained at her leash to get to me, pulling Dana up the walkway, I felt a little special.

"She likes you, Mom!" said Dana, either sincere or clever. Olive and I had our first physical contact—she exuberantly licking my shins, me patting her once on the head then moving away. This was Dana's gig, not mine. I'd said hello, now Dana was on duty.

Or not. Dana's nineteen. She sleeps in.

When I woke at six I realized that Dana's "I'm watching Olive" really meant that I was the one watching Olive. Olive hadn't been out since the night before, and Dana wouldn't be up until after noon. I realized with mild horror that a fair amount of the upcoming canine care would fall to me.

I called Olive's name. When the furry ball bounded out of Dana's room and down the hallway, I felt a little flutter. She didn't know me, but she nuzzled my legs and looked up with trust and anticipation that warmed me. Hmmm.

I noticed the training pad we'd put down—India had sent Olive's gear, including pads that smelled like grass to encourage duty-doing there rather than on the floor—was saturated with pee and piled with poop. I was delighted.

"Olive," I said, bringing her near the pad and stroking her back and head. "You're a good, good girl." In a strange house, with strange people who didn't get her out in time for her day's first constitutional, Olive had kept her business on a small plastic square. And, she hadn't barked since setting paw in our home. I was officially smitten.

It got worse as the days progressed. Olive worked some animal magic and cast a dog endearment spell on me. I started doing weird things—and enjoying them.

I became an ardent dog walker, confounding my neighbors, which I loved. I looked forward to our walks and the way Olive circled the kitchen in joyous frenzy when I jangled her leash to call her. As we walked, sometimes side by side, sometimes one pulling the other, I studied Olive's sniffing before choosing where to make her deposits.

I saved the plastic bags I bought my produce in and became

skilled at wearing them as gloves then turning them inside out after I'd retrieved Olive's neat little messes. I left the door between our kitchen and deck open all day. That way Olive could be outside whenever she wished and hang with me while I read my newspapers at the umbrella table, forgiving the flies that found their way into my house and bounced off walls. I spread a blanket on the deck, and Olive spent hours lying on it, lifting her head frequently to give me a happy gaze and a contented smile.

On a shopping trip to buy Dana back-to-campus items, I threw dog treats and chew toys into my cart. I perused my grocery store's pet aisle, comparing food labels to ensure Olive was getting the good stuff. I stopped wincing whenever Olive slurped my limbs and face, which was often. And, I, who heretofore would run for hand sanitizer anytime politeness dictated I pat someone's dog, developed a soothing chin stroke that made Olive close her eyes and grin. I even considered giving Olive a bath. I didn't, but I thought seriously about it.

"I'm taking Olive home in a few hours," said Dana one morning. "India's flight comes in tonight, and I'm picking her up at the airport."

The news hit me hard. This dog had achieved the impossible: she'd made me fall in love with her. I looked down at Olive, who was licking my toes. "I can't believe it's been nine days already. They went by so fast."

~Lori Hein

Buttons

It's good sportsmanship not to pick up lost balls while they are still rolling.
~Mark Twain

I had been visiting grand homes and gardens in northwestern Connecticut, where everything seems right in the world, especially in June. New ideas for improving my garden and my fitful golf game danced through my head as I opened the kitchen door to our home in Greenwich.

There I found my sixteen-year-old son, Sam, on the sofa with our adored Yellow Labrador, Buttons. He was tickling her tummy as she lay on her back looking at him with eyes that could melt the coldest of souls. Science has told us this is an evolutionary trick to ensure the survival of the canine species. It is an awfully good one.

Sam told me that he thought he could hear a grinding noise in her tummy. But as she seemed as well and as enthusiastically athletic as ever, I continued with dreams of peonies as big as dinner plates and holes in one.

Our Lab was called Buttons basically to make sense of our older Labrador's name, Zipper. Zippy was always quite sedate; Buttons was another kettle of fish entirely. She adored all sports that involved balls—even when they were on TV. She could catch a tennis ball as it rebounded from a wall; she went bananas when Sam taught himself to juggle.

As we lived near a golf course, we would take the dogs on an evening walk with seven irons in hand. Our golf lacked for direction but not necessarily for distance. However, we would happily watch Buttons race left and right as we hit off. Sometimes it was after a squirrel, but mostly after golf balls that we would retrieve from her. Often she would dive after golf balls we hit into the creek, sometimes swimming down such a distance only her wagging tail was visible.

Sam thought the mysterious grinding noise could be a couple of golf balls mashing against each other in her stomach. I thought it impossible, but he said it would be wise to take her to the vet before nightfall. He was a newly licensed driver, and newly assertive, so I agreed. The vet, when he presented Buttons, said it was "unlikely but if you insist we'll do an X-ray." Sam insisted.

When the film revealed thirteen golf balls in Buttons' stomach the vet thought the X-ray technician was playing a joke. But it was no joke, and they removed thirteen golf balls in surgery the next day.

Twelve were range balls and the thirteenth was a Titleist—which the vet kept.

Buttons recovered and retained her love of ball sports, although our walks with seven irons came to an end. My golf remains the joke.

~Rosita G. Trinca

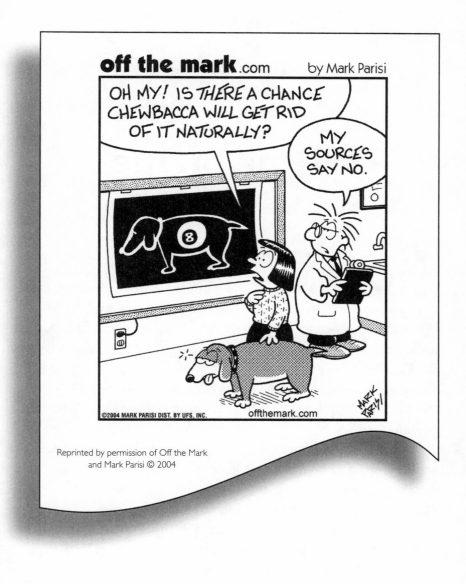

Reprinted by permission of Off the Mark
and Mark Parisi © 2004

White Stripe

Sometimes when you get in a fight with a skunk,
you can't tell who started it.
~Lloyd Doggett

J ust when I thought things were under control, our five-year-old Portuguese Water Dog proved me wrong. So long as he gets his two walks and two and a half meals a day, Oreo generally doesn't cause us too much trouble. Sure, there's the occasional roll in dead animal matter necessitating one or more baths. And there's also the ongoing expense of regular vet bills. But, Oreo doesn't get into too much trouble. Until, that is, a recent encounter with a nocturnal varmint.

Oreo is not a cat lover. We never introduced him to cats when he was a puppy and he retains his instinctive distaste for felines. Given the chance, he'd like to catch one and tear it to shreds. Little does he know that he'd likely be the loser in any such encounter.

Oreo has also never been accused of being overly bright. He's not stupid, but he's definitely not the wisest whippet on the block. Which might help to explain Oreo's latest misadventure.

One recent night he stood at our back door wanting to get out. Since this is a frequent request, I thought nothing of it, although I did notice that he seemed more eager than usual to get to the back yard. Given that I, too, as a sixty-year-old often have urgent bathroom visits, I figured Oreo's eagerness was just a function of his age. It turns out, however, that peeing was the last thing on his mind. When I opened the back door, Oreo took off like a shot, barking as if he were on a mission.

Opening that door was our first mistake.

Since it was dark out, I couldn't see what he was up to. I figured maybe he had spotted a squirrel and was futilely giving chase as he has done a hundred times before. But it turned out that Oreo had spotted something bigger than a squirrel. Something, that in his limited vision, probably looked like a cat. Except this cat had a white stripe down its back.

Before I could get back to the living room and the book I was quietly reading, I heard my wife Cheryl proclaim from the upstairs bedroom: "What is that horrible smell?"

Oreo's attack on what he thought was a cat turned out to be a kamikaze mission doomed to failure. This was no cat; this was a skunk. And as skunks will do, this one reared and fired. Oreo came staggering back to the door and Cheryl let him in.

That was our second mistake.

The poor dog looked like he'd been sucker punched and, to make matters worse, was foaming at the mouth. He wandered about the main floor of the house dripping skunk oil and finally plunked himself down on the living room carpet where he deposited even more of the foam.

Cheryl feared the worst and called the emergency animal hospital and, notwithstanding their warning that there was a minimum charge of $145, said she'd bring him right over. She then loaded him in the back of our car.

That was our third mistake.

Luckily for us, the technician at the animal hospital immediately recognized—by smell no doubt—that Oreo had been the victim of a wanton skunk attack. Thus, the $145 fee was waived and Cheryl was sent home with a hydrogen peroxide, baking soda, and dishwashing detergent recipe to apply to our dog's body as many times as needed.

The recipe worked, at least for Oreo. As for the carpet, the sofa, and our clothes, I'm not so sure. For days after, that distinctive skunk odor lingered throughout the house as a not-so-subtle reminder of our series of mistakes.

Weeks have passed and it seems like the worst is over. Oreo smells like a rose and we only get the occasional whiff of our absent Pepé Le Pew.

However, our third mistake lives on to haunt us. Cheryl's car has yet to fully recover from Oreo's skunk-scented ride to the animal hospital. We've tried fabric deodorizer, skunk smell remover, soap and water, and even incense. But try as we might, the odor lingers.

So if you see a dark blue, late model Toyota Matrix with all the windows down, you might want to give it a wide berth. Remember—you've been warned.

~David Martin

The Perfect Storm

Our perfect companions never have fewer than four feet.
~Colette

A t only eleven weeks old, Grady was an exceptionally tiny Bichon Frise puppy, weighing less than two pounds. He was born in a commercial kennel in Missouri with a patent ductus arteriosis heart murmur. There was a hole in his heart causing a leakage. He was failing to thrive and without immediate medical intervention this precious little baby would die.

The surgeon at Texas A&M told me that Grady, at that time, had been the smallest puppy on which they had ever performed the life-saving procedure. Thankfully, the procedure was a complete success, and Grady and I were now on our way back home.

Traveling with recovering surgical patients (with tails) has become customary for me as the Executive Director of Small Paws Rescue. I had driven to the Austin Airport for our return flight, noticing that odd hint of green in the skies, which is eerily familiar to anyone who lives in Tornado Alley. Weather reports were sketchy, but the skies were definitely darkening.

Flying with a donated airline pass, sometimes the only available seat is in first class, and that's where the "perfect storm" took place on that fateful April night back in the spring of 2002. Grady and I boarded the flight and he was a good little trooper, lying perfectly still and quiet in his soft-sided, under-the-seat airline approved bag. FAA rules dictated that he stay there for our entire time on the plane.

We had just pushed back from the gate when the pilot explained that while we would be taking off soon, weather-related issues had delayed our flight. We were free to move about the cabin and to use our cell phones.

The storm seemed to get worse and two long hours passed. Little Grady had become restless. He had also begun to howl loudly, his tiny voice reverberating throughout the entire cabin of the plane.

The wind was really blowing now, and the rain appeared to be coming down in sheets, sideways, as I gazed out the window of the plane onto the tarmac below. The captain continued to assure us of our safety, saying that we would be taking off as soon as the weather passed.

One small, white, furry puppy was now screaming to high heavens for me to let him out of the bag! As the storm continued to beat down, I tried to quiet Grady by patting the soft, see-through mesh of the bag. Then another commotion started in the back of the plane.

One of the passengers was experiencing some sort of medical problem. Concerned flight attendants and another passenger helped to bring her up to the less crowded first class cabin and put her in the empty seat directly in front of me.

The captain came on again, this time asking if there was a doctor on the flight, while little Grady's howls became even louder.

I saw that no doctor was coming forward and the rain and wind were now in direct competition with a very loud puppy and one young lady who was sobbing in the seat in front of me.

My mind was racing with concern for her as she had begun to hyperventilate, and Grady was screaming at my feet.

I watched as the flight attendant took the young girl's cell phone and began to speak to her mother. The girl was having a panic attack and her mother was requesting that the pilot return to the gate. She explained that once it got this far, medical attention was usually required to reverse her daughter's increasing physical symptoms.

I watched with interest as the flight attendant went to the cockpit, relaying the message from the girl's mother to the captain. It wasn't looking good for us to get permission to return to the gate.

The girl's sobs were drowning out the weather and Grady's howling.

One of the other passengers tried to lighten the mood with a chorus from the theme song from *Gilligan's Island* regarding a three-hour tour, as our time on the tarmac was fast approaching that.

It was then that the sheer chaos of it all caused me to take action. I decided that if I were to be arrested later, I would throw myself on the mercy of the court. I reached down in front of me and unzipped the wiggling bag. Grady popped his little head out and scrambled into my waiting arms. The howling stopped immediately. Before anyone had time to stop me, I stood up, leaned over, and plopped little Grady onto the lap of the young girl. It was done. I had just broken the FAA rule about keeping pets contained under the seat.

The panic attack which was in full swing only a few moments ago suddenly turned into the most beautiful of moments when the young girl realized she was now holding in her lap, a tiny, white, fluffy, live puppy.

Grady was thrilled with this new development, while the passengers on the plane broke into spontaneous applause. The puppy had stopped howling and the girl had stopped crying. Her mother, on the phone, was relieved as well, and the wind and rain had quieted, too.

The now familiar voice of the captain came on and asked the flight attendants to prepare the cabin for departure. We were to return our seats to an upright position and fasten our seat belts as we had been cleared for take-off. We were on our way home!

But wait. There was a problem.

I mouthed the words to the flight attendant from behind the young woman who was peacefully holding little Grady in her lap. I pointed and silently asked the flight attendant, "What do I do about the puppy?"

With very innocent-looking eyes, her silent lips answered back to me, "What puppy?"

The "perfect storm" had come and gone that night. As a precaution, an ambulance and the girl's parents were waiting upon our arrival into Dallas later that evening. Flights out had been cancelled due to the weather, and Grady and I flew home to Tulsa the next morning.

Grady had become a hero, and it came to me that just as Small Paws Rescue had healed his little heart, he, too, had become a heart healer. Grady was soon adopted by one of our supporters and he lives today in Florida where he is a happy, healthy ten-year-old Bichon with no sign of any health issues.

I wonder if Grady ever thinks about that night on the plane and the young girl that he helped to calm during the perfect storm.

I also wonder about that young girl who was moved up to first class and was given a puppy to hold during a most difficult moment in her life. Now as an adult, does she remember the little white dog who calmed her fears that stormy April evening?

~Robin Pressnall

Peter Pan

Blessed is the person who has earned the love of an old dog.
~Sydney Jeanne Seward

"Rex, drop that!" He stood in the family room with a piece of paper between his two front paws. He had taken methodical bites out of it, then spit out the pieces first to the left and then to the right. A scattering of white lay in his wake.

I expected this from a puppy. But Rex was ten. Would he ever grow up and become a mellow, calm dog?

"What happened to that puppy we rescued?" my husband asked one day. "The one that licked our faces and snuggled in our arms like a baby?"

We watched our seventy-five pound Golden Lab prance around the back yard. He barked at any bird that dared to flutter within sight and voiced his displeasure when a possum walked along the back wall.

"I don't know," I said. "Remember behavior training?"

"You'd come home exhausted and he'd still want to play."

"That was a total washout. He flunked!"

"And then you tried to find him a job," my husband added.

"Yup, that didn't work."

I wanted him to be a therapy dog. I thought he'd make a great one. But he was too high spirited and mischievous.

We both stared at the stature and regal pose of our beautiful dog.

With his nose high in the air and his body erect and standing stock still for a change, you could see the beauty and strength in his heritage. He was a mixed breed: part Golden Retriever, part Labrador. The vet said maybe even part Rhodesian Ridgeback.

"Even now when he's malicious, those golden eyes melt my heart. I remember when I could hold his squirming puppy body as he wiggled in my arms. He grew fast, didn't he?"

"Very. But I don't think he ever grew up."

But I always had hope. Those first few years we took long walks and went to more behavior training classes. Work kept me busy with long hours, but I took him with me to the office sometimes, and we walked to the park and went to the beach. We even signed him up for play dates with friends at a local doggie day care. He'd frolic with other dogs in a huge back yard filled with plastic swimming pools of sand and water, obstacle courses, rope toys, balls, and dog houses for relaxation. When I picked him up, I'd barely make it out the driveway before he stretched out on the back seat with his head on his front paws and his eyes closed.

Years passed. "Do you think Rex will ever become a mellow dog?" my husband asked me one day when Rex was about six. "You know, the kind that walk calmly at their owner's side, rest peacefully at their feet during dinner, and never tear through the house in a frenzy?"

"Don't get your hopes up," I replied.

More years passed and Rex is now seventy in dog years. He loves the potato chips my husband throws into the air and the challenge of catching them before they hit the ground. Besides his daily kibble, he especially enjoys a Kong toy stuffed with a little peanut butter or a treat or two.

Like us, Rex has developed simple pleasures. And like me, he's slowed down a bit. In the old days we could walk for more than an hour. Now, we tire more easily and we go to bed early, choosing sleep over staying up late. We're content, Rex and I, with the life we have.

But I swear, he's never grown up.

The other day it happened again. Rex snatched an envelope from my trashcan and ran into the family room.

"Rex, come back here," I yelled, then ran after him.

There he stood with the envelope held between his front paws. He methodically ripped it apart. He enjoyed each and every bite and tear. He spit the pieces to each side, then walked away with his head held high.

Did I stop him? No, I've learned to let him have his fun. After all, it's just a discarded envelope. He enjoys it, and I enjoy watching him act like a puppy again.

He never did grow up, or become that mellow dog we thought we wanted, and that's just fine with me.

~B.J. Taylor

Uncommon Courage

Courage is not the absence of fear, but rather the judgment
that something else is more important than fear.
~Ambrose Redmon

I wouldn't call my dog Henry a hero. Actually, Henry is a bit of a coward. Although he's a big, powerful German Shepherd, Henry greets the world with his tail between his legs. Cats make him tremble. Thunder will make him run for cover. Henry is afraid of his shadow. If he hears a knock at the door, he's under the bed. But Henry was a hero, once.

Henry and I go for walks on a wooded path that runs alongside my house. It's a peaceful place where my dog and I can get some fresh air, and all of the tensions of the world melt away. It's also a place where Henry doesn't have to face his many fears. Oh, there's the occasional dog with its owner, but most of them are of the Chihuahua type that make him go into hysterics only until they pass him by.

The day Henry decided to be a hero we went for a very long run. It had been a long week and I had a lot of tension I wanted to run off. Henry, too, seemed eager for an extended romp through the woods, so we took the long path that took us through the heart of the forested trail. By the time we finally turned for home it was getting late, and the sun was starting to set over the low hills.

We had run for a while when Henry suddenly stopped short. He sniffed the air several times and then began to whimper. I thought maybe we had run across another Chihuahua. Then I heard the angry growls of a pack of dogs. I pulled Henry close to me and bent down low to crouch behind some bushes. The light was beginning to fade, but through the shadows of the woods I saw the silhouettes of at least a dozen animals.

They moved through the woods as a focused pack. The glow of their eyes was angry and deadly. I could hear them growl and fight among themselves. The biggest animals easily outweighed Henry. They were angry and hungry. They were looking for someone or something to attack, and they had found us.

I could feel Henry tremble against me. He was scared, more scared than he'd ever been before. He sagged against me, and for a moment I thought he might faint. Then suddenly he squirmed in my arms and broke free. He took a few steps, looked back at me, and then ran for the woods. I sat there and watched my dog run to save himself and leave me at the mercy of those wild dogs. Part of me didn't blame him. I was scared, too.

The dogs got closer. I knew I couldn't outrun them, so I picked up a rock and prepared to defend myself. The lead dog stopped and raised its head, sniffing the air. I realized that I was downwind, and that it was getting my scent, tracking my location. I raised the rock and waited for the dogs to find me.

Then I heard barking, loud barking from deep in the woods. The dogs stopped and their ears perked up. They heard scrambling through the trees, and turned away from me. It took me a moment to figure it out, but as I watched the dogs break for the woods, I realized that it was Henry doing the barking and running back and forth through the woods. He was drawing them away from me. My coward of a dog, who couldn't face down a Schnauzer, was drawing a wild pack of dogs away from me and toward him.

Once the dogs were out of sight I ran for the edge of the woods. I was sure they had heard me and were on my heels, but as I broke free of the trees and stumbled onto the path leading back to my house, I saw that I was alone. I could hear barking in the distance, and then I heard a sound that froze my blood. I heard a terrified yelp. In that instant I knew the dogs had found Henry.

I didn't know what to do. There was no one on the path, no police to call, and I didn't want to run to the house to get help because I was afraid to leave Henry to the pack of dogs. I looked around and found a large branch and started back towards the forest. If Henry was willing to take them on to help me then I'd do the same for him.

Just then there was the sound of something moving through the trees. I raised the branch, ready to fight the dogs off, but then I saw Henry leap through the bushes. He limped up to me. I could see several scratches on him and there was a nasty gash where a dog must have bitten him on the leg. But he wagged his tail at me and smiled, as if to ask, "Are you okay?" I got down on my knees and hugged him.

Together my dog and I walked home. As I cleaned his wounds and patted his head, I wondered if Henry had suddenly become a courageous dog. But then the wind slammed a shutter against a window and Henry almost jumped out of his skin at the sound. I laughed and stroked his head, realizing that he was still a coward at heart. But that night he had summoned up every ounce of courage he'd had to save me. That made him a hero to me.

~John P. Buentello

A Baron with Dignity

A dog is the only thing on earth that loves you more than he loves himself.
~Josh Billings

I was home alone with our old Boxer, Baron. My husband Mike had gone out of town to his parents' home for the evening and decided to take our Bullmastiff, Josie. She was a young and playful girl, and unfortunately Baron hadn't been much of a playmate these past few months. My in-laws lived two hours away and their Boxer, Laila, was always up for a good romp.

So here we were: me with a glass of wine and a good movie playing, and Baron on his jumbo-sized orthopedic bed, which had been purchased specifically for his comfort during these final months. I decided to take him for his nighttime potty about an hour or so before I was actually ready to go to bed. There was a good reason for this.

I knew Baron like the back of my hand. Baron had spent twelve long years protecting me. I can say without a doubt that he would have gone to his death for me. Although in those last months he passed the protection "baton" to Josie, he would still check out the problem if Josie alerted us to possible danger, like the mailman arriving, but he was quieter than his younger, more rambunctious self.

Baron had also begun sleeping downstairs, since the stairs were a challenge for him, and he felt confident that Josie, upstairs, could handle any issues that might arise in the middle of the night.

However, on this particular night, the household dynamics had changed. Not only was Josie absent, but so was Mike, our alpha-male pack leader. I knew that the younger Baron would have gone upstairs with me, only allowing himself to sleep lightly so he could stay alert. But I did not want the twelve-year-old Baron to have to make this decision.

By the time I was ready to turn in, he was in a deep sleep and snoring heavily. I tiptoed around turning off lights, locking doors, and activating the alarm, but alas, it didn't work. Baron awoke, bright-eyed and ears up on alert. He began to slowly stand up.

"No, no, baby boy," I said to him as I knelt beside him and attempted to coax him back onto his bed. "I'll be okay tonight… you just relax."

But this was not going to happen. He wouldn't budge from his standing position. Baron looked me solemnly in the eyes and in his own way let me know he was going up those stairs and that was that. There we stood in the den staring at each other.

Then a solution came to me. The baby gate! I would have to just block him from the stairs. I turned away from our battle and came back with the gate in hand. That's when I saw something in his eyes that I will never forget.

It was dignity.

Gone was the puppy that would have made a getaway run up the stairs at this moment. Gone was the exuberant five-year-old who would have caused destruction by knocking the gate down after attempting to jump it. No, this was twelve-year-old Baron saying to me: "Please don't take this last stand of dignity away from me. I know I am old and ill, but I have always protected you and I always will. Now, let's go upstairs and go to bed."

So we went.

He took one slow step at a time while I followed behind carrying the jumbo orthopedic bed. I lay his bed on the floor by my side and both of us slept soundly.

In the morning I woke him from a deep sleep and thanked him for his protection during the night. Now it was my turn to help him. I firmly held his collar while he took the stairs down very slowly. He patiently waited at the landing while I went back upstairs to retrieve the trusty bed.

Then it was time for morning potty. It was a beautiful brisk January morning. The sun was shining. I went outside with him and stretched my arms to the sky as he did his business. I closed my eyes, welcoming the warmth of the sun. I looked around for the old guy and there he was: fur shining, a twinkle in his eye, and definite pep in his step. I patted him on the head and he looked up at me as if to say: "Thanks for last night. I needed that."

Baron passed away three weeks later.

~Carla Eischeid

81

Buffy to the Rescue

My dear old dog, most constant of all friends.
~William Croswell Doane

I t was community garage sale day, and Mom and I had been pricing clothing all afternoon. "It's a great way to earn extra money," she said, "and to pass along the things you and your sisters have outgrown."

I nodded.

Mom pushed her hand into the pocket of her sweatshirt and handed me a fresh page of brightly colored stickers. Twenty-five cents was stamped on the yellow ones. Fifty cents on blue. One dollar on green.

Buffy, our Terrier-Poodle mix, lay on the garage floor, under the ping-pong table that held neat stacks of toddler clothing. White paws rested under her chin, and her black ears grazed cool, gray cement. I bent at the knees, held the stickers in one hand, and rubbed Buffy's silky head with the other.

"Hey, sweet girl," I said. "You're lazy in your old age." Buffy's ears perked and her tail swished slowly. Her sweet brown eyes met mine. "I love you, girl."

I gently pushed my fingers through the thick, white fur on her neck and gave her an easy jostle. "C'mon, Buffy. Wanna play?" Buffy's eyes closed as she succumbed to slumber. That was all I was going to get from Buffy that day.

I returned to a box of pastel T-shirts. As I pressed stickers to soft cotton, I could hear the slow muffle of Buffy's snores.

Buffy had come to our family as a pup when I was a small girl. Mom and Dad decided that their four daughters had an abundance of love to share, more than could be showered on a multitude of baby dolls. We were responsible, too, and full of energy. They thought that just the right dog would fit right in.

And Buffy did, right from the start.

The moment Dad pulled our long, navy Oldsmobile into the drive, Buffy bobbing on Mom's lap, we were sold. When the passenger door opened and a tiny fur ball bounced out, nails tapping on the drive, we knew we'd found our Girls' Best Friend. Buffy licked our ankles and snuggled into our arms. When we rode our bikes, Buffy ran alongside. When we ran through the sprinkler, Buffy chased the wild spray. She was gentle, but Buffy had more spunk than all four of us girls combined. And twelve years later, she was still my darling. But she wasn't spunky anymore.

"I think we're done for the day," Mom finally said. "Let's have dinner. We want to get to bed early. Big day tomorrow. Ready?"

She didn't have to ask me twice. I beckoned to Buffy.

"C'mon Buffy-Girl," I said. I patted my hands against the fronts of my thighs.

Buffy roused. Stood on four paws. Stretched. Then took slow, gingerly steps.

I pulled the door to the garage shut, and Buffy and I meandered, her tail still swishing, up the hill to the front of our home.

The next day was warm and bright. Mom and I opened the garage door wide, and both sunshine and customers flooded in. We sat at a card table, the blue tackle box that served as a cash box between us. Buffy found a soft place in the shade of a tree near the house. From her stake she watched the morning unfold. At noon the flow was still steady and the tables were beginning to look sparse. The air had gone sticky and hot, and I was anxious to finish. Buffy had reclaimed her cool spot under the toddler table and indulged in an afternoon nap.

"How much longer, Mom?" I said, when we'd hit a lull. I'd had enough of the garage sale. "We've done well. Why don't we close up?"

Mom poked through the garage, making neat piles of picked-through clothing. "We don't have a lot left," she said. "But I advertised that we'd be open until three. I'd like to stay open until then."

I looked at Buffy, snoozing away, and smiled. It wasn't all bad, spending the day with my mom and my dog.

At about two a fresh throng of customers arrived. Mom and I counted quarters, chatted with friends, and began to talk about closing. A few of the customers made purchases, a few others left. Only one customer remained, a young man with a hard face and absent smile. He circled the tables slowly.

"Do you know that young man?" Mom asked me quietly.

I didn't. But he seemed close to my age. Maybe a little older. He didn't go to our high school. His hair was unwashed. And he wasn't friendly.

"How are you?" Mom shouted across the garage.

The young man didn't answer. He shuffled his feet on the hard cement.

"Hot today. It must be ninety."

The boy circled.

Mom made small talk about the weather, and I began to feel uneasy. I wished Dad were home, but he'd taken my sisters to the park.

"Mom," I whispered, "I think…"

From under the table, there came a low, deep rumble. Buffy sat arrow-straight, full alert, eyes on the boy. Her teeth were bared and her warning rumbled.

The boy looked at our growling dog, and then at our table. In an instant, he bolted toward the cash box. At the same moment, Buffy lunged after him. The boy crashed into the table. He scrambled to get up, but Buffy had a firm grip on the hem of his jeans. Mom and I, forgetting the box, ran for the door at the back of the garage.

We raced to the living room and peered out the bay window.

Buffy must've released the boy's jeans, because he ran like a shot down the long length of our drive. Buffy was on his heels all the way, growling, barking, and carrying on like a girl half her age. The boy pulled a bike from the ditch. He threw one leg over the bar and peddled hard. Buffy chased him as far as we could see.

Five minutes later, Buffy slowly and quietly ambled back up the road. Tired and spent. Mom and I ran down the front hill and met her at the garage.

"Buffy Girl," Mom said, eyes full of tears. "You protected us." Mom lifted Buffy. I hugged them both and stroked Buffy's soft fur as she panted long and hard. On the ground, near our feet, lay the cash box. Change spattered the floor, but the thick bundle of cash was there.

I'd never loved that dog more.

Buffy was no pup, but she'd given all she had for her family. I kissed the tip of her warm nose and whispered in her ear. "Thank you."

Mom and I learned later that the young man had visited several garage sales that day, and he'd stolen a few boxes of cash.

But not ours. Sweet Buffy had saved the day.

~Shawnelle Eliasen

I Can't Believe My Dog Did That!

Dog Gone Smart

82

Heaven Sent Protection

Most owners are at length able to teach themselves to obey their dog.
~Robert Morley

The crack of lightning made me jump. The flash of light struck across the skies. My husband and I stood in our carport watching the heavy rain, counting to see how far away the lightning was.

"One, two..." then we heard the thunder roll. It was close by. What an awesome sound, like a long drum roll across the sky.

"It's going to get worse," I shouted to John.

He nodded. "The drains are going to overflow again. It's too much rain."

Our three dogs moved closer to us as the rain splattered all over the carport and sprayed us. All three of them are afraid of lightning, and they seemed more nervous about this storm than usual. The rain thundered down so heavily we could hardly hear ourselves speak.

The wind started blowing fiercely, picking up dead leaves and whirling them around. We shifted our stance slightly to keep from having the leaves fly into our faces. John laughed and said, "I'd better get raking tomorrow."

There were more cracks and flashes of lightning. I smiled and cuddled up to my husband and spoke close to his ear so he could hear me.

"It's amazing how quickly it gets going. Those trees are really getting hammered," I said. The trees were bending and swaying in the wind so vigorously.

The sky grew darker. Another crack of lightning and we heard the familiar click as the carport lights went out. Our only light was from the flashes of lightning across the sky.

As we watched the storm, the carport started to flood. The drains could not handle the huge volume of water. Our dogs huddled closer.

The storm got even fiercer and the lightning moved closer. Suddenly, our driveway's automatic gate broke free of its connector and began to open. We were always very careful with the gate because of our dogs.

Without hesitation, John ran toward the front of the carport into the rain to close it and lock it back into place. He grabbed a plastic bag to put over his head to protect him from the rain as he ran.

Our German Shepherd Sheba leaped after him with such speed I was startled. As John began to run into the rain up the driveway, Sheba bounded in front of him, blocking him. John tried to move around her. Again, she blocked him. The rain was pouring down. I went to the front of the carport and yelled to him, "You're going to get drenched!"

John tried again to get around Sheba and move forward toward the gate. This time Sheba ran around him and jumped up, pushing him backward. She then pressed against his legs and kept pushing John back.

Startled, he slid on the wet driveway and almost lost his balance. He moved backward shaking his head. Sheba had pushed him back into the carport beside me. John patted her on the head and told her, "Stay here," before going back out into the rain.

Again, Sheba leapt forward to get in front of John. This time she jumped up and put her paws on his chest before dropping down and giving him a hard push back into the carport.

At that instant, there was a blinding flash of lightning and an immediate deafening crash of thunder. We watched in amazement as the lightning struck the gate just where John would have been standing to lock it into place.

We stood in stunned silence as we realized that John would have been killed had Sheba not kept pushing him back into the safety of the carport. I gave him a hug of relief and then bent down to cuddle Sheba.

I smiled up at John and said, "Praise God, she was heaven sent to save your life today."

How she knew what was going to happen, only God can tell us. I am so grateful for Sheba's prompt action and bravery. Dogs are truly man's best friend.

~Michelle Johns

Good Nuisance

To your dog you are the centre of the universe.
~Pam Brown

Nuisance must have inherited a double dose of his mum's intelligence. She was never happier than when doing tricks for an appreciative audience. She would jump through a hoop and roll over on command, her Maltese Terrier body quivering with excitement.

Nuisance, on the other hand, was an observer. This became clear one day when he had watched our home movies showing a very successful visit to the game reserve. At the end of the film he crept up to the screen growling fiercely and bravely looked behind it for the strange beasts that had invaded our living room.

Nuisance was David's particular pet. What bond is there stronger than that between a nine-year-old boy and his dog? They went everywhere together. His brother Curly was Alice's dog, as affectionate as any six-year-old girl could want, but lacking that spark of intelligence that was so obvious in his sibling Nuisance.

One Saturday afternoon, in our VW Kombi, we drove up the rough track following the Tugela River. The Kombi was an excellent vehicle for carting the family, dogs, picnic table, chairs and food over rough roads. We turned off the main track onto a short bumpy strip to the picnic spot, which was between high banks with green grass and trees—a refreshing relief after the arid dry season and thorn brush of the rest of the valley. We had a wonderful family picnic together; the dogs explored all the strange scents and even swam the river to check the other side. Apart from collecting many grass seeds in their fluffy coats, they were having just as much fun as we humans.

As the sun went down behind the hills we decided to pack up. Nuisance was missing! We searched and called over and over but there was no movement or bark. He had disappeared in this strange environment. Our thoughts turned to all the predators and snakes he might have met with in the South African bush.

As the evening set in, I despaired of seeing Nuisance again and David was beside himself with anxiety. We said prayers that Nuisance would be found. When night had fallen and it was pitch dark, I overruled the family's pleas and said we would have to return home, but that we would come back the next day to continue the search.

We were very sad passengers in the Kombi as we bounced back to the main track, stopping once at David's insistence to call again for Nuisance into the darkness. We rejoined the main track and travelled about a mile downstream. David again asked that we stop, but I pointed out to him that there was no chance that Nuisance could be anywhere near.

However, because of the desperate pleas, I stopped and David rolled back the sliding door and called out again into the night. Within half a minute Nuisance jumped into the vehicle, just as if he'd been waiting at a bus stop. He was dusty and covered in seeds and thorns but happy to be back with his family.

We were at least a mile and a half from the picnic spot, and well clear of the river. There was no reasonable explanation to how he got there. He could not have kept up with the Kombi over such a long distance. He might have been carried downstream in the current, but would then have been far from our route.

The biggest puzzle of all was how David knew that this was the right place to stop. I can only put it down to some sort of telepathy between dog and boy, which overruled my adult logic, and to an intervention from Him who even knows when the sparrow falls.

~John McCutcheon

84

Do You Do Windows?

The meal's complete when the kitchen's neat.
~Author Unknown

Kate and Valley, our two Newfoundlands, spent their time observing and outfoxing me. Kate learned to open sliding doors; Valley's nose tripped screen door latches. Both tried to open the refrigerator, but were thwarted when I stopped hanging my hand towel through the handle. Valley could flip the gravity latch on the fence gate, and when I put an S-hook through the bolthole, it only took a day before both of them could remove it.

Both dogs had a number of toys and were gentle enough with them that even latex squeaky animals lasted for years. The stash of balls and toys were kept in a bucket on our deck, and Valley was very possessive of her soft hedgehog. So much so that when she finished tossing and pouncing on it, she would put it away in the bucket.

The girls were fed in separate two-quart stainless steel bowls that rested side by side in openings in a raised platform feeder. After they ate dinner, I'd come with a bowl of fresh water and nest one food dish in the other to make a place for the water dish. Sometimes I didn't pick up the food dishes right away, but left them until I was ready to wash them.

One night I went to put the water dish down and the two food bowls were already stacked, one inside the other. Hmmm, I thought. I must have done that and then gotten distracted before I got the water.

A few nights later, the same thing happened. I thought I was having a premature senior moment. Again, a few nights later, the dishes were stacked.

Now I was sure I wasn't losing my mind and watched from a distance while the Newfs quickly cleaned their food bowls. Then Valley took the rim of one dish in her front teeth, picked it up and placed it inside the other dish.

I wonder how long it would take to teach her to hold a dust cloth in her teeth and swish it over the end tables.

~Ann E. Vitale

85

Barney

Dogs have a way of finding the people who need them,
Filling an emptiness we don't even know we have.
~Thom Jones

Twelve years ago, Muffin arrived in our yard, and six months later, Barney joined him. Both dogs had roamed the area for months before adopting us. The vet guessed that each was approximately two years old and that they were part Chow. Muffin, however, had short legs, long golden hair and the face of a lion cub, while Barney appeared to have some Setter genes too, with his long legs and reddish-brown coat. Perhaps it was their shared Chow heritage that bonded them immediately.

Muffin was relatively healthy, just leery of strangers, but Barney was in terrible shape. He had obviously been mistreated, and he ran with his left back leg held up. It took weeks to gain his trust. He was clearly afraid of being hurt again. Our entire neighborhood was relieved when they saw him settle in at our place. No one had been able to get close enough to help him.

Flash forward eight years. As we did several times a year, we took Muffin and Barney to be washed and trimmed in a town five miles away. My husband dropped me off at my hairdresser for the same purpose. One hour later he walked into the beauty shop, his face ashen, and told me that Barney had escaped from the dog-grooming place. As usual, both dogs had been placed in the same large cage, waiting their turn to be washed. Apparently, after Muffin was taken out, the latch hadn't closed, and Barney realized he could get out. He bounded through the shop and hit the front door so hard that it opened. They had chased him, first on foot and then by car, until they lost sight of him.

Everyone began searching and praying for him. After a few days, our hope began to wane. It was the not knowing that was so hard. I couldn't bear to think of him wandering around, lost again, as he had been years ago. I prayed that if we couldn't find him, someone would take him in and love him as we had done. We placed ads in two papers and on the Internet. We posted flyers in the area and talked to everyone we met on the street and in the stores throughout the town. Each day we woke with heavy hearts and renewed our search. We took Muffin with us, hoping Barney would sense his best friend. Muffin began to eat less and less, and we worried about him. Was he confused? Was he lonely? We tried to give him extra loving attention.

One positive aspect of this stressful time was the people we met. The camaraderie of animal lovers is wonderful. Strangers become instant, concerned friends. One woman made copies of our flyers and distributed them herself. (We received a Christmas card from her ten months later.) We visited the Humane Society every day, where again we met kind, compassionate people who understood our feelings about our lost dog.

As we talked to people, we heard encouraging stories of animals that had found their way home after long periods of time. One woman knew of a family that had lost their dog while camping more than fifty miles away from their home. To reach the campsite, you have to drive through a mountain pass and up 5,000 feet to the high desert of California and then out into the wilderness. They were very upset when they had to go home without their beloved pet. Three months later, he showed up on their doorstep. We appreciated hearing the stories, but they sounded more like miracles than reality, and as each day passed we became more resigned to never seeing Barney again.

Nine days later, a dog matching Barney's description appeared on the "dead on arrival" list at the Humane Society. The driver who had picked up the dog was not available and the bodies had already been taken away, so we went to the area and talked to several children.

They studied Barney's picture and decided that it matched the dog they had seen hit by a car. The Humane Society promised to show Barney's picture to the driver the following morning and call us to confirm. Our hearts were broken.

That evening, we took Muffin for his walk, feeling sad and a bit disoriented because neither of us could believe that our sweet dog was dead. I kept thinking about all the times I had hugged him and promised that no one would ever hurt him again, that he was safe with us. We went to bed emotionally exhausted.

The next morning at around 6:30 a.m. my husband opened the back door to let Muffin out—and there sat Barney on the back stoop, his tail wagging. Sometime during the night he had arrived and patiently waited for us to open the door. He had walked five miles through a metropolitan area of houses, businesses and heavy traffic to find his way back to us. He didn't appear to be particularly hungry or thirsty and looked none the worse for wear, just very happy to see us. After enduring much hugging and tears, he went to his favorite spot in the living room and lay down. Muffin followed and licked him all over. His friend was back.

I spent the next few hours calling everyone. The people at the grooming shop clapped and cheered when they heard the words "Barney's home." The manager quietly said, "Our whole church was praying for him."

It has been twelve years since Barney entered our life, making him around fourteen years old today. Sadly, Muffin died of natural causes two years ago. Barney is still doing well. He never ran away again.

For the rest of our lives, when difficulties arise, we will remind one another that miracles do happen, that God does move in mysterious ways—that Barney found his way home.

~Libby Grandy

Mischa's Mind

Genius is the ability to put into effect what is on your mind.
~F. Scott Fitzgerald

Mischa is an Australian Kelpie, a herding dog capable of traveling miles in a day. They are extremely intelligent and used to working on their own without any humans near to tell them what to do. But I had no idea of all that when I got her. She was sold to me as a Labrador cross. As a puppy she was a small fuzzy black thing with ears that hung down. As she got older her ears began to turn upward.

Mischa learned quickly and even calling her "bad" would send her into fits of pacing, sucking up and looking woefully apologetic as she did her best to work her way back into my good graces.

She first showed me what a smart dog she was at nine months. We were playing in the snow in our back yard. I tossed a Frisbee for her, and she returned it. But only when she was good and ready would she allow me to have the Frisbee back. She loved to play keep-away. She'd touch the Frisbee to my hand and then jerk it away.

Mischa was returning with the Frisbee after a throw, and she saw a plastic bottle, another wonderful toy that would be fun to play with. Mischa dropped the Frisbee and picked up the bottle. She was about to come to me with the bottle when she paused, this time exchanging the bottle for the Frisbee.

It was clear she faced a quandary. She wanted both toys and she didn't dare leave one behind. She tried to pick up both in her mouth, but it didn't work. She then went back to picking one up in her mouth, only to put it down and go for the other.

Then she paused and I could have sworn I saw a cartoon light bulb click on over her head. Her next moves were so precise, there was no doubt what she was doing, and it was clear that there was no more confusion in her mind as she worked.

Mischa flipped the Frisbee upside down and placed it on the ground. The rim that runs around the underside of the Frisbee was now pointing up. She then picked up the bottle and dropped it onto the upturned Frisbee. She then carefully gripped the Frisbee in her teeth and trotted toward me, her tail wagging joyfully, both toys with her, the bottle held by the edge of the Frisbee.

I was stunned. Mischa was sitting there acting like she hadn't done anything particularly special. She was just waiting for me to throw her toy. I told her how good she was, and what a smart girl she was, but inside I have to admit I felt a little chill. That was the first inkling I had of how smart she would prove to be over the years.

Sometime after that, at an agility class, the instructor had set up the teeter for the dogs to try. So the teeter would not go all the way down, she set the table under it so it wouldn't drop all the way down as the dogs were getting used to it.

For those not into agility, the teeter is much like a child's playground teeter-totter, only the dog walks up the board, rides it down and gets off. Mischa didn't like the teeter and the way it moved. No amount of coaxing or bribery could get her onto it. Not so much as one foot touched that board. She wanted nothing to do with it.

The instructor felt Mischa needed the right incentive so she took her training toy and placed it at the top of the upraised teeter. Then she looked at Mischa and announced "You want it, you come and get it!"

Mischa accepted the challenge. She ran around the teeter, jumped up on the table, and reachd for the toy, without ever touching the teeter.

The whole class howled with laughter and even the instructor shook her head and said, "You have a smart one on your hands."

For the record, Mischa does the teeter just fine now. Her intelligence, though, sometimes really has me wondering who's training whom.

~Loretta Olund

Insight

What we see depends mainly on what we look for.
~John Lubbock

He had been beaten blind as a puppy. When Mickey entered our lives, his eyes had already been surgically sewn shut. But, even though he could not see, Mickey always knew exactly where life was taking him.

When we first met, I was struck by how happy and unafraid he seemed. Mickey was then in the foster care of another family. Less than a year old, and only recently removed from his physical and emotional trauma, he showed none of the symptoms one would naturally expect.

Before our family agreed to expand to include Mickey, we had a test weekend in our house. Not only was he able to adapt to us immediately, and to show us love and affection, he seemed to have an uncanny ability to quickly memorize his surroundings.

He moved about our house, bumping into a chair or a couch, then bumping into it again. But never it seemed quite head on. Always, he exhibited a sense that something was in his way and so he would, even from the first, adjust.

Within what seemed like minutes, he would avoid the chair altogether, and then the couch. You could see him memorize his world. When he moved up or down a flight of stairs, he went through the same mental exercise. First there were mishaps, but none too great.

Then there were fewer. Then there were none. We adopted him at the end of the weekend, and he adopted us.

Over the next dozen years Mickey became an integral part of who we were. And wherever we were, there was Mickey. He adapted no matter what. Once we were visiting friends who had just moved into a new house with a pool. As we gathered for a swim, Mickey was the first in the pool. Not intentionally of course. But, after a few short dips, he understood the dimensions of the pool, and for the rest of the day Mickey ran happily in circles around the pool's perimeter without falling in.

Through the years, our other dog, Shadow, became best of friends with Mickey. He acted as a seeing-eye dog of sorts. But the truth is, on many of our walks, both of them were off leash and there was really no way to tell which of the dogs was blind.

Late in Mickey's life, our family circumstances changed and we were forced to find other housing for both dogs. After much searching we were able to locate a wonderful woman, Shirley, who agreed to take Shadow, at that point old and in the early stages of decline. We were going to have to separate the two comrades. A very dear friend had agreed to take on the responsibility of bringing Mickey into his home.

On the day that Shadow was leaving, we brought Mickey along to say his last goodbyes. When we reached Shadow's new residence, we lingered for some time. Mickey roamed through the house and soon was making his way around without any hint of difficulty. Shirley was astounded. She had never met Mickey and so was unaware of his amazing capability. As we were about to go, Shirley asked if we would consider leaving both dogs with her. I went out into her driveway and cried.

Mickey and Shadow spent the rest of their days together. After Shadow passed away, Shirley gave Mickey a loving and wonderful home for the rest of his life.

While Mickey had no vision, he had the ability to see the world as few others could. Loving, playful and forever happy, Mickey's early problems left physical scars, but what remained was a dog who saw life's path clearly and followed it no matter the obstacles in his way.

~Robert Nussbaum

88

Great Scott

We are impossibly conceited animals, and actually dumb as heck.
Ask any teacher. You don't even have to ask a teacher. Ask anybody.
Dogs and cats are smarter than we are.
~Kurt Vonnegut, Jr.

I once heard a Westminster Kennel Club Dog Show announcer say, "The Scottish Terrier is the only breed of dog that knows he is smarter than his master." I didn't have a clue as to what he meant at the time, but that was before my nine-year journey with McDuff, my Scottish Terrier therapy dog. That was before a dog with off-the-chart intelligence and you-wouldn't-believe stubbornness that time after time outsmarted and frustrated me to tears. That was before the first volley was fired in the battle of The Pill War.

Looking back I realize how naïve I was. I'd taken McDuff to the vet for whatever. I can't even remember why now. The vet gave me seven pills, a week's supply, to give him. No problem. Why should giving McDuff pills be any different from giving pills to my other dogs? Scotty was content to wolf down a wiener with a pill tucked inside. Dawn relished the mound of cheese surrounding the concealed tablet. Just hide the pill in something tasty and give it to him. Right?

McDuff watched while I turned my back to him and slipped a pill inside the wiener. With a wide grin on my face, I turned and offered him the meat. "Here, Duff."

Cautiously taking it from my hand, he chewed once, dropped it on the floor, picked it up, chewed once, dropped it on the floor and repeated the process until the pill popped out. After devouring the wiener, McDuff looked up at me, turned, and walked away licking his chops. The pill lay on the floor. The smile slowly faded from my face.

The next day I told a colleague at work about it. "Judy, just put the pill far back in McDuff's mouth, hold it shut, then rub his throat until he swallows. That always works with my dog."

I couldn't wait to get home and try it. I'd fix him. But, I hit a snag she never encountered. McDuff saw me put the pill in my clenched hand. He knew what was going on. When I tried to force his mouth open, he clamped his jaws shut tighter than a vise. Have you ever tried to pry open the mouth of a Scottie with a severe case of lockjaw? It's like trying to open a bear trap with a straw.

After telling another friend the next day about my problems with McDuff, she suggested putting the pill in peanut butter. McDuff loves peanuts. I gave him the pill in a gigantic blob of peanut butter.

He smacked his mouth and smacked his mouth and smacked his mouth until the peanut butter dissolved—and then spat out the pill. I could still hear him smacking long after he left the room.

Three days had gone by without McDuff taking any medication. Desperate, I called his vet and told him everything that had happened. "Put the pill in his dog food, Judy." Why hadn't I thought of that?

I made an adjustment because I fed McDuff dry dog food, and in this case, canned would work better. I bought the most expensive brand on the supermarket shelf.

Above the hum of the can opener, with fiendish delight, I described to McDuff the delicious gourmet dinner coming his way. He watched me intently, nose twitching, mouth beginning to drool. It smelled so good I was tempted to take a bite.

When McDuff wasn't looking, I buried a pill deep in the middle of his dog food and casually strolled away. Sneaking back later, I found the bowl licked clean and the pill nowhere in sight. I had outsmarted him at last. Sure, it hadn't been easy, but after all, I'm a human; he's a dog. Six more days passed by with the same results. Dog bowl licked clean, pill gone.

Canned dog food is messier than the dry. I decided to give the bowl a good cleaning after a week and picked it up from its place next to our pet fountain. That's when I found the seven blue pills lined neatly in a row. McDuff had been hiding them between the dog bowl and pet fountain all week.

Frantic, frustrated and in tears, I ran to the phone and dialed the vet. "McDuff hid the pills. He hasn't taken a single pill since you gave them to me ten days ago. He'll never get well," I said between sobs.

After he finally stopped laughing, the vet said, "That McDuff sure is one smart dog. Calm down, Judy. Come to the office and I'll give you capsules. You can break them apart and mix the medicine in with his dog food." I was afraid it wouldn't work. He would smell the medication and refuse to eat. But that didn't happen.

The final battle in The Pill War ended in victory for me. I should have felt elated. So tell me something. Why did I feel I'd won the battle, but lost the war?

~Judy McFadden

89

Because of Max

No animal I know of can consistently be more of a
friend and companion than a dog.
~Stanley Leinwoll

Max has always been an in-your-face kind of dog—never pesky, but always around watching and listening, absorbing and observing and never missing out on anything. So when I was diagnosed with Stage II breast cancer, I wasn't at all surprised that Max knew something was radically wrong with me, nor was I or anybody else surprised at his actions. During that time he hardly left my side, watched my every move, and often nestled next to me, cuddling and licking my bald head, letting me know he was there for me in his loving, overprotective doggy sort of way.

One day when my daughter came by, I wrote out a list of things I needed and sent her to the store. To be perfectly honest, I really wasn't feeling well and wasn't up to having company. I told her that she didn't have to rush back with the items—the next day would be fine.

After an hour or so of conversation and feigned laughter, I told her I was tired and was going to take a nap. After doing a few things around the house, she left and I went downstairs to get some water. All of a sudden, everything went black. I had passed out and woken up in a pool of blood. From time to time Max would run throughout the house barking and then come back and lie beside me. At that point I knew he was the only one who could help me. As I lay there wondering what my dog could do, my world suddenly became black again.

I awoke to hear the phone ringing, unable to reach it. Max barked loudly and frantically. A few minutes later the phone started ringing again. Max barked. The third time it started ringing, I weakly whispered, "Go get it boy; get the phone," but all he did was run around barking. When the phone stopped ringing, he would stop barking and lie back down beside me.

I could feel myself growing weaker and weaker, and it seemed as if he sensed this too. Every time I drifted off, he'd lick my face and bark until I opened my eyes. It was as if he was doing what he could to keep me from falling into an eternal sleep.

The phone started ringing again, and I weakly whispered in the most commanding voice that I could muster, "Go get it boy; get the phone." He ran off, then came back and continued to lie beside me, licking my face and barking. Time passed and I no longer heard the phone ring. As I tried to raise my head and body, in pain, weak and with absolutely no strength at all, I'd sink back into a world of darkness and despair.

I don't know how much time passed before I faintly remember my daughter leaning over me—and then being rushed to the hospital. It was a few days later when I became conscious enough to find out what had happened. I had become dehydrated and anemic. My blood pressure had dropped dangerously low while my temperature rose dangerously high.

My daughter had gone to the store and realized that she had forgotten the list of things I needed. She called several times. At first when I didn't answer, she thought I was still sleeping. The second time she thought I was talking on the phone and just didn't click over, which was a bad habit of mine, or that I was sitting in the yard with Max and didn't hear the phone.

She said she thought of all the usual reasons why it often took several tries before reaching me. After the third time that I didn't answer she started getting concerned, but didn't get alarmed until the fourth time she called. Since I have call waiting, she knew something was wrong when she got a busy signal the last time she called. So she dropped everything and rushed over.

As she was putting the key in the door, she said all she could hear was Max barking. When she opened the door, he anxiously jumped all over her and pushed her into the kitchen, where she found me passed out on the floor and the phone off the hook. Max had knocked the phone off the hook and that busy signal was the sign that I needed help.

My daughter and I often talk about that time. She said she wasn't going to wait until the next day to bring the things that I needed, but she was planning to come back later that evening. Had she waited until that time, it might have been too late. It was definitely because of the busy signal that she returned in time to save my life.

~Francine L. Baldwin-Billingslea

Our Buddy

*We derive immeasurable good, uncounted pleasures, enormous security,
and many critical lessons about life by owning dogs.*
~Roger Caras

B uddy, our Beagle, never asked to go out in the middle of the night, so when he came to our bedside and began to claw at the blankets, my thought was that he seriously needed to go outside. I spoke softly to him and gently stroked him while he stood on his hind legs, but he kept pawing the bed with an agonizing frenzy.

I forced myself up and he surged ahead of me down the hall, way beyond his usual romping run, ignored the outside door, and zoomed straight to the cellar stairs. He insistently nodded his head toward the stairs and then nudged me to descend. Obediently, I followed the jittery dog to the basement.

Nearly to the bottom step, I suddenly jolted fully awake. I smelled smoke!

Our twelve-year-old son had made the basement his new bedroom. He had recently rigged up an egg hatchery under the basement stairs for the robin eggs he found in the yard. The light bulb that he had extended above the hatchery to warm the eggs had fallen into his birdie bedding and nesting twigs, and had heated them—creating a flaming fire!

Our son's head was still burrowed in his crumpled pillow. We, being upstairs and at the other end of the house, would have had no knowledge of the blue eggs cooking in the middle of the night had Buddy not alerted us.

So when I say our alert Buddy saved the night, I guess I could declare that he also saved the basement, our son, our house, and although on the night shift, he also saved the day—make it days. The next days could have been filled with grief and mourning.

Some different sparks flew when my infuriated husband woke up and assessed our son's burning birds blunder. But after the scorching fiasco and Dad's chastising lecture, our dazed family discussed the rescue and it was our hearts that were burning then, melting with accolades for a Beagle, not usually considered a bird dog. We all laughed at that, hugged a lot, thrust a thousand thank yous toward Heaven, and decreed great acclaim to our devoted—and perfectly named pet. He surely was our Buddy.

~June K. Blake

91

Follow Moses

Thorns may hurt you, men desert you, sunlight turn to fog;
but you're never friendless ever, if you have a dog.
~Douglas Mallock

Life with my Australian Shepherd and Labrador mix, Moses, was always a wild and crazy ride—because he was such a wild and crazy dog. He was so different from any other dog I'd owned. So intelligent, so independent—and so untrainable, I was repeatedly informed. Even getting Moses on a leash was a challenge.

But it was okay because instead of my husband and I teaching him, he taught us. And we learned a lot. How to relax, to stop worrying, and how to "just be Moses."

Every day my husband and I, or one of us, would walk Moses along the gravel road near our home in rural Bend, Oregon. We led him to the open land and let him roam off the leash for half an hour or so. As long as there was plenty of space for him to run free, he'd be happy.

Most days, it worked well. Not every day.

Winters in Bend are bitterly cold. Being high desert, the weather can change quite suddenly. One minute the skies can be clear, and the next, a storm could blow through.

That winter day I had stayed behind and my husband had taken Moses out. I had nothing on my mind besides preparing a salad to go along with our main dish. Crock-Pot roast beef was a family favorite, and by the time I had the table set and the beverages poured, I expected to hear David unzipping his down jacket in the foyer, and Moses slurping water from his bucket out back of the house.

But no footsteps sounded in the hall, no dog woofed for his dinner at the back door. I dressed the salad and brought it to the table. Checked the clock. A little late. I was getting worried. They should have been home.

I heard the wind roaring, bits of hail slamming against the window.

I tried to focus on slicing the garlic bread and cutting the roast, but decided to put on my boots and hat, just in case. I peeked out the front window and gasped. The world hadn't turned into a glistening snowy postcard, as I'd hoped. It was a full-blown whiteout—seeing more than a few feet was impossible. I couldn't see past the edge of our front porch. I shuddered as I imagined David out in the open spaces with a dog unwilling to be leashed, let alone follow commands.

In these conditions, there was no telling where Moses might have led him; there was no way to sense direction. They could have been walking in circles, freezing or hurt. They might have found their way to the road, only to be hit by a motorist who either didn't see them or even worse, saw them but couldn't swerve to avoid hitting them. The thoughts that ran through my mind were terrifying. I struggled not to panic.

I shrugged on my jacket and grabbed the keys to the SUV, determined to find them. Driving down the lane, I fought to keep the car on the icy pavement.

Nearing the area where David walked Moses, I strained for a glimpse of them through the sleet. I pulled over to the side of the road to check the drainage ditch that ran along it. With relief, I saw it was empty. I called out. No response. The snow muffled any sound that the wind hadn't stolen away. The skies were getting darker. I didn't know what to do next.

Just then, I caught a glimpse of movement up ahead, a blur in the gray. Out of the darkness came my husband with Moses leading him. I cried tears of relief. I was so grateful to see them and give them a hug.

We got into the car and headed home. David leaned in to give me a quick kiss as I drove.

"I would never have found the road if it hadn't been for Moses—he kept dragging me in this direction," he said, ruffling our pet's fur.

I checked the rear-view mirror. There was Moses, smiling his cockeyed smile.

Pulling into our driveway, I turned to face David.

"I was so worried. I thought you might have..." I heard the tremor in my voice.

"Me, too," he said, and cleared his throat. "What's for dinner?"

I just shook my head and smiled.

Outside the car's window, the winds had died down. The storm had transformed the yard into a sweet, muted watercolor. I looked at our cozy little house, soft lights glowing in the dusk. Sitting together in the car, gazing through the windows, I felt as though I were being given a peek into someone else's life. A very lovely life. Safe, secure, warm.

Home is all those things to me. It's the arms of the man I've loved for so many years, the rough fur of a dog who loves me in spite of my imperfections. A dog who taught me to work hard and play like I mean it. It's knowing how precious and fragile life is—even if I need a storm to remind me.

Many years have passed now, and my husband and I have a new dog to teach us. But I'll never forget my Moses, the blizzard and the night I thought I had lost it all.

~Heidi Gaul

I Can't Believe My Dog Did That!

Chapter 10

My Best Friend

92

Canine Cop

The dog, in life the firmest friend, the first to welcome, foremost to defend.
~Lord Byron

Someone banged on the front door, startling me awake. It was the middle of the night... who could it be? Our tiny six-month-old Terrier puppy, Heidi, bounced up and down on the bed barking furiously—a bark I'd never heard her use before. Her bark was usually a high-pitched beginner's yelp. This deep, gruff sound might as well have been coming from a full-grown Great Dane.

My husband worked nights, and Heidi, although she'd only been a member of the family for two months, was already taking on a protective role. When he was away, she would sleep at the foot of the bed as if guarding me, her ears perking up at the slightest sound.

After she accomplished her task of rousing me on this particular night, Heidi ran to the door and scratched at it while still "arrfing" at the top of her lungs.

"Who is it?" I asked, squinting through the peephole.

"I just had an accident right outside your house. Can I come in and use the phone?"

This was before the days of a cell phone in every pocket. I saw a man leaning against the doorframe, not looking at all as if he was scared or in trouble. So in my sleepy daze I gave an answer I would regret the moment it came out of my mouth: "No... I'm alone right now. I can't let you in."

Immediately I winced, knowing it was the wrong thing to say. I scooped Heidi up into my arms and held my breath, waiting for him to kick down the door.

Thankfully, Heidi kept barking and the knocking stopped. I heard footsteps fade as he walked away.

But that wasn't the end.

The following week, on the same night of the week, at the same time, the banging started again. Only this time, when Heidi and I got to the door, I saw the doorknob turning. Someone was trying to get into the house. Heidi jumped up and down, growling and snarling. I ran and dialed 9-1-1.

"Help—someone's trying to break into my house!"

"I'm going to stay on the phone with you until an officer gets there," the dispatcher said, and began giving me instructions.

"Do you have a room where you can lock yourself in?"

"Yes, the master bedroom... I'm in there now."

"What kind of dog is that barking?"

"A West Highland White Terrier," I whispered, not wanting the burglar to possibly hear that Heidi only weighed about ten pounds and stood less than a foot tall.

"What? I can't hear you."

"A little Terrier," I said louder, figuring I had blown Heidi's cover.

"Well," the dispatcher laughed, "It sounds like a much bigger dog. You are probably safe. Thieves don't like dogs."

"Then why is he still rattling on my door?"

"Well... ummm... an officer is on the way. But until they get there, if the guy gets in, try to get a good look at him before you lock yourself in your room, so we can get a description."

"What?" I couldn't believe he was telling me to do this. Then, the wiggling of the front door stopped and I heard the footsteps go around to the back of the house. Heidi followed the sound, still woofing her little heart out.

The person was now trying the sliding glass door at the porch entrance.

Heidi pulled out all the stops. She couldn't see through the vertical blinds (and thank goodness neither could our mysterious visitor), but she jumped about two feet in the air and scratched at the door with all her might, her little paws pushing the blinds up against the glass.

No police officer yet…

Finally, the banging and rattling stopped. Heidi's bark calmed down. The invader had walked away.

It turned out that the police were sent to a neighborhood with a similar name. I could have been dead three times over by the time they arrived. I'm sure I owe my life and the safety of our home to Heidi, our very own canine cop.

My husband and I cherished that little dog for the next thirteen years. This precious companion, who grew to all of two feet tall and fifteen pounds, provided not only protection, but also love, humor and warmth in our lives, and we gave her the same with all our hearts.

Heidi retired from being our private police squad when she was ninety-one dog years old. We haven't yet replaced her in our hearts or our home. We figure the next dog is going to have some pretty big paws to fill.

~Sheryl Young

93

The Dirty, Stinky Stray

The best kind of friend is the one you could sit on a porch with,
never saying a word, and walk away feeling completely understood.
~Author Unknown

The old farmhouse had been too big and too lonely since Martin died. I roamed the empty rooms searching for something to do. The vegetable patch was overgrown with weeds. The hours that I used to spend canning and freezing Martin's harvest now dragged on endlessly. It wasn't fun to drive into town for ice cream on Sunday afternoons anymore. As a matter of fact, nothing was fun without Martin.

My daughter Jane lived in another town about fifty miles away. It wasn't a great distance, but she was busy with a job and two young boys. I tried hard not to get upset when weeks went by without a visit from her. I knew she would come more often if she realized I needed her. I did need her. I needed to see her face, hear her voice, feel her hug, and spend a little time with someone who cared for me. But Jane didn't know that. The farm was paid for, I had enough coming in to pay my bills, and my health was fairly good for someone my age. Jane thought I was doing fine. I wasn't.

One morning, while sweeping off the porch I saw a skinny little dog coming from behind the house. His tail and his head were lowered and he watched me with wary eyes as he slowly approached. If he hadn't been so dirty he would have probably been white, but he was so caked with mud and brambles it was hard to tell. Sighing, I went into the kitchen to look for a scrap of food to feed the dog. I didn't need a dog. I didn't want a dog. But I couldn't let him go hungry. I would feed him and then I would call animal control to come and get him.

I cut up a few slices of bologna and put them on a paper plate. Knowing that the dog was probably thirsty I filled a cereal bowl with water before going back outside. At the sound of the screen door scraping open, the dog lifted his head, a hopeful look in his chocolate eyes. I placed my meager offerings at the edge of the porch and watched him for a moment. He eyed the plate of bologna hungrily and lifted one paw as if to step forward, but he was afraid. I went back inside the house, knowing he would quickly devour the food once he felt safe.

When I went out to get the mail I saw that the dog was curled up on the rug on the porch in a deep sleep. He opened one eye and watched me, trying to decide whether he should run or not.

"I won't hurt you," I murmured softly. "But I won't let you stay here either." He heard no threat in my voice, closed the one eye that had been fixed on me and was asleep again by the time I had taken three steps.

I shuffled through the mail, feeling certain that I would find a card from Jane. Saturday had been my birthday. Apparently she had been too busy to come by or call. I found no card from Jane.

I sat down in the rocker on my porch and started to cry. Suddenly I felt a rough tongue licking my cheeks. Startled, I looked into the upturned face of the dirty mutt, who had stretched as far as he could to reach my tears. His front paws rested on the arms of the rocker, and his expressive brown eyes seemed to be filled with understanding. He had such a sincere, concerned look on his little face that I found myself chuckling. I smiled down at him and patted his head. He gave a small whimper as if to tell me that he also needed a little love and affection.

I looked down at the malnourished dog, amazed that he had put aside his own suffering to offer me comfort. He had been on his own, alone, hungry and afraid. He had no way of knowing how I might react to his display of affection. He could have been shoved away and shouted at, but he gave me what he sensed that I needed. He was dirty and smelly, but at that moment he was the most beautiful dog I had ever seen.

I thought of Martin and how he always let me know that I was loved. He was affectionate and sweet natured every day of his life. I thought that Martin would be a good name for this warm, friendly dog.

Martin and I have a strong bond. We both know we are loved, and the affection and camaraderie is appreciated by both of us. I am greeted warmly when I wake up every morning. I go for long walks again with Martin at my side. I read or watch TV in the evenings with him at my feet. He seems to enjoy the sound of my laughter and is always doing funny antics for my amusement. He will lie on his back and juggle his beach ball in the air with his front paws. He can only keep it in the air for a few seconds, but that is long enough to get a giggle out of me. His favorite game is to catch flies in his mouth, which he eats. The vet says it won't hurt him.

I have not shed a single tear in self-pity since Martin came into my life. I laugh every day. I am shown affection and love every day. I no longer peer out the window watching for the mailman, hoping for a letter or a card from Jane. I no longer stare at the phone trying by sheer willpower to make it ring and hear Jane's voice when I pick it up. Oh, I still wish she would visit or call more often. But I am no longer consumed by it. Martin has put joy back into my heart again. I found a purpose to live in Martin. He has filled the lonely, sad voids in my life. And when he lays his head on my knees and gazes up at me in pure adoration, I know that he realizes I have done the same for him.

~Elizabeth Atwater

94

Share and Share Alike

Love is the greatest refreshment in life.
~Pablo Picasso

"That's kind of kismet, isn't it, Casey? Your baby and ours being the same age," I stated when I realized that our friend's baby, Austin, and our Yorkie puppy, D-Dog, were both nine months old.

Casey and her husband Jerry had brought their first baby on a fishing trip to our fishing camp on the San Bernard River. Roy and I had not seen them since their wedding two years before. It was the first chance they had to slow down and relax since the wedding, new house, and new baby. It was also the first time we got to show off our newly purchased fishing camp. We were anxious to meet Austin, and the young couple was excited to visit the camp and meet our new puppy.

It was obvious from the minute Austin entered our camp house that the two "babies" would get along well. D-Dog was put on the couch with Casey and Austin for a trial encounter. D-Dog sniffed Austin, and he, in turn, petted D-Dog with gentle hands—it was an instant bond. For the rest of the weekend, the two were inseparable. It was almost as if they knew that in their youth, they were different from the surrounding adults. Casey and I had no problem afterward putting the two on a blanket on the floor together while we made lunch for our menfolk.

D-Dog was a puppy—with all that entails. He was teething at the time of Austin's visit, so I decided I should give him a new rawhide chew stick to encourage him not to teethe on Austin's tiny toes. I called him into the kitchen; he took the chew stick and carried it directly back to the blanket where Austin lay.

Austin was a very good baby—he had not cried once, or even fretted, since the start of the visit. But just as we began making gumbo, he started to fret. Casey laughed.

"Austin's teething, too. I'd better go get something for his gums before we get too involved with the gumbo."

Austin's fretting seemed to calm as soon as Casey left to get the medicine, but I didn't think much about it at the time. Casey got the medicine from the diaper bag in the spare bedroom while I cut up vegetables in the kitchen. When she got back to the living room, she said, "Jan, come here—you have to see this."

There on the blanket sat Austin blissfully chewing on D-Dog's brand new rawhide chew stick. D-Dog lay there with his head in Austin's lap chewing on his own old, slobbery piece of a chew stick. D-Dog thought it wasn't necessary to use the teething medicine—his new chew stick would do the trick. D-Dog figured out Austin was having the same teething problem that he was experiencing, and knew what helped him—so he shared it with his friend. Casey and I could not believe that D-Dog comprehended Austin's fretting and would give him his treasured new chew stick. That display of empathy was amazing, but D-Dog was not through sharing with his friend that weekend.

At the time of the visit, Austin was learning to crawl. He could get up on his hands and knees and rock backward and forward, but he just could not lift his little diapered behind up and master the art of locomotion. While he didn't fuss about this, we adults could all see the frustration in his little face as he attempted to crawl time and time again.

We were watching a movie while D-dog and Austin alternately

slept and played on the blanket on the floor in front of us. After a while, Austin decided it was time to try crawling again—he pulled up on all fours and started rocking. D-Dog watched intently as Austin made another attempt to crawl—another failure. He fell over again. I could almost see the cogs turning in his brain as D-Dog appraised the situation. Then, when Austin again struggled to the all fours position, D-Dog got behind him, put his head under Austin's diaper and pushed up and forward, up and forward until it happened—Austin crawled a couple of feet. When he fell over this time, he sat up and locked his wide eyes with D-Dog's, as if to say, "What just happened here?"

Not long after this incident, Austin, Casey and Jerry returned home to Louisiana. Austin had not crawled prior to his visit to our camp, but Casey later told me that he was soon crawling on his own after D-Dog's lesson—shortly before he decided it was time to walk.

A nine-month-old baby and a nine-month-old dog shared an understanding that we adults had long lost. How my puppy knew to befriend and share his experiences with that baby still amazes me.

~Janice R. Edwards

95

Someone to Love

It is astonishing how little one feels alone when one loves.
~John Bulwer

When it became obvious that my once solid marriage was coming to an end, I was devastated. The man of my dreams had turned out not to be. Finally, after enough fights, tears and pain, I had to admit to myself and to him that it wasn't working anymore. I filed for divorce and moved out.

At the time, I was working as a manager for a very busy retail store. I often worked over fifty hours a week, and sometimes eighty or more. I devoted myself to my work for the next ten years. I was so busy working that I didn't have time to be lonely or depressed.

Then the unthinkable happened. The recession hit. Suddenly, our product was considered a luxury when people were struggling to pay their mortgage and buy food. Sales dropped. Then they dropped some more. Finally, the store was forced to close its doors.

I applied for unemployment and dragged myself out of bed each morning to look for a job. I believed that with my credentials, finding new employment would be relatively easy.

I'll never forget the first job interview I went to. There were just a few openings, but over one hundred people showed up. The turnout was so large, the employer was interviewing people in groups instead of individually. I didn't get that job. Or the next. Or the next.

One night, I'd had it. I was overwhelmed with fear and depression.

Through tears, I yelled at God at the top of my lungs. My marriage had failed. I'd lost my job. Unemployment didn't pay all the bills I had stacked neatly on top of the refrigerator—most of them unopened. It didn't seem fair. I'd worked hard all my life. Here I was, middle aged, divorced, alone and couldn't find a job.

"Please God," I begged through tears. "Find someone who will love me. Someone who will treat me with respect and share the good and the bad times with me. Someone who will love me forever; a relationship that will last."

A month or so later, I was scanning the want ads in the local newspaper for job openings when I spotted her. She was a black cocka-peeka-poo puppy who was absolutely adorable. She reminded me of a dog that I'd had twenty years earlier who eventually died of old age.

Realistically, the last thing I needed was a puppy. I was struggling to feed myself, and buying dog food on my meager budget was out of the question. But something told me to drive to the shelter and "just see." I had no intention of bringing home a puppy that day. I just wanted to explore what they had available.

When I inquired about the dog featured in the newspaper, I was told she'd been adopted. More disappointed than I thought I'd be, I started walking toward the front door of the shelter.

"Wait," the woman said brightly. "We have another baby in back. We didn't advertise her because she needs a special home. I don't know if you have what she needs but it wouldn't hurt to fill out an application and see."

I completed the paperwork in short order.

After scanning the paperwork, the woman said with a smile, "Follow me."

She led me to a small hallway.

"Wait here," she instructed.

A minute later, she returned with the smallest puppy I'd ever seen.

Black and white with a curled up tail, the puppy fit in the palm of her hand. The small little bundle of fur began whimpering. Slowly, she set it down on the floor and it wobbled over to me.

I picked the dog up and eyed it suspiciously. I had planned on getting a large dog like a German Shepherd or a Labrador. I'd had large dogs before and enjoyed the protection they afforded me. This was a little ragamuffin who might be a small yapper. I knew it wouldn't do to have an ankle-biter in my home and certainly not one who would disturb me, and my neighbors, with incessant barking.

It whimpered again. I picked the dog off the floor and cradled it in my arms. So tiny, so small. So what I didn't have in mind. It licked my face. It licked me again. Enthusiastically, it began licking my face all over, with large wet kisses. That did it. My cold heart instantly melted and I was in love.

"The owner brought her to us saying he didn't want her. She was less than a month old. We've had to hand feed her, but isn't she beautiful? We weren't sure of her breed but the vet told us she's a cross between a Pekingese and a Japanese Chin. Her black-and-white markings are classic Chin."

I didn't care what I had to do or how much money I had to spend, that dog was coming home with me.

I've had Bella for a year now. She is my joy, my inspiration, my companion, and my life. When I get up in the morning, she's lying on the bed beside me. When I go to sleep at night, she dutifully crawls in bed with me, to sleep right next to me and keep me company in the darkness of the night.

When I take trips in the car, she's right beside me on the passenger seat. She likes to put her paws on the dash and gaze out the window as the miles go by. When I'm at home, watching television, she's beside me on the couch, watching the same show. Bella is so much a part of my life now, I can't imagine ever having lived without her.

That's not to say my life has been easy. I have the same old problems. I'm still unemployed. I still struggle to pay my bills. But with Bella at my side, we'll face whatever it is we have to face, together. We're a team.

Just recently, I thought back to that night so long ago; the night

I cried out to God in pain and anguish. I'd begged Him to bring me someone to love; someone who would stand by me. I realized with a start that God had answered that prayer, though not in a way I expected.

I looked over at Bella, rubbed her affectionately between the ears, and grinned.

~Pam Phree

Reprinted by permission of Off the Mark
and Mark Parisi © 2007

96

Schnitzel Come Home

Dogs are not our whole life, but they make our lives whole.
~Roger Caras

When Lonny and I were first married, we had a miniature Dachshund named Schnitzel. Lonny was a college student. I worked in the office of an elementary school. I'd dreamed, for years, of having a doxie. So had Lonny. We ate Ramen noodles for a semester in order to save enough money to buy our purebred beauty.

She was easy to choose at the breeder's. She was shorthaired, black with rich brown markings. Her coat was shiny as marble and soft as silk. And she was sweet as could be. She took immediate hold of my heart. Lonny loved her, too, but she became my dog.

"Why does she love you more?" Lonny asked, peering over a thick textbook. He was sprawled over the living room floor. Schnitzel and I were curled together on the loveseat. She was a tiny, black comma on my lap.

"Because I'm sweeter," I said.

"Got me there," Lonny said. Then he winked. I stroked Schnitzel's sleek back and wondered how I could love a four-legged creature so much.

I think that Lonny knew that I needed something to love. Of course I loved him first. But that first year of marriage was tough.

Lonny was consumed with study. We were away from family. I enjoyed my job at the elementary school, but I finished work at three and Lonny spent every evening immersed in books. I struggled to find friends. My co-workers were kind but they were much older than me. The other married couples in our apartment complex were students. I was lonely.

Until Schnitzel came along.

We lived only a block from the school where I worked, so I walked home to spend lunch hour with my girl. I'd hold her close to my face and she'd pat my cheeks with tiny paws. She'd cry with joy and burrow into my arms. If the weather was good, we'd take a walk to stretch her tiny legs. My mom sent her a red nubby knit sweater for the cold Illinois winter. "For my Granddog," the tag read. During visits home, she'd fallen in love with my little pup, too.

By the time Lonny's graduation came near, Schnitzel and I were inseparable. She trotted around the apartment at my heels. I took her to parks and she even rode on my lap when I ran errands around town. When Lonny had a job interview out of state, and I'd been invited to join him to tour the community, I didn't know how I'd leave my dog.

I shared my struggle with Kathy, a kind young teacher at the elementary school. She immediately offered to help.

"We'll babysit," she said. "My little boy will love it. We have a big back yard with a fence. It will be a blessing to us."

Kathy lived in a small community near the university town. She was amazing with her fourth grade students. I knew she'd be amazing with Schnitzel, too. So I agreed. But as the plane lifted from the ground, Lonny squeezed my hand. I squeezed my eyes shut. I was praying for my little dog.

Lonny and I spent three days in Michigan. He interviewed. I fell in love with the community. There was even a sweet pet shop in town. I'd stopped to buy a rawhide twisted in the shape of a pretzel for Schnitzel. But on the last evening, when we returned to our hotel room, the light on our phone blinked red.

We called the front desk for the message: Call Kathy.

I dialed the number while my heart beat hard in my chest. Kathy began to cry at the sound of my voice.

"Schnitzel ran away. I left her in the yard, for just a minute, while I took my son inside. She squeezed under the slats of the fence. We've looked everywhere."

I knew that she had gone looking for home. Looking for me. But our apartment was miles away from Kathy's country home. Schnitzel would never find her way.

I didn't sleep that night. I twisted and turned in the hotel-crisp sheets. Lonny tried to console me, but all I could think about was my dog. Cold. Hungry. Lost. Or worse.

When we returned to Illinois, Lonny and I didn't go home. We went straight to Kathy's neighborhood.

"Hang these signs around town," Lonny said. "I'm going to put an ad in the paper."

I shivered as I hammered cardboard signs into posts. I talked with business owners and taped signs in windows. Lonny and I scoured the streets until the sun sunk low and the wind blew hard. Then, hand in hand, in silence, we walked to our car and drove home.

Morning revealed a thick, white frost. The trees were covered. The ground was crisp and harsh. I stood in the window and pulled my robe tight. Schnitzel was so small. She'd never survive the cold. The apartment was heavy with traces of my girl. A chew toy in the corner. Her blue paisley bed. I padded back to the bedroom and slipped in beside Lonny. He wrapped his arms around me, and he held me while I cried.

Something inside me broke, and I knew I had to let go.

I was startled when the phone rang loud and sharp. Sleep must've come, because the green digitals blinked late morning and the sun was up strong. After a minute, Lonny came to the bedroom, holding his jacket. He sat firm on the bed.

"Shawnelle," he said. "Kathy called. They found Schnitzel."

My heart went cold.

Lonny took my hands. "A custodian found her. Curled up on

the football field at the high school. He'd heard that Kathy had been looking for a Dachshund pup."

Football field? High school. Schnitzel had been traveling our direction. She had been heading home. And she'd traveled miles in the cold looking for me. Tears burned hot on my cheeks.

"No, Shawnelle," Lonny said. "Schnitzel's cold, but she's alive." He handed me his jacket. "Let's go to Kathy's."

Twenty minutes later, Schnitzel was in my arms. She was weak and shaking. But her tiny paws patted my face and she squealed and cried like mad. Her tail beat a steady rhythm and her heart pounded a song. I'd never held such joy. In my arms, or in my heart.

Sweet, sweet Schnitzel was going home.

~Shawnelle Eliasen

97

Get 'em Boy

*What counts is not necessarily the size of the dog in the fight;
it's the size of the fight in the dog.*
~Dwight D. Eisenhower

His name couldn't be Killer. It didn't fit a dog who always looked happy. Demon wouldn't work either since his brown eyes were too kind. Bruiser, my husband Mark's last choice, was too ridiculous for such a handsome silver-and-black German Shepherd. But when I called to him with the name I picked, Bruno, the puppy responded immediately. So Bruno stuck from the first day.

That was the day Mark rescued Bruno from an abusive owner who was so cruel he'd actually fed the puppy screws and nails. Besides feeling like a savior, Mark was excited because he had always wanted a guard dog. Even better, a purebred German Shepherd.

I had always protested getting a dog. I was too busy with work and nursing school—until I saw the emaciated, shivering puppy. My heart went out to this creature, with his tail between his legs and his matted, dirty fur. The tender look on his face hooked me right away.

After three trips to the veterinarian and a lot of love and healthy food, Bruno filled out. As soon as he was strong enough, Mark began training him, hoping to turn Bruno into the warrior animal he'd always wanted.

Week after week Mark trained him. And as Bruno grew, he took on the appearance of a fighter and could certainly pose as one with teeth bared, but it was a charade. He may have looked ferocious, but his heart was too tender—he was too sweet-natured and trusting. He patiently followed Mark's commands, but without fail, when the lesson ended, Bruno would run to me and push his snout into my hip, his way of asking for a hug.

While he obeyed Mark and appeared to respect him, I clearly had Bruno's heart. He was my protector and dear friend. He was a loving dog, often lying at my feet, or as he preferred, placing his large head on my lap as I scratched behind his ears.

When Mark worked late, Bruno and I ate dinner together. Although his plate sat on the floor next to me, he'd always give an appreciative wag of his tail for the opportunity to be my lone dinner date.

On one of those nights, I heard the fence door slam outside. I froze as Bruno jumped up and stood at the glass patio door with a low, teeth-baring growl I'd never heard before. It chilled me. I turned on the outside light, but since our yard was so deep, I couldn't see beyond the concrete patio. Bruno continued showing his teeth and growling, while I became increasingly frightened. My heart thumping, I yanked open the glass door, yelling, "Go get 'em boy."

Bruno tore out of the house, barking furiously and bolting into the darkness. Then suddenly his barking stopped. I couldn't be sure, but thought I heard a whimper. Then nothing.

I debated calling 911, but decided against it since I didn't actually see anything or anyone. Trembling, I pulled a butcher knife from the kitchen drawer and waited, terrified. I felt so guilty sending Bruno out alone. Tears rolled down my face, thinking I'd ordered Bruno, my loving, trusting friend, to face some unknown fiend.

For twenty minutes all was quiet. Then I heard a light scratch at the front door.

With measured breaths and knife in hand, I tiptoed to the door and looked through the peephole. Bruno. Tongue hanging out, and tail wagging.

I swung the door open and he leapt at me, nearly knocking me down. So elated and relieved to see him, for a moment I forgot the danger that had loomed in the back yard.

Then I wondered what had gone on out there. How had Bruno gotten past the backyard fence? When my husband got home, we took out flashlights and explored the yard, finding the gate open. The next day we found footprints in the muddy area around the patio.

No doubt Bruno saved me from an intruder. My starved, straggly puppy was not only brave enough to trust and love again after suffering so much abuse, but he protected me from it, too.

~Carole Fowkes

Fancy That

I can no other answer make, but, thanks, and thanks.
~William Shakespeare

My husband and I were told that we couldn't have children. We decided to get a dog, a Great Dane named Fancy. She was our "baby" and went everywhere with us, slept by our bed, and was pampered.

Three years later, a miracle occurred. I became pregnant. After celebrating, we started to realize that Fancy would no longer be our baby. She would have competition, and we worried about how she would handle it.

We brought our daughter, Caroline Jeanne, home from the hospital, put her in the bassinet, watched and waited to see what would happen.

Fancy slowly approached the bassinet and looked down into it, inhaled the new smells and became a slave to this new human. She did not exist except to wait on Caroline. If Caroline fussed at all, Fancy would start to pace and soon would come to get one of us. Her mouth would close over one of our hands and she would lead us to Caroline so we would do something.

When Caroline started to crawl, Fancy would lie on the floor and crawl after her. When Caroline had a bottle, if she was on the floor, Fancy would lie behind her, a leg on each side and guard her. Caroline took her first steps by hanging on to Fancy by some loose skin or the collar. Caroline would grab onto her, then Fancy would slowly stand up, taking Caroline with her. As soon as they were steady, Fancy would start moving, taking a step at a time, careful not to knock Caroline over or go too fast.

When Caroline was a toddler, I took her out to play in the yard. The rear of the house had over an acre of land, with fields behind that. On one side were more fields and the other side had a six-foot fence separating the yard from a deep ditch and the Ohio turnpike high above. When Caroline started to go toward the front of the house heading for the driveway and road, I picked her up and carried her to the back yard. I only did that twice. The third time, Fancy beat me there, picked up Caroline by her diaper-covered bottom and carried her to the back yard.

I always watched, but I never really worried as long as Fancy was close to Caroline. Fancy didn't allow anyone to pick up Caroline except us—not even her grandparents—and Fancy had previously adored them BB (before baby). If someone wanted to hold the baby, we had to pick her up and hand her to them while Fancy watched. Fancy would tolerate that, but paced the entire time until Caroline was back in her bassinet or crib.

Caroline is grown now with a family of her own. Fancy has long since departed this earth, but we always remember her in our hearts. We still wonder sometimes what would have happened if someone driving on the turnpike had looked down into our yard and seen a Great Dane with a toddler in its mouth. Fancy that!

~Bonita Chambers

Who's Your Daddy?

Call it a clan, call it a network, call it a tribe, call it a family.
Whatever you call it, whoever you are, you need one.
~Jane Howard

Everyone has read articles, seen stories on television, or watched videos on social websites about mother animals adopting babies of another species: mother cats nursing puppies and visa versa, cat and dog mothers adopting and nursing squirrels, fox cubs, coyotes, rabbits and skunks—I once saw a story about a dog that nursed and raised an African lion cub. All are amazing. My Sparky adds a little twist to this nurturing instinct that appears to be very strong in all types of mothers... regardless of species.

From the time I rescued him, I knew my Pug-Beagle mix was a cat lover. That's why he fit right into my little family of three cats. Wherever he came from, he had obviously shared his life with cats. He wanted to be friendlier with them than they preferred, but the two old toms and one queen accepted the little dog with resigned dignity, hopping out of his reach if he got too affectionate.

I learned quickly that Sparky takes accepting cats farther than any other dog I have owned. He adores them. If it were up to him, he would take every cat he saw home with us when we go on our walks. He cries, he moans, he begs with sad eyes focused on them, then on me... for more cats. This makes him quite the dog in our neighborhood. Everyone jokes about him.

In his first year with me, one cat in particular became his best friend on our walks. She was just a simple gray-striped little tabby and she would run out to greet us from her yard as we passed by each day. She would rub against Sparky and he'd lick her, and they would tumble on her front lawn until I had to pull him away. He would follow me reluctantly.

One day, I saw the moving trucks in front of the cat's house and told Sparky, "It looks like your Miss Kitty is moving away."

Unfortunately, within a few days after the trucks left Miss Kitty appeared again. I don't know if she was abandoned or if she snuck back home after the move. The good news was that the people next door to the now vacant house said they would take her because she was so loveable.

The bad news was that they did not spay her. Within a few months, I could tell she was very, very pregnant. Sparky seemed to think the whole idea was wonderful because they still played together every time they met on our walks.

Miss Kitty had her kittens under a rosebush in a front yard driveway and was immediately disowned by her new hosts because a cat with kittens was simply too much to deal with. With her friendly attitude toward dogs, and with dogs that were definitely not like Sparky running loose in the neighborhood, I couldn't leave this little family under a rosebush two feet from the main sidewalk. I'd seen too often what happened to kittens when roving dogs found them or if they wandered into the street.

Once we had the mother and kittens safely settled in a spare bedroom, Sparky stepped in. Overwhelmed with delight, he became the surrogate father to the three kittens. He moved in with Miss Kitty and her babies, gently washing them, letting them snuggle up to him and allowing the little blind squeakers to crawl all over him. Miss Kitty could go rest by the window when she wasn't nursing her crew, safe in the knowledge that Sparky would take good care of them.

As the kittens grew, I wondered what they thought. Did they think that Sparky was some weird looking—and weird smelling—cat? Did they think that they were puppies? I couldn't imagine.

All I knew was that the little family grew up, rolling and playing together like puppies, not cats… and yet they still kept all their feline instincts and actions with the other cats in the household. I assume they thought, and still think, that they are some type of cross-species creatures.

That was three years ago and they are all still together, all safely spayed and neutered. The young tom, Ringo the Third, is taller than his daddy, Sparky. They still roll, play and chew on each other like dogs, with Ringo keeping his claws retracted. The two girls, Duchess and Friday (named Friday because she was born a day later than the other two), still sleep on top of their daddy, Sparky.

In the last three months, another throwaway rescue dog has come into our house and he seems to take it all in stride. Although he does look at Sparky with a questioning face when he sees the cats pile on top of him to sleep on the couch.

Sparky is a protective father even though the kittens are all grown. If one of the older cats picks on Miss Kitty or one of his "family," or if the new dog growls when Duchess or Friday try to jump on him, Sparky is at the ready with a bark, leap and a quick snap at the offending animal, as if to say, "Nobody messes with my kids!"

Talk about a mixed relationship. However strange, the one thing that is very clear is that they love each other. And I guess that says it all. In the end, it's always love that really counts, isn't it?

~Joyce A. Laird

A Star
Named Lucy

Fifteen years ago we decided to adopt a dog. After scanning the Sunday paper, I found an ad for one that seemed to be just the dog we were looking for. It was a small Yorkshire Terrier, and the ad said the people were moving out of state and unable to take the dog. They had actually advertised two dogs — the other was a Labrador/Chesapeake Bay Retriever mix.

After calling to inquire if I could drop by to see the Yorkshire Terrier, I drove over to look at the dog. When I arrived I discovered that another family had arrived before me and were taking the little dog.

As I turned to leave, the woman who owned the dogs asked me if I would be interested in the other dog. She practically begged me to take a look at the dog. The big dog was not on my periscope that day — until they told me her story.

Star was her name. They had raised her from a pup, and then given her to their daughter and son-in-law who lived on a farm fifty miles away. She said that a couple of months earlier, the son-in-law had tried to harm their daughter and her baby in a drunken rage.

Star had jumped into the fight to receive a knife wound intended for their daughter. The woman was able to escape with their grandchild, and the dog was left to fend for itself. Eventually, the wounded dog managed to get all the way back to Kansas City to the parents' home.

Star had been tracking her way home for several weeks when, within blocks of the parents' house, she collapsed at a gas station on the interstate. As she described the scene and named the station location, my heart skipped a beat. I knew the very dog she was describing.

My husband had come home from work one evening very upset, around the same time of this dog's journey. On his route home that day, he had passed by that same gas station and this was the very scene he had described to me. He said that he had seen a badly starved and beaten black Lab mix collapse. He had stopped to try to assist the dog. The dog was terribly frightened and would not let anyone approach her.

Finally a woman had come along and said she recognized the dog as her neighbor's missing dog. The frightened animal offered no resistance when the woman called to her, and the dog allowed the woman to load her in the truck.

Impossible as it seemed, the dog had survived more than a fifty-mile trek across Missouri.

My husband had worried about the fate of that dog every day since it had happened. Now I was being given the opportunity to save her. She had heartworms and the couple was moving. They had no money to care for her and did not want to have to put her to sleep. I just could not abandon her.

When I came home with this pitiful, scrawny piece of canine fur, my husband said, "Good Lord! She looks just like the Lab I saw at the gas station." Of course when I explained it was the very same one, he was instantly in love.

After several rounds of treatment for her heartworms, she regained her health. In the meantime, she quickly learned that my husband Gene was her champion. He held her and cuddled her through all the misery she had to endure with the treatments.

After a couple of weeks, Gene decided we should change her name from Star to Lucy. She wasn't responding to her name, and he decided that the man must have used it when beating her. She seemed to associate the name Star with pain. Sure enough she instantly came to accept the name Lucy and it stuck.

She quickly worked her way into every fabric of our lives. For the first few months, we thought they had removed her voice box, as she never made a sound. But one day as we were walking her a child unexpectedly ran onto the path, startling her, and she let out a bark. Then she cringed as though she expected a beating. My husband and I hugged her over and over, praised her and told her it was okay. From then on, she got her doggie voice back. And within days, she would prove to be a hero.

During the night, that first November after we adopted her, she woke us by barking and growling. She jumped at the window, then ran to the front door and barked some more. We turned on the lights and looked around but could not discover the reason she was so upset. We were puzzled, but she finally calmed down and we went back to sleep. The next day we discovered a burglar had broken into two houses on our block during the night. We were pretty sure Lucy had run them off from our house.

Six years after she came to live with us, she began to show signs of kidney failure. Her kidneys had been damaged in her earlier years of abuse and it would finally prove irreversible. But she still managed one last heroic deed before her star burned out.

In early October of that year, she had gotten into a habit of jumping up and licking my husband's neck. She would shiver and whine and bark. This was something she had never done before. I finally asked my husband why she was doing that. He said he had no idea. He did finally admit though, that he had a sore in his mouth and his neck hurt. I convinced him to see a dentist. The dentist recommended an immediate biopsy, which tested positive for oral cancer. The cancer required extensive surgery, but thanks to Lucy, they were able to stop it from spreading.

One year later, Lucy's earthly light burned out. We knew we had been blessed to have owned her. She was a hero and her deeds will never be forgotten. Now all we have to do is look up to see our special star Lucy in the sky.

~Christine Trollinger

Fishmongrel

Fishing is boring, unless you catch an actual fish, and then it is disgusting.
~Dave Barry

Some dog owners have become very picky. They want their dogs clean and devocalized. They don't want an animal that sheds, barks, knocks over furniture, or growls at strangers. They're looking for a pooch you can carry in your purse or use as a fashion accessory, a designer dog.

Not me. I enjoy real dogs. When it comes to mutts I'm not the least bit finicky. I like a yappy pooch that chews up house slippers and leaves a trail of hair wherever it goes. I prefer an animal with bug-filled fur, Frisbee-snatching teeth, and big floppy ears; one that drools and stretches its head out the window and snaps at the passing wind when I take it for a car ride.

That's exactly what I got when I found an abandoned dog wandering the streets near our home. It was raining and the little guy was wet and cold. I dried him off and fed him. He looked to be a Beagle/Corgi mix.

My wife, Linda, named him Snack because he had a love of all things gastronomic. Eating was all he seemed to think about. Snack loved pizza, chips, chicken fingers, mozzarella sticks, Oreo cookies or whatever else dangled from the unsuspecting hand of our two-year-old daughter. He would gobble down anything, with the possible exception of dog food.

Snack was a smart dog, sweet and independent-minded. Even

though he couldn't talk, he was a great communicator. He could make his wishes known by using a combination of scratching, barking and whining. His brown eyes covered a wide range of emotions from happy to sad to guilty.

During his time with our family, Snack taught us a lot about unconditional love. He also taught us how to relax more and enjoy life with the windows rolled down. Through Snack I learned not to stress about my job. No matter how tough my day was, he always put me in a happy mood when I arrived home.

Among Snack's favorite activities besides eating were playing ball in the back yard and cuddling on the couch. He also enjoyed gardening. Whenever he saw me grab a hoe or a shovel, he would scamper for the back yard. Before long, soil was flying everywhere. After an afternoon of digging with Snack, it usually took a few days to get the dirt out of my hair.

In Snack's world, life was something to experience and chase, chew up and swallow. When I was training for marathons we would run together in the hills behind our home. I would choose the steepest training routes and take off at a sprint. Snack would never falter or fall behind.

As we moved along the trail, Snack would flush quail and roll in the remains of dead animals. Sometimes he would course far ahead, long tongue lolling and short legs churning. Perhaps he had caught the pungent trail of a raccoon, or a bobcat. Whatever it was, he saw the world nostrils first, experiencing it in layers of Technicolor scents.

The thing that amused me most about Snack was how he loved to fish. We went to the river often and he was always the first one out of the car. Snack would dash straight for the water, wade in belly deep, and fish for hours on end, strolling along and snapping up minnows as he went.

Sometimes he would bring his catch back to shore. Panting and pleased with himself, he would place the fish at my feet and raise his wet mug for a reward. After a pat on the head, several words of encouragement and a sandwich, he would head back to the river to resume his fishing.

Snack was not a dog who required a heated bed, weekly grooming, or special medication to ward off some exotic illness. He didn't fit into a purse, wear a Burberry outfit, or have weekly appointments with a pet psychologist. Snack had no pedigree and thanks to a steady diet of human food his body jiggled like a San Andreas Jell-O factory. But if love and devotion could win a beauty pageant, he would have been walking around with a gold sash around his tummy.

Snack may have been a plain old dog to some folks. But to me he was the best dog money couldn't buy. And he could catch dinner too.

~Timothy Martin

I Can't Believe My Dog Did That!

Meet Our Contributors
Meet Our Authors
Thank You
About Chicken Soup for the Soul

Meet Our Contributors

Monica Agnew-Kinnaman was born in England and came to America after World War II. She lives in Colorado, and for many years has adopted abused and abandoned dogs. Now aged ninety-three, she lives with Jess, a ten-year-old Border Collie who was the victim of gross abuse, and an abandoned sheepdog.

Elizabeth Atwater lives in an idyllic village in North Carolina, which affords her a peaceful, quiet, soul-soothing place to write. She spends a great deal of her time in utter bliss nurturing her love of words and phrases and happily weaving stories out of the air.

Francine L. Baldwin-Billingslea is a mother, a grandmother, and a breast cancer survivor who has recently found a passion for writing. She has been published in over fifteen anthologies and has published her memoir titled *Through It All*. She loves writing, traveling and spending quality time with Max and her loved ones.

Kerrie R. Barney lives with her always-entertaining Border Collie, Mythos, in Pullman, WA, where the two enjoy hiking, playing fetch, and cheering for the WSU football team (Go Cougs!) Her first collection of personal essays, *Life, the Universe, and Houseplants*, will be available for the Amazon Kindle in 2012.

June K. Blake belongs to two writing clubs. This heroic dog story was a writing assignment to applaud a pet. Her usual writing thrust is humor.

Jeanne Blandford has found her dream job as an editor at Chicken Soup for the Soul. When she is not reading inspirational submissions, she and her husband Jack are producing documentaries, creating children's books or running SafePet, a partnership between Outreach for Pets in Need and Domestic Violence Crisis Center.

Lil Blosfield is the Chief Financial Officer for Child and Adolescent Behavioral Health in Canton, OH. She has been published several times in *Chicken Soup for the Soul* anthologies. Lil loves sunny days and peaceful nights. E-mail her at LBlosfield40@msn.com.

Carol A. Boas is a retired teacher and children's book author. She loves cooking, walking, traveling and Dalmatians. Her four grandchildren love taking her to school for show-and-tell on visits to Chicago and Denver. She lives in Connecticut with her husband, renowned proofreader Rick. E-mail her at cboas4@gmail.com.

Long Beach, WA author **Jan Bono** is a retired schoolteacher turned full-time writer. Her specialty is humorous personal experiences. She has had several collections published, and has seen nine one-act plays hit the stage. Her books and play scripts are available at www.JanBonoBooks.com.

Marcia E. Brown, of Austin, TX, has enjoyed sharing her family stories in magazines, newspapers and anthologies, including the *Chicken Soup for the Soul* series, for eighteen years. She especially loves writing about the dogs and cats that have graced her life. She is a member of the National League of American Pen Women.

Sallie Wagner Brown lives on Hood Canal in Washington State with three dogs and her husband. All the dogs in her life, twenty-seven years teaching high school and five grown children provide endless topics for her stories, two of which were published in previous *Chicken Soup for the Soul* anthologies.

John P. Buentello is a writer who publishes novels, essays, short stories and poems. Currently he is at work on a book about writing and a mystery novel. He can be reached at jakkhakk@yahoo.com.

Leah M. Cano is a teacher/writer living in Laguna Beach, CA. She has written for *Transitions Abroad* magazine, *MAMM* magazine and has been featured on The Experiment in International Living's website. She is also a contributor to recent *Chicken Soup for the Soul* anthologies.

Mary C. Chace, a seasoned Army wife, writes from Northern California where she shares life with her favorite pilot, Doug, their six children, and many pets. Besides freelancing, Mary helps students improve their college admission essays and timed writing skills. E-mail Mary at mary.chace@gmail.com.

Bonita Chambers is an office manager for St. John Lutheran Church in Angleton, TX. She is also a freelance writer/photographer for *Image Magazine* of Brazoria County, TX. E-mail her at bonitachambers@comcast.net.

Emily Parke Chase is a popular conference speaker and author of six books, including *Help! My Family's Messed Up* (Kregel, 2008) and *Standing Tall After Falling Short* (Wingspread, 2012). She and her husband reside in Mechanicsburg, PA. Visit her at www.emilychase.com.

Janet Ann Collins has written for newspapers and is the author of books for children. She has also been a teacher, a parent, and a foster parent of kids with special needs, and is now a grandmother. Learn more at www.janetanncollins.com.

Linda Cox is a retired secretary from the Illinois Department of Natural Resources. She, her husband Gerald, and their two indoor/ outdoor mutts live on a farm in southern Illinois. She has had short stories as well as devotions published and is also a regular contributor at www.divinedetour.com.

Aeriel Crook is a high school student; she was in tenth grade when this story was written. Aeriel likes reading, drawing and writing short stories. Her creative writing teacher, Mrs. Fegan, had her write this story and submit it as an assignment. Aeriel thanks Mrs. Fegan; she's an amazing teacher.

Martha Deeringer writes for children and adults from her home on a central Texas cattle ranch. Her large, loving family provides endless material for her articles and stories. Visit her website at www. marthadeeringer.com.

Janice R. Edwards received her BAT degree, with honors, from Sam Houston State University in 1974. She taught English and journalism before working for Texaco. Now she writes freelance for *Image Magazine*, showcasing Brazoria County, TX. Her first Chicken Soup for the Soul story was in *Chicken Soup for the Soul: My Dog's Life*.

Carla Eischeid received her B.S. degree in psychology from the University of Tennessee. She works in construction sales in Chattanooga, TN. Carla enjoys traveling, running, reading and spending time with her husband Mike and their two dogs, Bella and TT.

Shawnelle Eliasen and her husband Lonny raise their five sons in Illinois. Shawnelle home teaches her youngest boys. Her writing has been published in *Guideposts*, *MomSense* magazine, *Marriage Partnership*, *Cup of Comfort* books, numerous *Chicken Soup for the Soul* books, and other anthologies. Follow her adventures at Shawnellewrites.blogspot.com.

Claire Field received her B.A. degree from the University of Vermont. She is married and the mother of three kids. She is a full-time homemaker, hockey mom and coach. She enjoys traveling, skiing, skating and playing tennis and paddle tennis.

Malinda Fillingim lives in Leland, NC with her husband David, and they enjoy long, quiet walks with Patch. An ordained Baptist minister, she is a frequent speaker at churches and other places where folks gather. E-mail her at fillingam@ec.rr.com.

Pat Fish has been a blogger for almost ten years and writes for The Morton Report. She has written a few books and vows to write till death does part her from the keyboard. Pat loves to write about current events and enjoys reviewing movies, books and, of course, TV shows. E-mail her at patfish1@aol.com.

Jennifer Flaten is an author and jewelry artist who lives in Wisconsin with her husband, three children, three cats, and, of course, her dog Pepper. E-mail her at JennFlaten@gmail.com.

Carole Fowkes is a freelance journalist and food and restaurant reviewer. Her articles and short stories have appeared in several anthologies and news publications. She has also published a novella and five short story books. E-mail her at cgfowkes@yahoo.com.

Heidi Gaul lives in Oregon, and is currently writing her second novel. When she is not busy writing articles and devotionals, she spends her time with her husband, dog, and small, but manageable, herd of cats.

Dalia Gesser toured her children's shows under the name Compact Theatre for over twenty years. Since 2000 she has been sharing her love and experience of the theatre with children through her workshops and classes. She lives north of Kingston in beautiful lake country and can be e-mailed at daliag@kingston.net.

After a twenty-year career as an R.N. and hosting/producing a radio show, **Pamela Goldstein** began writing. She has short stories published in various anthologies, including several in the *Chicken Soup for the Soul* series. She has written fiction and young-adult manuscripts, and two plays. E-mail Pam at boker_tov2002@yahoo.ca.

T'Mara Goodsell is a lifelong dog lover who writes and teaches in St. Charles, MO. She is published in several *Chicken Soup for the Soul* books as well as other anthologies, newspapers, and publications.

Libby Grandy lives in Claremont, CA with her husband Fred. She has published articles in magazines such as *Mature Living, Writers' Journal, Woman's World*, and other *Chicken Soup for the Soul* books. Learn more at www.libbygrandy.com.

Bill Halderson received a B.A. degree from California State Polytechnic University, and an M.A. degree from Claremont Graduate University a long time ago. A retired corporate manager and trainer, he lives with his wife and dog Max in Cookeville, TN. E-mail him at billandmonica1943@frontiernet.net.

Talia Haven is a children's author. Her most recent work appeared in *Stories for Children Magazine, The Scareald*, Loconeal publications, and *Chicken Soup for the Soul: My Cat's Life*. B-A-L-L is her third story for the *Chicken Soup for the Soul* series.

Jonny Hawkins' cartoons have been in *Reader's Digest, Parade* magazine and in over 600 other publications. He draws from his home in Sherwood, MI with his wife and three kids alongside. His *Dog Cartoon-a-Day* calendar and *Jonny Hawkins Unleashes the Dog* ebook are available online. His e-mail is jonnyhawkins2nz@yahoo.com.

Between and during writing and filmmaking projects, **Harley Hay** has worked as a professional drummer, a paralegal, a high school English teacher, a photographer and a TV videographer. He lives in Red Deer,

Alberta, Canada with his wife Nina, their children Jesse and Jenna Lee, and Scamp, their slightly deranged Shih Tzu.

Lori Hein is the author of *Ribbons of Highway: A Mother-Child Journey Across America*. Her freelance work has appeared in publications such as *The Boston Globe* and several *Chicken Soup for the Soul* anthologies. Visit her at LoriHein.com or her world travel blog, RibbonsofHighway. blogspot.com.

Diane Helbig is a business coach, speaker, author, and radio show host. She has contributed to other *Chicken Soup for the Soul* books and has her own book, *Lemonade Stand Selling*. Diane enjoys helping business professionals succeed, as well as raising her two children. E-mail her at diane@seizethisdaycoaching.com.

Karen R. Hessen has been published in *Chicken Soup for the Soul: Divorce and Recovery*, *Chicken Soup for the Soul: Food and Love*, *Guideposts*, *Vista* and many publications. She and her husband Douglas live in Forest Grove and Seaside, OR. E-mail her at karenwrites@frontier.com or visit her website at www.karenrhessen.com.

Camille Hill is an animal communicator who lives in Canada with her partner Ed and a variety of animal companions. She has contributed several stories to the *Chicken Soup for the Soul* series, written a pet column for a local newspaper and is currently working on her first book of animal stories. E-mail her at chill@hilladvisory.com.

Mariane Holbrook has received degrees from both Nyack (NY) College and High Point (NC) University. She is a retired elementary school teacher and lives in coastal North Carolina with her husband John. She enjoys writing, music, reading and painting. E-mail her at Mariane777@bellsouth.net.

Nancy Ilk is a writer living in Oak Creek, WI. Her short stories, poetry and essays have appeared in anthologies as well as in several online publications. She is currently working on a book featuring a collection of her essays.

Gayle Mansfield Irwin is a writer who enjoys sharing about the pet-human bond. Her works include several children's books, stories in other *Chicken Soup for the Soul* anthologies, and a nonfiction book about her blind dog to be released Fall 2012. She's won two Wyoming Writers Inc. awards. Learn more at www.gaylemirwin.com.

Jennie Ivey lives in Tennessee. She is a newspaper columnist and the author of numerous works of fiction and nonfiction, including stories in several *Chicken Soup for the Soul* anthologies. Visit her website at www.jennieivey.com.

Marilyn Jensen, a voracious reader, vowed to one day write as well as read books. Her freelance writing as a stay-at-home mom led to her becoming a newspaper columnist and editing a magazine for veterinarians. Her published work includes four books on California history and a biographical novel.

Michelle Johns received her Bachelor of Arts degree from Victoria University of Wellington, New Zealand in 1985. She home schools her children and enjoys crafts, outdoor activities and youth ministry. She is currently writing an inspirational book on making a lifestyle change to better health. E-mail her at mjsda2011@gmail.com.

Recently retired, **Yvonne Kays** lives in the high desert of Central Oregon with her husband and two dogs. A member of Oregon Christian Writers, she writes short stories and poetry. She loves spending time with her grandchildren, traveling, hiking, fishing, camping and working with youth.

Kristy Kehler, originally from East Grand Forks, MN, graduated from the University of North Dakota with a B.Sc. degree in psychology. She currently lives in Manitoba with her husband and two dogs. She is in the process of completing her first book targeted towards young adults. E-mail her at KristyKehler@hotmail.com.

Pamela Kent received her Diploma in Creative Writing when she was sixty. Twenty years later she still writes every day. Her articles and stories have won awards and appeared in magazines, newspapers and online.

Joyce Laird is a freelance writer living in Southern California with her menagerie of animal companions. Her features have been published in many magazines including, *Cat Fancy*, *Grit*, *Mature Living*, *I Love Cats* and *Vibrant Life*. She contributes regularly to *Woman's World* and to the *Chicken Soup for the Soul* series.

Cathi LaMarche is the author of the novel *While the Daffodils Danced* and has contributed to numerous anthologies. She currently teaches composition and literature. Living in St. Louis, she shares her home with her husband, two children, and three spoiled dogs.

Sharon Landeen, a retied elementary teacher, believes working with children helps keep her young. This great-grandmother stays busy volunteering at schools as a reading mentor and art teacher, making blankets for Project Linus, and being a 4-H leader. She also finds time to be a good pal to her dog, Dusty.

Beth Levine is a Connecticut-based freelance writer who spends way too much time talking to her dog. She has previously been published in *Chicken Soup for the Soul: Food and Love*, *Chicken Soup for the Soul: Family Matters* and *Chicken Soup for the Soul: All in the Family*. Learn more at www.bethlevine.net.

Lisa Mackinder received her Bachelor of Arts degree at Western Michigan University. A freelance writer, she lives in Kalamazoo, MI with her husband and rescue animals. Besides writing, Lisa enjoys photography, traveling, reading, running, hiking, biking, climbing, camping and fishing. E-mail her at lisa_mackinder@yahoo.com.

Gail MacMillan is a graduate of Queen's University, Kingston, Ontario. She is the author of three books on the Nova Scotia Duck Tolling Retriever, one of Canada's unique dog breeds. Gail enjoys reading, writing, and walking her dogs. She lives in New Brunswick, Canada with her husband and three dogs. E-mail her at macgail@ nbnet.nb.ca.

David Martin's humor and political satire have appeared in many publications including *The New York Times*, the *Chicago Tribune* and *Smithsonian Magazine*. His latest humor collection, *Dare to be Average*, was published in 2010 by Lulu.com. David lives in Ottawa, Canada with his wife Cheryl and their daughter Sarah.

Tim Martin's work has been featured in numerous *Chicken Soup for the Soul* books. He is the author of *Wimps Like Me* and *Summer With Dad*. Tim has two books due out in 2012: *Scout's Oaf* and *Third Rate Romance*. E-mail him at tmartin@northcoast.com.

Sarah McCrobie received her Bachelor of Arts degree in journalism, with honors, from SUNY Oswego in 2006. She has served as editor of *The Palladium-Times*, a daily community newspaper in Oswego, NY. Sarah enjoys writing and spending time with her family (human and canine). E-mail her at smccrobie@gmail.com.

John McCutcheon retired recently after years as a medical administrator and now works part-time in a clinic for AIDS patients in the Limpopo province in South Africa. He writes a column for a local newspaper and enjoys new challenges. E-mail him at j.mcc@webmail.co.za.

Judy McFadden, author of *Life with McDuff: Lessons Learned from a Therapy Dog*, lives in Henderson, NV, and speaks to audiences about the benefits of volunteering in animal assisted therapy and reading programs like Therapy Dogs International and Reading with Rover. Visit www.lifewithmcduff.com for more information about Judy and McDuff.

Dianne Moen earned her Bachelor of Arts degree in art from California Lutheran University. She is a published freelance writer and attends writing workshops. Her inspiration is derived from nature. Dianne especially enjoys writing fiction and nonfiction for young readers. E-mail her at diannemoen@hotmail.com.

Nell Musolf lives in Minnesota with her husband, two sons and assorted animals. Her work has appeared in a variety of magazines, newspapers and books. E-mail her at nellmus@aol.com.

Jan Nash lives in Minnesota right on Lake Superior. She has MS and lives alone, so her dog Angel is her little soul mate. Jan and Angel enjoy playing outside in the snow, visiting other tenants and their pets, and taking walks along the lake. Angel sits on Jan's bed and whines when she knows it's time for Jan to rest. They take care of each other.

This is **Robert Nussbaum's** fourth story published in the *Chicken Soup for the Soul* series. A lawyer by day and a writer in the early morning hours, Robert is also a regular contributor to the letters pages of *The New York Times*. Learn more at tooearlytocall.blogspot.com.

Loretta Olund enjoys spending time with her pets, being with her family, reading and writing stories. She had a short story included in a book produced by the SPCA titled *How I Learned to Speak Dog and Other Animal Stories*.

Penny Orloff played featured parts on Broadway and sang twenty principal soprano roles for the New York City Opera. She is a published playwright, librettist and arts journalist. Her comic novel, *Jewish Thighs on Broadway*, is available at Amazon.com. She is currently completing a PhD in spiritual psychology.

LaVerne Otis lives in Southern California, where she loves writing, photography, bird watching, reading and spending time with family. LaVerne is recently retired, taking classes at a local community college. She has been published several times in *Chicken Soup for the Soul* books and various magazines. E-mail her at lotiswrites@msn.com.

Mark Parisi's award winning "off the mark" cartoon appears in newspapers worldwide. His work also appears on calendars, cards, books, T-shirts and more. Visit www.offthemark.com to view 7000+ cartoons. Mark resides in Massachusetts with his wife and business partner Lynn, along with their daughter Jen, three cats and a dog.

A.R. Parliament, a misplaced Canadian, currently lives near Montgomery, AL. She is a university student who will graduate with a degree in psychology and English. She's been published in the *Southern Women's Review* for photography and is the assistant editor for the 2012 Auburn University Montgomery's *Filibuster*. E-mail her at a.parliament16@gmail.com.

Novelist, blogger, and award-winning food writer, **Perry P. Perkins** is a stay-at-home dad who lives with his wife Victoria and their four-year-old daughter Grace in the Pacific Northwest. Perry has written for hundreds of magazines and is the author of two novels, four cookbooks, and numerous short-story collections.

Pam Phree is co-author of the book, *Betrayal, Murder and Greed: The True Story of a Bounty Hunter and a Bail Bond Agent* (New Horizon Press). www.betrayalmurderandgreed.com. She is currently writing the sequel with Mike Beakley and has a novel about heaven in the works. Pam lives in Puyallup, WA.

Kathleen Whitman Plucker lives and writes in the Midwest. She also enjoys cooking, knitting, figure skating, and taking pictures. She dreams of being on a game show and of making over her family room. E-mail her at pluckfam@comcast.net.

Robin Pressnall is Executive Director of Small Paws Rescue, twice featured on Animal Planet. She is a five-time guest on *Fox & Friends*, and also appeared on *Inside Edition* to talk about her story in *Chicken Soup for the Soul: Find Your Happiness* with Deborah Norville. Robin is a frequent contributor to the *Chicken Soup for the Soul* series.

Victoria Radford became interested in writing in the fourth grade when she wrote and published a poem about a pet monkey her family acquired. She enjoys writing about life in general and looks forward to the completion of her first fictional, preteen book. E-mail her at vicki1363@gmail.com.

Susan Randall is a hospice nurse in Montgomery County, MD, and has been taking creative writing classes. One of her stories was published in *Spotlight On Recovery* magazine. She writes heartwarming nonfiction stories of her experiences. E-mail her at rnsue19020@aol.com.

Passionate about the frail elderly and end-of-life care, **Carol McAdoo Rehme** spends several days each month providing interactive arts programs in long-term care facilities across northern Colorado. Her Toy Poodle Jazzy, who considered every lap an open invitation, attended with her for thirteen years. Carol is a full-time author and editor.

Dan Reynolds' work is seen by millions of people throughout the United States via greeting cards for American Greetings, Papyrus, NobleWorks, and other companies. He's the most frequent cartoon contributor to *Reader's Digest*, and regularly appears in *Esquire*, *Christianity Today*, *The Saturday Evening Post*, *Catholic Digest*, and many other titles.

J.F. Ridgley has loved dogs, horses, and animals all her life. She can't imagine not having their beaming faces, licking tongues, and happy tails around her. She hopes to make their lives as wonderful as they have made hers. A writer about ancient Rome, she lives in the Midwest with her wonderful hubby. E-mail her at jfridgley@jfridgley.com.

Rachel Rosenthal received her B.A. degree in English literature from Fort Lewis College. She lives in Durango, CO with her husband, and teaches middle school. She is working on a children's book based on her lovable childhood dog. Rachel enjoys traveling, hiking with her dog, and running. E-mail her at rnrosenthal@hotmail.com.

David Michael Smith, from Delaware, believes all pets go to heaven, including his cucumber-eating Golden Retriever, Brandy. He is happily married to Geri, and the proud daddy of Rebekah and Matthew, both of whom desperately want their own dogs. Maybe soon. E-mail David at davidandgeri@hotmail.com.

Lauren Smith spent five years living in Thailand working as a freelance writer before returning to her native England with her two dogs, Wishbone and Nibbles (Nobs). Lauren enjoys writing, cupcakes and wine, and is still searching for a job that combines all three! E-mail her at lsmith136@gmail.com.

B.J. Taylor finds Rex adorable, even when he's capricious. She is an award-winning author whose work has appeared in *Guideposts*, more than thirty *Chicken Soup for the Soul* books, and numerous other publications. Contact B.J. at www.bjtayloronline.com and check out her dog blog by Charlie Bear at www.bjtaylorblog.wordpress.com.

Richard Temtchine graduated from College Colbert in Paris, France. He is currently finishing a feature film, which will be a sequel to his previous one. E-mail him at Quadrantent@yahoo.com.

A lifelong animal lover, **Jean Tennant** has had her writing published by Silhouette, Warner Books, and Kensington. She lives in northwest Iowa with her husband Grover and an ever-rotating menagerie of dogs, cats, birds and whatever else might need a temporary or forever home. E-mail her at jeandtennant@hotmail.com.

The cartoons of **Andrew Toos** have been anthologized in numerous cartoon collections, such as *Lawyers! Lawyers! Lawyers!*, *Cats, Cats, Cats* and *Modern Employment*. His cartoons appear in textbooks, trade paperbacks and books published by Cambridge University Press, Simon & Schuster, Warner Books, Contemporary Publishing, Gibbs Smith and many others.

Rosita Trinca was born in Melbourne, Australia and moved to Connecticut with her family in 1982. A retired journalist, she has spent too much of her time cooking for and watching dogs and their antics. She met many of her best friends through her dogs.

Christine Trollinger is from Kansas City, MO. Her stories have been published in several *Chicken Soup for the Soul* books over the years as well as many other publications.

Ann Vitale has been a microbiologist, a dog trainer, and a car dealer. Previously published by an educational press, in the *Chicken Soup for the Soul* anthologies, and in newspaper columns, she is writing a mystery novel. Her interests are wildlife, teaching in adult schools, and art. E-mail her at ann.e.vitale74@gmail.com.

Stephanie Winkelhake holds two degrees in engineering, but her real passion lies in reading and writing young adult literature. She is a member of YALitChat and RWA. Stephanie also enjoys traveling and photography, and she hopes to one day share the words and stories painted in her novels.

Carol Witmer lives in Maryland but hopes to someday return to Virginia where she was born. She has three grandchildren and loves animals, especially dogs and ferrets. She just recently got a Lab puppy named Delila. She enjoys traveling, reading and writing, mostly songs and poems.

Sheryl Young has been freelance writing since 1997 for magazines, newspapers and websites. She's written two books, most recently *God,*

Am I Nobody? about valuing God's plans ahead of personal success. It's available on Amazon.com in paperback and Kindle, and also for the Nook. Visit or contact her at 20-20faithsight.blogspot.com.

Mom of seven, Nana to nineteen grands and eight great-grands, **Lynne Zielinski** lives, laughs and loves in Huntsville, AL. She believes that life is a gift from God and what we do with it is our gift to God. E-mail her at Arisway@comcast.net.

Patti Zint is a freelance writer and private college program director. Home is shared with numerous pampered cats and two "wish-we-were-cats" dogs. She is the proud mother of one amazing teenage daughter, one inspiring Marine son, and one awesome twenty-something son. E-mail her at pwzint@cox.net.

Meet Our Authors

Jack Canfield is the co-creator of the *Chicken Soup for the Soul* series, which *Time* magazine has called "the publishing phenomenon of the decade." Jack is also the co-author of many other bestselling books.

Jack is the CEO of the Canfield Training Group in Santa Barbara, California, and founder of the Foundation for Self-Esteem in Culver City, California. He has conducted intensive personal and professional development seminars on the principles of success for more than a million people in twenty-three countries, has spoken to hundreds of thousands of people at more than 1,000 corporations, universities, professional conferences and conventions, and has been seen by millions more on national television shows.

Jack has received many awards and honors, including three honorary doctorates and a Guinness World Records Certificate for having seven books from the *Chicken Soup for the Soul* series appearing on the New York Times bestseller list on May 24, 1998.

You can reach Jack at www.jackcanfield.com.

Mark Victor Hansen is the co-founder of Chicken Soup for the Soul, along with Jack Canfield. He is a sought-after keynote speaker, bestselling author, and marketing maven. Mark's powerful messages of possibility, opportunity, and action have created powerful change in thousands of organizations and millions of individuals worldwide.

Mark is a prolific writer with many bestselling books in addition to the *Chicken Soup for the Soul* series. Mark has had a profound influence in the field of human potential through his library of audios, videos, and articles in the areas of big thinking, sales achievement, wealth building, publishing success, and personal and professional development. He is also the founder of the MEGA Seminar Series.

Mark has received numerous awards that honor his entrepreneurial spirit, philanthropic heart, and business acumen. He is a lifetime member of the Horatio Alger Association of Distinguished Americans.

You can reach Mark at www.markvictorhansen.com.

Jennifer Quasha is an award-winning writer and editor. She is a published author of more than forty books, including three dog books: *Don't Pet a Pooch... While He's Pooping: Etiquette for Dogs and their People*, *The Dog Lover's Book of Crafts: 50 Home Decorations that Celebrate Man's Best Friend*, and *Sew Dog: Easy-Sew Dogwear and Custom Gear for Home and Travel*.

She graduated from Boston University with a B.S. in Communication and has been writing ever since. Jennifer has been a contributing editor at *Dog Fancy* and *Dogs for Kids* magazines, and has written monthly columns on rescue dogs, etiquette, and travel. Jennifer has also been published in Chicken Soup for the Soul books and is thrilled to be a co-author of *Chicken Soup for the Soul: I Can't Believe My Cat Did That!* and *Chicken Soup for the Soul: I Can't Believe My Dog Did That!* She also was a co-author of *Chicken Soup for the Soul: My Dog's Life* and *Chicken Soup for the Soul: My Cat's Life*.

In her free time Jennifer loves to read, travel and eat anything anyone else prepares for her. She lives with her husband, kids, and two dogs, Sugar and Scout. You can reach her by visiting her website at www.jenniferquasha.com.

Thank You

Hello again dog lovers! As we go to print on the second dog book I have co-authored for Chicken Soup for the Soul, I want to extend my sincerest thanks to each and every one of you who sent us a story, or in some cases, many stories.

This particular Chicken Soup for the Soul title lent itself to submissions that were laugh-out-loud funny. I never knew just what crazy, completely canine tale I was going to get to read. Thank you for putting a smile on my face!

As always, all of us at Chicken Soup for the Soul appreciate the time and energy that you spent crafting your story and sharing your lives with us. As is often the case, we could only publish a small percentage of the stories that were submitted, but we read every single one. Even the stories that do not appear in the book influenced us and affected the final manuscript.

A special thank you goes to Chicken Soup for the Soul editors Barbara LoMonaco and Jeanne Blandford, who read all the stories and poems with me. This book could not have been made without their diligence, input, and well-oiled knowledge of what makes a great Chicken Soup for the Soul story. Amy Newmark, Chicken Soup for the Soul's whip-smart publisher had my back during every stage of creating this book and guided me gracefully and with quick replies. I also want to thank Assistant Publisher D'ette Corona for managing the whole production process, and editor Kristiana Glavin for all her help with creating the final manuscript and getting it off to the printer.

Thank you to cartoonists Jonny Hawkins, Mark Parisi, Dan Reynolds, and Andrew Toos for giving us eleven reasons to giggle throughout the book. Lastly, I owe a very special thanks to our creative director and book producer, Brian Taylor at Pneuma Books, for his brilliant vision for our covers and interiors.

~Jennifer Quasha

Improving Your Life
Every Day

Real people sharing real stories—for nineteen years. Now, Chicken Soup for the Soul has gone beyond the bookstore to become a world leader in life improvement. Through books, movies, DVDs, online resources and other partnerships, we bring hope, courage, inspiration and love to hundreds of millions of people around the world. Chicken Soup for the Soul's writers and readers belong to a one-of-a-kind global community, sharing advice, support, guidance, comfort, and knowledge.

Chicken Soup for the Soul stories have been translated into more than forty languages and can be found in more than one hundred countries. Every day, millions of people experience a Chicken Soup for the Soul story in a book, magazine, newspaper or online. As we share our life experiences through these stories, we offer hope, comfort and inspiration to one another. The stories travel from person to person, and from country to country, helping to improve lives everywhere.

Share with Us

We all have had Chicken Soup for the Soul moments in our lives. If you would like to share your story or poem with millions of people around the world, go to chickensoup.com and click on "Submit Your Story." You may be able to help another reader, and become a published author at the same time. Some of our past contributors have launched writing and speaking careers from the publication of their stories in our books!

Our submission volume has been increasing steadily—the quality and quantity of your submissions has been fabulous. We only accept story submissions via our website. They are no longer accepted via mail or fax.

To contact us regarding other matters, please send us an e-mail through webmaster@chickensoupforthesoul.com, or fax or write us at:

Chicken Soup for the Soul
P.O. Box 700
Cos Cob, CT 06807-0700
Fax: 203-861-7194

One more note from your friends at Chicken Soup for the Soul: Occasionally, we receive an unsolicited book manuscript from one of our readers, and we would like to respectfully inform you that we do not accept unsolicited manuscripts and we must discard the ones that appear.

Chicken Soup for the Soul.

I Can't Believe My Cat Did That!

101 **Stories** about the **Crazy Antics** of Our **Feline Friends**

Jack Canfield,
Mark Victor Hansen
& Jennifer Quasha

We all rejoice in the simple absurdities, funny habits, and crazy antics of our cats. They make us smile every day, but sometimes they really outdo themselves. You will love reading all the heartwarming, inspirational, and entertaining stories in this book. We know after reading the stories you'll say, "I can't believe a cat did that!"

978-1-935096-92-4

Classics for Cat Lovers

Chicken Soup for the Soul.

What I learned from the Dog

101 Stories about Life, Love, and Lessons

Jack Canfield,
Mark Victor Hansen & Amy Newmark

With a foreword by Wendy Diamond,
pet lifestyle expert as seen on *Today* and *Greatest American Dog*

An old dog might not be able to learn new tricks, but he might teach his owner a thing or two. Dog lovers will recognize themselves, or their dogs, in these 101 new tales from the owners of these lovable canines. Stories of learning how to be kinder, overcome adversity, say goodbye, love unconditionally, stay strong, and tales of loyalty, listening, and family will delight and inspire readers, and also cause some tears and some laughter.

978-1-935096-38-2

Classics for Dog Lovers

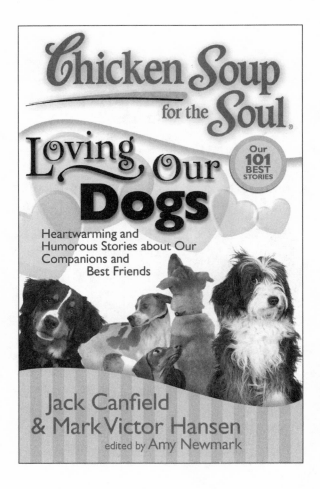

Chicken Soup for the Soul®

Loving Our Dogs

Our 101 BEST STORIES

Heartwarming and Humorous Stories about Our Companions and Best Friends

Jack Canfield
& Mark Victor Hansen
edited by Amy Newmark

We are all crazy about our dogs and can't read enough about them, whether they're misbehaving and giving us big, innocent looks, or loyally standing by us in times of need. This new book from Chicken Soup for the Soul contains the 101 best dog stories from the company's extensive library. Readers will revel in the heartwarming, amusing, inspirational, and occasionally tearful stories about our best friends and faithful companions—our dogs.

978-1-935096-05-4

Classics for Dog Lovers

Chicken Soup for the Soul.

My Dog's Life

101 Stories about All the Ages and Stages of Our Canine Companions

Jack Canfield,
Mark Victor Hansen & Jennifer Quasha
Foreword by Wendy Diamond

From puppyhood antics to the twilight years and saying goodbye, this collection of heartwarming and inspiring stories focuses on all the memorable ages and stages of our lovable canines' lives. It also pays special attention to senior dogs and grieving when our dear friends leave us. All dog lovers will laugh, cry, and recognize themselves and their furry friends in these heartwarming and inspiring stories.

978-1-935096-65-8

Classics for Dog Lovers

www.chickensoup.com